P9-EJZ-609

AMERICAN
SIGN LANGUAGE
CONCISE
DICTIONARY

AMERICAN SIGN LANGUAGE CONCISE DICTIONARY

Martin L. A. Sternberg, Ed.D.

ILLUSTRATED BY HERBERT ROGOFF

Abridged edition of *American Sign Language*

PERENNIAL LIBRARY

Harper & Row, Publishers, New York
Grand Rapids, Philadelphia, St. Louis, San Francisco,
London, Singapore, Sydney, Tokyo, Toronto

To Joseph V. Firsching

This work is an abridgment of *American Sign Language: A Comprehensive Dictionary*, published in hardcover by Harper & Row, Publishers.

AMERICAN SIGN LANGUAGE CONCISE DICTIONARY. Copyright © 1990 by Martin L. A. Sternberg. All rights reserved. Printed in the United States of America. No part of this book may be used or reproduced in any manner whatsoever without written permission except in the case of brief quotations embodied in critical articles and reviews. For information address Harper & Row, Publishers, Inc., 10 East 53rd Street, New York, N.Y. 10022.

First PERENNIAL LIBRARY edition published 1990

Designed by Lydia Link

Library of Congress has catalogued the hardcover edition of this title as follows:

Sternberg, Martin L   A
  American sign language.
  Bibliography: p.
  Includes indexes.
  1. Sign language—Dictionaries.   I. Title.
HV2475.S77 1981   001.56   75-25066
ISBN 0-06-014097-6

ISBN 0-06-080996-5 (pbk.)
  91 92 93 94 CC/OPM 10 9 8 7 6 5 4 3 2

Contents

Foreword

This dictionary of the language of signs is a significant addition to the published works on manual communication and brings further dignity to the communication medium of deaf people.

Presentation of the components of the language of signs in true dictionary form complete to entry titles, pronunciation, parts of speech, rationale description, and cross references with other entries, imparts to the volume important values. Its usefulness to rehabilitation as a language training tool is readily apparent. The deaf reader with language problems will be greatly benefited in his search for word knowledge by the finely executed word-sign illustrations. The hearing reader who is learning the language of signs so that he may better serve deaf people will find helpful the alphabetical word-sign order.

It is interesting to know that the development of the dictionary was generative. A supposed 2,000 American sign vocabulary expanded in research to over 5,000 entries.

The Vocational Rehabilitation Administration is very pleased to have had a part in making available to deaf people and to hearing people who serve them this advanced reference document on the language of signs. My special thanks go to Martin L. A. Sternberg and Dr. Edna S. Levine of New York University and the many other persons who labored to make this dictionary possible.

Mary E. Switzer
Commissioner of Vocational Rehabilitation

Acknowledgments

The original work from which this abridged edition is derived, *American Sign Language: A Comprehensive Dictionary,* is the culmination of a period of endeavor that goes back to 1962. Dr. Elizabeth Peet, late Dean of Women and Professor of Romance Languages at Gallaudet College, Washington, D.C., first inspired me to compile this work, and she offered the initial guidance and encouragement.

Dr. Edna S. Levine, Professor Emeritus at New York University, provided continuing help and support after Dr. Peet's death. She assisted in the design of the dictionary format, and was instrumental in obtaining a two-year grant from the Rehabilitation Services Administration to demonstrate the feasibility of the project.

Herbert Rogoff, an illustrator of uncommon ability, labored with me for many years on the illustrations in this book, which were drawn from Polaroid photographs depicting the signs. His style and approach to illustration in this demanding area have influenced the work of many other people in the field.

Both Norma Schwartz and Jean Calder kept the thousands of drawings and entry cards in their homes for several years while they worked on mounting and checking. Judith Clifford also provided shelter for much of the manuscript. All these people made unique sacrifices, and it is difficult to express my thanks in adequate terms.

My publishers, Harper & Row, deserve a medal of honor for the patience and encouragement that have marked their long relationship with me while the book was taking shape. Harold Grove, my long-suffering editor, heads the list of people to whom I am indebted. Carol P. Cohen, Editorial Director, Mary Kay Linge, William

Monroe, Lydia Link, Dolores Simon, Millie Matacia, and Barbara Hufham also deserve special mention.

Theodora S. Zavin provided valuable legal assistance from the very beginning of this project. Leo Rosen and Kenneth S. Kauffman shared their expertise in copyright and related matters, and helped keep this very considerable undertaking on a businesslike basis.

My friends Dr. Salvatore diMichael and Dr. Boyce R. Williams both merit a very special thank-you. It was they who provided the very earliest guidance in the shaping of this project, and, through the years, have maintained a lively interest in its development.

An undertaking of this scope, and covering such a long period of time in its development, cannot escape certain built-in hazards. Among these are new signs and new applications for old ones. It has not always been possible to include them. Older signs, too, tend sometimes to fall into disuse. Their inclusion in the dictionary may be useful, however, as historical benchmarks in sign development. Like a history book, this work will never really be finished. I accept full responsibility for what is included and for what is not, and urge my colleagues everywhere to draw my attention to material which I may include in a later edition.

Martin L. A. Sternberg, Ed.D.

General Editorial Committee

Editorial Staff

Edna S. Levine, Ph.D., Litt.D., *Project Director;* Professor Emeritus, New York University, New York, N.Y.

Martin L. A. Sternberg, Ed.D. *Principal Research Scientist and Editor-in-Chief;* Former Adjunct Assistant Professor, New York University; Adjunct Associate Professor, Adelphi University, Garden City, N.Y.; Adjunct Assistant Professor, Hofstra University, Hempstead, N.Y.

Herbert Rogoff, *Illustrator;* Former Associate Research Scientist, New York University; Member, Society of Illustrators; Former Director of Public Relations, M. Grumbacher, Inc., New York, N.Y.

William F. Marquardt, Ph.D., *Linguist;* Late Professor of English Education, New York University.

Joseph V. Firsching, *Project Secretary*

Consulting Committee

Elizabeth E. Benson, Litt.D., *Chief Consultant;* Late Dean of Women and Professor of Speech, Gallaudet University, Washington, D.C.

Leon Auerbach, L.H.D., *Senior Consultant;* Professor Emeritus of Mathematics, Gallaudet University, Washington, D.C.

Special Consultants

Charles L. Brooks, *Vocational Signs*
Nancy Frishberg, Ph.D., *Editorial*
Emil Ladner, *Catholic Signs*
Max Lubin, *Jewish Signs*
The Rev. Steve L. Mathis III, *Protestant Signs*
Jerome D. Schein, Ph.D., *Editorial*
Edward L. Scouten, *General Signs*
William C. Stokoe, Ph.D., *Editorial*
Joseph P. Youngs, Jr., LL.D., *General Signs*

Illustration Assistants

Ann Silver, *Senior Illustration Assistant*
Jack Fennell
Jean Worth

Illustration Processing

Norma Schwartz, *Senior Illustration Processor*
(Mounting)
Jean Calder, *Illustration Processor* (Mounting)

Editorial Assistants

Lilly Berke, Edna Bock, Jean Calder *(Senior),* Nancy
Chough, Judith M. Clifford, Arlene Graham, Pat Rost,
Norma Schwartz, Patrice Smith, Mary Ellen Tracy

Secretarial/Clerical/Typing

Edna Bock, Carole Goldman, Carole Wilkins

Abbreviations

adj.	Adjective
adv.	Adverb, adverbial
adv. phrase	Adverbial phrase
arch.	Archaic
colloq.	Colloquial, colloquialism. Informal or familiar term or expression in sign
eccles.	Ecclesiastical. Of or pertaining to religious signs. These signs are among the earliest and best developed, inasmuch as the first teachers of deaf people were frequently religious workers, and instruction was often of a religious nature.
e.g.	*Exempli gratia.* L., for example
i.e.	*Id est.* L., that is
interj.	Interjection
L.	Latin
loc.	Localism. A sign peculiar to a local or limited area. This may frequently be the case in a given school for deaf children, a college or postsecondary program catering to their needs, or a geographical area around such school or facility where deaf persons may live or work.
obs.	Obscure, obsolete
pl.	Plural
poss.	Possessive
prep.	Preposition
prep. phrase	Prepositional phrase
pron.	Pronoun

q. v.	*Quod vide.* L., which see
sl.	Slang
v.	Verb
v. i.	Verb intransitive
viz.	*Videlicet.* L., namely
voc.	Vocational. These signs usually pertain to specialized vocabularies used in workshops, trade and vocational classes and schools.
v. t.	Verb transitive
vulg.	Vulgarism. A vulgar term or expression, usually used only in a colloquial sense.

Pronunciation Guide

Symbol	Example	Symbol	Example
a	cat	o͞o	groove
ā	name	ou	plow, clout
â	hair, rare	th	think, wrath
ä	balm, palm, father	tͪh	those, neither
e	berry, pet	u	cup, hut
ē	eat, tee	û(r)	turn
ēr	hear	zh	visionary
i	kitten, sit	ə	Indicates sound in
ī	kite, like		unaccented
n͡g	ring, fling		syllables, as:
o	pop, rotten		a in about
ō	coat, open		e in the
ô	pall, claw		i in readily
oi	boil		o in calorie
o͝o	took, hook		u in circus

Condensed and adapted from *The Random House College Dictionary*. Revised Edition. New York: Random House, 1968, 1975. Used by permission.

Explanatory Notes

Sign rationale

This term, admittedly imprecise semantically, refers to the explanatory material in parentheses which follows the part of speech. This material is an attempt to link the entry-word iconographically with the sign as described verbally. It is a device to aid the user of the dictionary to remember how a sign is formed.

Verbal description

The sign and its formation are described verbally. Such terms as "S" hand, "D" position, "both 'B' hands," refer to the positions of the hand or hands as they are depicted in the American Manual Alphabet on page xvi.

Terms such as "counterclockwise," "clockwise," refer to movement from the signer's orientation. Care should be taken not to become confused by illustrations which appear at first glance to contradict a verbal description. In all cases the verbal description should be the one of choice, with the illustration reinforcing it. The reader should place himself or herself mentally in the position of the signer, i.e., the illustration, in order to assume the correct orientation for signing a word.

Sign Synonyms

Sign synonyms are other words for which the same sign is used. They are found at the end of the verbal description, following the words, "See also," and are given in SMALL CAPITAL LETTERS.

It is important to remember that the words listed after the "See also" do not carry an equivalent sense in and of themselves. Because meaning for the deaf person springs from the sign, apparently unrelated words can be expressed by similar movements.

Illustrations

A. Illustrations appearing in sequence should not be regarded as separate depictions of parts of a sign. They are fluid and continuous, and should be used in conjunction with the verbal description of a sign, for they illustrate the main features of the sign as one movement flows into the next.

B. Arrows, broken or solid, indicate direction of movement. Again, they are designed to reinforce the verbal description and, where confusion may arise, the reader is cautioned to review the verbal description, always keeping himself or herself mentally in the position of the illustration (the signer).

C. As a general rule, a hand drawn with dotted or broken lines indicates the sign's initial movement or position of the hand. This is especially true if a similar drawing appears next to it using solid lines. This indicates terminal position in the continuum.

D. Groups of illustrations have been arranged as far as possible in visually logical order. They are read from left to right, or from top to bottom. Where confusion is possible, they have been captioned with letters A, B, C, etc.

E. Small lines outlining parts of the hand, especially when they are repeated, indicate small, repeated, or wavy or jerky motions, as described in the verbal section of an entry. ANTICIPATE is an example.

F. Arrows drawn side by side but pointing in opposite directions indicate repeated movement, as described in the verbal section of an entry. APPLAUD is an example.

G. Illustrations giving side or three-quarter views have been so placed to afford maximum visibility and to avoid foreshortening problems. The user of the dictionary should not assume a similar orientation when making the sign. As a general rule, the signer faces the person he or she is signing to.

H. Inclusion of the head in the figures permits proper orientation in the formation of certain signs. The head is omitted where there is no question of ambiguity.

American Manual Alphabet

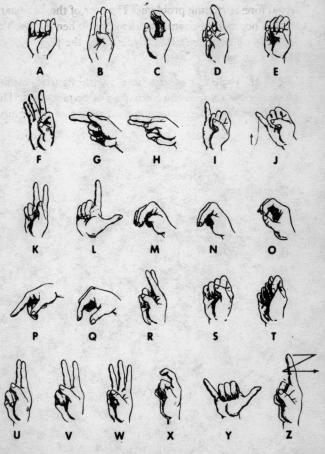

A

ABOUT (ə bout′), *prep.* (Revolving about.) The left hand is held at chest height, all fingers extended and touching the thumb, and all pointing to the right. The right index finger circles about the left fingers several times.

ACCEPT (ăk sĕpt′), *v.*, -CEPTED, -CEPTING. (A taking of something unto oneself.) Both open hands, palms down, are held in front of the chest. They move in unison toward the chest, where they come to rest, all fingers closed.

ACHIEVE (ə chēv′), *v.*, -CHIEVED, -CHIEVING. (Penetrating the heights.) The "D" hands, palms back, are held at each side of the head, near the temples. With a pivoting motion of the wrists, the hands swing up and around, simultaneously, to a position above the head, with palms facing out. See also SUCCEED, TRIUMPH.

1

ACROSS (ə krôs′, ə krŏs′), *prep., adv.* (A crossing over.) The left hand is held before the chest, palm down and fingers together. The right hand, fingers together, glides over the left, with the right little finger touching the top of the left hand. See also CROSS 2, OVER.

ACT (ăkt), *v.,* ACTED, ACTING, *n.* (Motion or movement, modified by the letter "A" for "act.") Both "A" hands, palms out, are held at shoulder height and rotate alternately toward the head. See also PERFORM 2, PERFORMANCE 2, PLAY 2, SHOW 2.

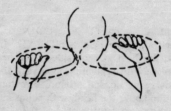

ADD 1 (ăd), *v.,* ADDED, ADDING. (To bring up all together.) The two open hands, palms and fingers facing each other, with the left hand above the right, are brought together, with all fingers closing simultaneously. This sign is used mainly in the sense of adding up figures or items. See also SUMMARIZE 2, SUMMARY 2, SUM UP.

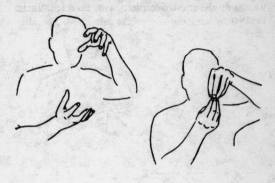

ADD 2, *v.* (Adding on.) The index and middle fingers of the right "H" hand, palm up, are swung up and over until they come to rest on the index and middle fingers of the left "H" hand, held palm down. See also GAIN, INCREASE, RAISE.

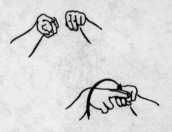

ADDITION (ə dĭsh' ən), *n.* See ADD 1.

ADDRESS (ăd′ rĕs), *n., v,* -DRESSED, -DRESSING. (Same rationale as for LIFE 1, with the initials "L.") The upturned thumbs of the "A" hands move in unison up the chest. See also ALIVE, LIFE 1, LIVE 1, LIVING.

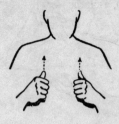

ADVICE (ăd vīs′), *n.* (Take something, *advice,* and disseminate it.) The left hand, held limp in front of the body, has its fingers pointing down. The fingers of the right hand, held all together, are placed on the top of the left hand, and then move forward, off the left hand, assuming a "5" position, palm down. See also INFLUENCE.

ADVISE (ăd vīz′), *v.,* -VISED, -VISING. See ADVICE.

AFRAID (ə frād'), *adj.* (The heart is suddenly covered with fear.) Both hands, fingers together, are placed side by side, palms facing the chest. They quickly open and come together over the heart, one on top of the other. See also FEAR 1, FRIGHT, SCARE(D), TERROR 1.

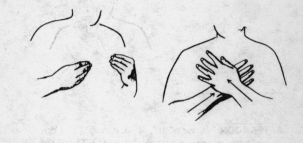

AFTER (ăf' tər, äf'-), *prep.* (Something occurring *after* a fixed place in time, represented by the hand nearest the body.) The right hand, held flat, palm facing the body, fingertips pointing left, represents the fixed place in time. The left hand is placed against the back of the right, and moves straight out from the body. The relative positions of the two hands may be reversed, with the left remaining stationary near the body and the right moving out.

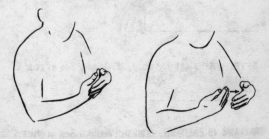

AFTER A WHILE (hwīl), *adv. phrase.* (A moving on of the minute hand of the clock.) The right "L" hand, its thumb thrust into the palm of the left and acting as a pivot, moves forward a short distance. See also LATER 1.

AFTERNOON (ăf´ tər nōōn´, äf´ -), *n., adj.* (The sun is midway between zenith and sunset.) The right arm, fingers together and pointing forward, rests on the back of the left hand, its fingers also together and pointing somewhat to the right. The right arm remains in a position about 45° from the vertical.

AFTERWARD (ăf´ tər wərd, äf´ -), *adv.* See AFTER A WHILE.

AGAIN (ə gĕn´), *adv.* The left hand, open in the "5" position, palm up, is held before the chest. The right hand, in the right-angle position, fingers pointing up, arches over and into the left palm. See also REPEAT.

AGAINST (ə gĕnst′, -gānst′), *prep.* (Opposed to; restraint.) The tips of the right fingers, held together, are thrust purposefully into the open left palm, whose fingers are also together and pointing forward. See also OPPOSE.

AGREE (ə grē′), *v.*, -GREED, -GREEING. (Of the same mind; thinking the same way.) The index finger of the right "D" hand, palm back, touches the forehead (the modified sign for THINK, *q.v.*), and then the two index fingers, both in the "D" position, palms down, are brought together so they are side by side, pointing away from the body (the sign for SAME). See also CONSENT.

AGREEMENT (-mənt), *n.* See AGREE.

AIM (ām), *v.,* AIMED, AIMING, *n.* (A thought directed upward, toward a goal.) The left "D" hand, palm facing the body, is held above the head, to represent the goal. The index finger of the right "D" hand, after touching the forehead (modified sign for THINK, *q.v.*), moves slowly and deliberately up to the tip of the left index finger. See also GOAL.

AIRPLANE (âr′ plān′), *n.* (The wings of the airplane.) The "Y" hand, palm down and drawn up near the shoulder, moves forward, up and away from the body. Either hand may be used. See also FLY 1, PLANE 1.

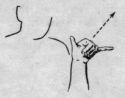

ALIKE (ə līk′), *adv.* (Matching fingers are brought together.) The outstretched index fingers are brought together, either once or several times. See also LIKE 2, SAME 1, SIMILAR.

ALIVE (ə līv′), *adj.* (The fountain [of LIFE] wells up from within the body.) The upturned thumbs of the "A" hands move in unison up the chest. See also ADDRESS, LIFE 1, LIVE 1, LIVING.

ALL (ôl), *adj., n., pron.* (Encompassing; a gathering together.) Both hands are held in the right angle position, palms facing the body, and the right hand in front of the left. The right hand makes a sweeping outward movement around the left, and comes to rest with the back of the right hand resting in the left palm. See also ENTIRE.

ALL ALONG (ə lông´, əlŏng´), *adv. phrase.* (From a point up and over.) In the "D" position, palms down, both index fingers touch the right shoulder and then are brought up and over, ending in a palm-up position, pointing straight ahead of the body. See also EVER SINCE, SINCE, SO FAR, THUS FAR.

ALLOW (ə lou´), *v.,* -LOWED, -LOWING. (A permissive upswinging of the hands, as if giving in.) Both hands, palms facing and fingers pointing away from the body, are held at chest level, almost a foot apart. With an upward movement, using their wrists as pivots, the hands sweep up until the fingers point almost straight up. See also GRANT 1, LET, LET'S, LET US, MAY 3, PERMISSION 1, PERMIT 1.

ALL RIGHT (rīt), *phrase.* (A straightening out.) The right hand, fingers together and palm facing left, is placed in the upturned left palm, whose fingers point away from the body. The right hand slides straight out along the left palm, over the left fingers, and stops with its heel resting on the left fingertips. See also O.K. 1, RIGHT 1, RIGHTEOUS, YOU'RE WELCOME 2.

ALMOST (ôl′ mōst, ôl mōst′), *adv.* The left hand is held at chest level in the right angle position, with fingers pointing up and the back of the hand facing right. The right fingers are swept up along the back of the left hand.

ALONE (ə lōn′), *adj.* (One, wandering around in a circle.) The index finger, pointing straight up, palm facing the body (the number *one*), is rotated before the face in a counterclockwise direction. See also LONE, ONLY.

ALSO (ôl′ sō), *adv.* (A likeness; a sameness.) Both index fingers, held together at one side of the body near waist level, point forward. As they travel to the other side of the body they separate an inch or two and come together again.

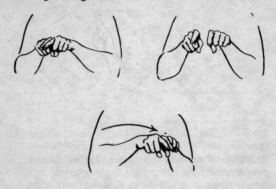

ALWAYS (ôl′ wāz, -wǐz), *adv.* (Around the clock.) The index finger of the right "D" hand points out-ward, away from the body, with palm facing left. The arm is rotated clockwise.

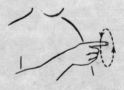

AM 1 (ăm; *unstressed* əm), *v.* (Part of the verb to BE.) The tip of the right index finger, held in the "D" position, palm facing left, is held at the lips, and

the hand moves straight out and away from the lips.
See also ARE 1, BE 1.

AM 2, *v.* (The "A" hand.) The tip of the right
thumb, in the "A" position, palm facing left, is held
at the lips. Then the hand moves straight out and
away from the lips.

AMAZE (ə māz′), *v.*, -MAZED, -MAZING. (The eyes
pop open in amazement.) Both hands are held in
modified "O" positions with thumb and index fingers of each hand near the eyes. These fingers suddenly flick open, and the eyes simultaneously pop
open wide. See also SURPRISE.

AMAZEMENT (-mənt), *n.* See AMAZE.

AMBITIOUS (ăm bĭsh' əs), *adj.* (Rubbing the hands together in zeal or ambition.) The open hands are rubbed vigorously back and forth against each other. See also EAGER, EAGERNESS, ENTHUSIASM, ENTHUSIASTIC.

AMERICA (ə mĕr' ə kə), *n.* (The fences built by the early settlers as protection against the Indians.) The extended fingers of both hands are interlocked, and are swept in an arc from left to right as if encompassing an imaginary house or stockade.

AMOUNT (ə mount'), *n.* (Throwing up a number of things before the eyes; a display of fingers to indicate a question of how many or how much.) The right hand, palm up, is held before the chest, all fingers touching the thumb. The hand is tossed straight up,

while the fingers open to the "5" position. See also
HOW MANY?, HOW MUCH?.

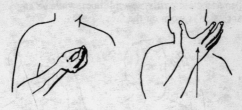

AND (ănd; *unstressed* ənd; ən), *conj.* The right "5"
hand, palm facing the body, fingers facing left,
moves from left to right, meanwhile closing until all
its fingers touch around its thumb.

ANGER (ăn' gər), *n.* (A violent welling-up of the
emotions.) The curved fingers of the right hand are
placed in the center of the chest, and fly up suddenly
and violently. An expression of anger is worn. See
also FURY, MAD, RAGE.

ANGRY 1 (ăn′ grĭ), *adj.* (Wrinkling the brow.) The "5" hand is held palm toward the face. The fingers open and close partly, several times, while an angry expression is worn on the face.

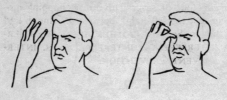

ANGRY 2, *adj.* See ANGER.

ANNOUNCE (ə nouns′), *v.*, -NOUNCED, -NOUNCING. (An issuance from the mouth.) Both index fingers are placed at the lips, with palms facing the body. They are rotated once and swung out in arcs, until the left index finger points somewhat to the left and the right index somewhat to the right. Sometimes the rotation of the fingers is omitted in favor of a simple swinging out from the lips.

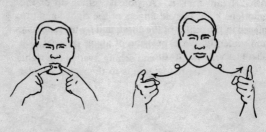

ANNOUNCEMENT (-mənt), *n.* See ANNOUNCE.

ANNOY (ə noi'), *v.*, -NOYED, -NOYING. (Obstruct, block.) The left hand, fingers together and palm flat, is held before the body, facing somewhat down. The little finger side of the right hand, held with palm flat, makes one or several up-down chopping motions against the left hand, between its thumb and index finger. See also BOTHER, DISTURB, INTERFERE, INTERFERENCE, INTERFERE WITH, INTERRUPT, PREVENT, PREVENTION.

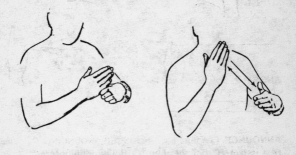

ANNOYANCE (ə noi' əns), *n.* See ANNOY.

ANOTHER (ə nŭth' ər), *adj.* (Moving over to *another* position.) The right "A" hand, thumb up, is pivoted from the wrist and swung over to the right, so that the thumb now points to the right. See also OTHER.

ANSWER (ăn' sər; än' -), *n., v.*, -SWERED, -SWER-
ING. (Directing a reply from the mouth to someone.)
The tip of the right index finger, held in the "D"
position, palm facing the body, is placed on the lips
while the left "D" hand, palm also facing the body,
is held about a foot in front of the right hand. The
right index finger, swinging around, moves toward
and stops in a pointing position a few inches from the
left index fingertip. See also REPLY, RESPOND, RE-
SPONSE 1.

ANY (ĕn' ĭ), *adj., pron.* The "A" hand, palm down
and thumb pointing left, pivots around on the wrist,
so the thumb now points down.

APART (ə pärt'), *adv.* (The hands are moved *apart.*)
Both hands, in the "A" position, thumbs up, are
held together, with knuckles touching. With a deliberate movement they come apart. See also DIVORCE
1, SEPARATE 1.

APOLOGIZE 1 (ə pŏl′ ə jīz′), v., -GIZED, -GIZING.
(The heart is circled, to indicate feeling, modified by
the letter "S," for SORRY.) The right "S" hand,
palm facing the body, is rotated several times over
the area of the heart. See also REGRET, REGRETFUL,
SORROW, SORROWFUL 2, SORRY.

APOLOGIZE 2, v. (A wiped-off and cleaned slate.)
The right hand wipes off the left palm several times.
See also EXCUSE, FORGIVE, PARDON.

APOLOGY 1 (ə pŏl′ ə jĭ), n. See APOLOGIZE 1.

APOLOGY 2, n. See APOLOGIZE 2.

APPEAR (ə pǐr′), *v.* -PEARED, -PEARING. (Popping up before the eyes.) The right index finger, pointing up, pops up between the index and middle fingers of the left hand, whose palm faces down. See also POP UP.

APPLAUD (ə plôd′), *v.,* -PLAUDED, -PLAUDING. (Good words coming from the mouth; clapping hands.) The fingertips of the right hand, palm flat and facing the body, are brought up to the lips, so that they touch (part of the sign for GOOD, *q.v.*). The hands are then clapped together several times. See also CONGRATULATE 1, CONGRATULATIONS 1, PRAISE.

APPLAUSE (ə plôz′), *n.* See APPLAUD.

APPLE (ăp′ əl), *n.* (A chewing of the letter "A," for *apple.*) The right "A" hand is held at the right cheek, with the thumb tip touching the cheek and palm facing out. In this position the hand is swung over and back from the wrist several times, using the thumb as a pivot.

APPOINTMENT (ə point′ mənt), *n.* (A binding of the hands together; a commitment.) The right "S" hand, palm down, is positioned above the left "S" hand, also palm down. The right hand circles above the left in a clockwise manner and is brought down on the back of the left hand. At the same instant both hands move down in unison a short distance.

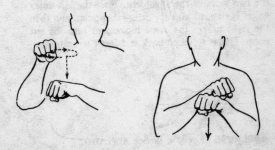

Are 1

ARE 1 (är), *v.* (Part of the verb to BE.) The tip of the right index finger, held in the "D" position, palm facing left, is held at the lips, and the hand moves straight out and away from the lips. See also AM 1, BE 1.

ARE 2, *v.* This is the same sign as for ARE 1, except that the "R" hand is used. It is an initialized version of ARE 1.

ARGUE (är′ gū), *v.*, -GUED, -GUING. (An expounding back and forth.) The index fingers here represent the two sides of the argument. First the left index finger is slapped into the open right palm, and then the right makes the same movement into the left palm. This is repeated back and forth several times.

 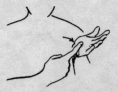

ARGUMENT (-mənt), *n.* See ARGUE.

ARRANGE (ə rānj′), *v.,* -RANGED, -RANGING. (Placing things in order.) The hands, palms facing, fingers together and pointing away from the body, are positioned at the left side and held about a foot apart. With a slight up-down motion, as if describing waves, the hands travel in unison from left to right. See also ORDER 2, PLAN, PREPARE 1, PUT IN ORDER, READY 1.

ARRANGEMENT (ə rānj′ mənt), *n.* See ARRANGE.

ARRIVAL (ə rī′ vəl), *n.* (Arrival at a designated place.) The right hand, palm facing the body and fingers pointing up, is brought forward from a position near the right shoulder and placed in the upturned palm of the left hand (the designated place).

ARRIVE (ə rīv′), *v.*, -RIVED, -RIVING. See ARRIVAL.

ASHAMED (ə shāmd′), *adj.* (The color rises in the cheek; an attempt is made to hide the head.) The backs of the fingers of the right hand, held in the right angle position, are placed against the right cheek. The hand moves up along the cheek, pivoting at the wrist, so that the fingers finally point to the rear. See also BASHFUL, SHAME 1, SHAMEFUL, SHAME ON YOU, SHY 1.

ASK 1 (ăsk, äsk), *v.*, ASKED, ASKING. (Pray tell.) Both hands, held upright about a foot in front of the chest, with palms facing and fingers pointing straight up, are positioned about a foot apart. Moving toward the chest, they come together until they touch, as if in prayer. See also REQUEST.

ASK 2 *(colloq.), v.* (Fire a question.) The right hand, held in a modified "S" position with palm facing out, assumes a position with the thumb resting on the fingernail of the index finger. The index finger is flicked out and forward, usually directed at the person being asked a question. Reversing the direction so that the index finger flicks out toward the speaker indicates the passive voice of the verb, *i.e.,* to be ASKED. See also INQUIRE.

ASLEEP (ə slēp´), *adv.* (The eyes are closed.) The fingers of the right open hand, facing the forehead, are placed on the forehead. The hand moves down and away from the head, with the fingers closing so that they all touch. The eyes meanwhile close, and the head bows slightly, as in sleep. See also SLEEP 1.

ASSIST (ə sĭst'), *n., v.,* -SISTED, -SISTING. (Helping up; supporting.) The left "S" hand, thumb side up, rests in the open right palm. In this position the left hand is pushed up a short distance by the right. See also HELP.

ASSISTANCE (ə sĭs' təns), *n.* See ASSIST.

ASSUME (ə sōōm'), *v.,* -SUMED, -SUMING. (To take up.) Both hands, held palms down in the "5" position, are at chest level. With a grasping upward movement, both close into "S" positions before the face. See also PICK UP 1, TAKE UP.

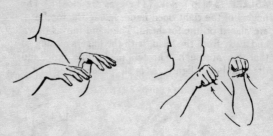

ATTACH (ə tăch'), *v.,* -TACHED, -TACHING. (Joining together.) Both hands, held in the modified "5" position, palms out, move toward each other. The thumbs and index fingers of both hands then connect. See also BELONG, CONNECT, JOIN.

ATTEMPT 1 (ə tĕmpt′), *n.*, *v.*, -TEMPTED, -TEMPT-ING. (Trying to push through.) The "A" hands, palms facing before the body, are swung around and a bit down, so that the palms now face out. The movement indicates an attempt to push through a barrier. See also EFFORT 1, TRY 1.

ATTEMPT 2, *n.*, *v.* (Trying to push through, using the "T" hands, for "try.") This is the same sign as ATTEMPT 1, except that the "T" hands are employed. See also EFFORT 2, TRY 2.

ATTITUDE (ăt´ ə tūd´, -tōōd´), *n.* (The letter "A"; the inclination of the heart.) The right "A" hand describes a counterclockwise circle around the heart, and comes to rest against the heart.

ATTRACT (ə trăkt´), *v.*, -TRACTED, -TRACTING. (Bringing everything together, to one point.) The open "5" hands, palms down and held at chest level, draw together until all the fingertips touch.

ATTRACTION (ə trăk´ shən), *n.* See ATTRACT.

ATTRACTIVE (ə trăk´ tĭv), *adj.* See ATTRACT.

AUNT (ănt, änt), *n.* (A female, defined by the letter "A.") The "A" hand, thumb near the right jawline (see sign for FEMALE), quivers back and forth several times.

AUTOMOBILE (ô′ tə mə bēl′, ô′ tə mō′ bēl, -mə bēl′), *n.* (The steering wheel.) The hands grasp an imaginary steering wheel and manipulate it. See also CAR, DRIVE.

AUTUMN (ô′ təm), *n.* (A chopping down during harvest time.) The right hand, fingers together and palm facing down, makes several chopping motions against the left elbow, to indicate the felling of growing things in autumn.

AVOID 1 (ə void′), *v.*, -VOIDED, -VOIDING. (Ducking back and forth, away from something.) Both "A" hands, thumbs pointing straight up, are held some distance before the chest, with the left hand in front of the right. The right hand, swinging back and forth, moves away from the left and toward the chest. See also EVADE, EVASION.

AVOID 2, *v.* (To push away and recoil from; avoid.) The two open hands, palms facing left, are pushed deliberately to the left, as if pushing something away. An expression of disdain or disgust is worn. See also HATE.

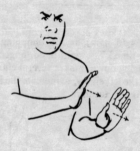

AWAKE (ə wāk′), *v., adj.,* -WOKE or -WAKED, -WAKING. (Opening the eyes.) Both hands are

closed, with thumb and index finger of each hand
held together, extended, and placed at the corners of
the closed eyes. Slowly they separate, and the eyes
open. See also WAKE UP.

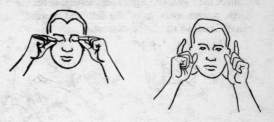

AWAKEN (ə wā′ kən), *v.*, -ENED, -ENING. See
AWAKE.

AWFUL (ô′ fəl), *adj.* (Throwing out the hands.)
Both hands, their fingertips touching their respective
thumbs, are held, palms facing each other, near the
temples. They are thrown out before the face, assuming "5" positions, palms still facing. See also TERRI-
BLE.

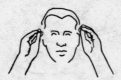

AWKWARD (ôk′ wərd), *adj.* (Clumsy in gait; all thumbs.) The "3" hands, palms down, move alternately up and down before the body. See also CLUMSINESS, CLUMSY.

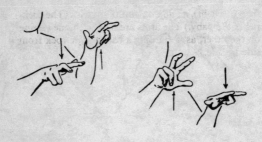

AWKWARDNESS, *n.* See AWKWARD.

B

BABY (bā′ bǐ), *n., adj., v.,* -BIED, -BYING. (The rocking of the baby.) The arms are held with one resting on the other, as if cradling a baby. They rock from side to side.

BAD (băd), *adj.* (Tasting something, finding it unacceptable, and turning it down.) The tips of the right "B" hand are placed at the lips, and then the hand is thrown down.

BANANA (bə nan′ ə), *n.* (The natural sign.) Go through the motions of peeling a banana, the left index representing the banana and the right fingertips pulling off the skin.

BASEBALL (bās′ bôl′), *n.* (Swinging a bat.) Both "S" hands, the right behind the left, grip an imaginary bat and move back and forth over the right shoulder, as if preparing to hit a baseball.

BASHFUL (băsh′ fəl), *adj.* (The color rises in the cheek; an attempt is made to hide the head.) The backs of the fingers of the right hand, held in the right angle position, are placed against the right cheek. The hand moves up along the cheek, pivoting at the wrist, so that the fingers finally point to the rear. See also ASHAMED, SHAME 1, SHAMEFUL, SHAME ON YOU, SHY 1.

BASKETBALL (băs′ kĭt bôl′), *n*. (Shooting a basket.) Both open hands are held with fingers pointing down and somewhat curved, as if grasping a basketball. From this position the hands move around and upward, as if to shoot a basket.

BATH (băth, bäth), *n*. (The natural sign.) The closed hands move up and down against the chest as if scrubbing it. See also WASH 2.

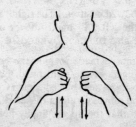

BATHE (bāth), *v.*, BATHED, BATHING. See BATH.

BE 1 (bē; *unstressed* bǐ), *v.*, BEEN, BEING. (Part of the verb to BE.) The tip of the right index finger, held in the "D" position, palm facing left, is held at the lips, and the hand moves straight out and away from the lips. See also AM 1, ARE 1.

BE 2, *v.* (The "B" hand.) This is the same sign as for BE 1 except that the "B" hand is used.

BEAT (bēt), *v.*, BEAT, BEATEN, BEATING. (Forcing the head into a bowed position.) The right "S" hand, placed across the left "S" hand, moves over and down a bit. See also DEFEAT, OVERCOME.

BEATEN (bē' tən), *adj.* (The head is forced into a bowed position.) The right "S" hand, palm up, is placed under and across the left "S" hand, whose palm faces down. The right "S" hand moves up and over, toward the body. This sign is used as the passive voice of the verb BEAT.

BEAUTIFUL (bū' tə fəl), *adj.* (Literally, a good face.) The right hand, fingers closed over the thumb, is placed at or just below the lips (indicating a tasting of something GOOD, *q.v.*). It then describes a counterclockwise circle around the face, opening into the "5" position, to indicate the whole face. At the completion of the circling movement the hand comes to rest in its initial position, at or just below the lips. See also PRETTY.

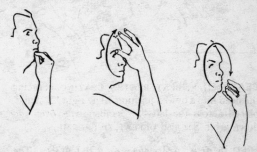

BEAUTY (bū' tǐ), *n.* See BEAUTIFUL.

BE CAREFUL (kâr′ fəl), *v. phrase*. (The "K" for *keep* in the sense of *keeping carefully.*) Both "K" hands are crossed, the right atop the left. The right hand moves up and down a very short distance, several times, each time coming to rest on top of the left.

BECAUSE (bĭ kôz′, -kŏz′), *conj*. (A thought or knowledge uppermost in the mind.) The fingers of the right hand or the index finger, are placed on the center of the forehead, and then the hand is brought strongly up above the head, assuming the "A" position, with thumb pointing up. See also FOR 2.

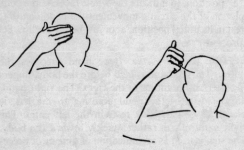

BED (bĕd), *n*. (A sleeping place with four legs.) The head is tilted to one side, with the cheek resting in the palm, to represent the head on a pillow. Both index fingers, pointing down, move straight down a short distance, in unison (the two front legs of the bed), and then are brought up slightly, and move down again a bit closer to the body (the rear legs).

BEER (bĭr), *n.* (Raising a beer stein to the lips.) The right "Y" hand is raised to the lips, as the head tilts back a bit.

BEFORE (bĭ fōr'), *adv.* (One hand precedes the other.) The left hand is held before the body, fingers together and pointing to the right. The right hand, fingers also together, and pointing to the left, is placed so that its back rests in the left palm. The right hand moves rather quickly toward the body. The sign is used as an indication of time or of precedence: *He arrived before me.*

BEG 1 (bĕg), *v.*, BEGGED, BEGGING. (Holding out the hand and begging.) The right open hand, palm up and fingers slightly cupped, is moved up and down by the left hand positioned under it.

BEG 2, *v.* (An act of supplication.) With the right hand clasped over the left, both hands are shaken gently before the body. The eyes often are directed upward.

BEGIN (bĭ gĭn'), *v.*, -GAN, -GUN, -GINNING. (Turning a key to open up a new venture.) The right index finger, resting between the left index and middle fingers, executes a half turn, once or twice. See also ORIGIN, START.

BEHIND (bĭ hīnd'), *prep.* (One hand is after or behind the other.) Both hands, in the "A" position, are held knuckles to knuckles. The right hand moves back, describing a small arc, and comes to rest against the left wrist.

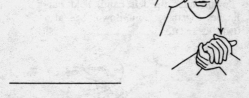

BELIEF (bĭ lēf'), *n.* (A thought clasped onto.) The index finger touches the middle of the forehead (where the thought lies), and then both hands are clasped together.

BELIEVE (bĭ lēv'), *v.*, -LIEVED, -LIEVING. See BE-LIEF.

BELONG (bĭ lông', -lŏng'), *v.*, -LONGED, -LONGING. (Joining together.) Both hands, held in the modified "5" position, palms out, move toward each other. The thumbs and index fingers of both hands then connect. See also ATTACH, CONNECT, JOIN.

BELOW 1 (bĭ lō′), *adv.* (The area below.) Both
hands, in the "5" position, palms down, are held
before the chest, the right under the left. The right
hands moves under the left in a counterclockwise
fashion. See also FOUNDATION.

BELOW 2, *adv.* (Underneath something.) The right
hand, in the "A" position, thumb pointing straight
up, moves down under the left hand, held outstretched, fingers together, palm down. See also
UNDER 1, UNDERNEATH.

BE QUIET 1 (kwi′ ət), *v. phrase.* (The natural sign.)
The index finger is brought up against the pursed
lips. See also QUIET 1, SILENCE 1, SILENT.

BE QUIET 2, (Quiet and peace.) The open hands are crossed before the mouth, the right palm facing left, left facing right. Then both hands, held palms down, move down from the mouth, curving outward to either side of the body. See also CALM, QUIET 2, SILENCE 2.

BE SEATED, *v. phrase.* (The act of sitting.) The extended right index and middle fingers are draped across the back of the same two fingers of the downturned left hand. The hands then move straight downward a short distance. See also CHAIR, SEAT, SIT.

BEST (bĕst), *adj.* (The most good.) The fingertips of one hand are placed at the lips, as if tasting something (*see* GOOD), and then the hand is brought high up above the head into the "A" position, thumb up, indicating the superlative degree.

BE STILL, *v. phrase.* See BE QUIET 2.

BETTER (bĕt' ər), *adj.* (More good.) The fingertips of one hand are placed at the lips, as if tasting something (*see* GOOD). Then the hand is moved up to a position just above the head, where it assumes the "A" position, thumb up. This latter position, less high up than the one indicated in BEST, denotes the comparative degree. See also PREFER.

BETWEEN (bĭ twēn'), *prep.* (Between the fingers.) The left hand, in the "C" position, is placed before the chest, all fingers facing up. The right hand, in the "B" position, is placed between the left fingers and

moves back and forth several times. This sign may
also be made by pointing the left fingers to the right,
with the left thumb pointing up, and the right hand
making the same back and forth motion as before,
with the right little finger resting on the left index
finger.

BICYCLE, (bī′ sə kəl), *n.*, *v.*, -CLED, -CLING. (The
motion of the feet on the pedals.) Both hands, in the
"S" position, rotate alternately before the chest.

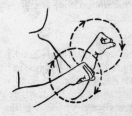

BIG 1 (bĭg), *adj.* (A delineation of something big,
modified by the letter "L," which stands for
LARGE.) Both "L" hands, palms facing out, are
placed before the face, and separate rather widely.
See also LARGE.

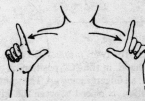

BIG 2, *adj.* (The height is indicated.) The right right-angle hand, palm facing the left, is held at the height the signer wishes to indicate. See also HEIGHT 2, HIGH 2, TALL 2.

BIRD (bûrd), *n.* (The shape and movement of a beak.) The right thumb and index finger are placed against the mouth, pointing straight out. They open and close.

BIRTH (bûrth), *n.* (The baby is brought forth from the womb.) Both cupped hands, palms facing the body, are placed at the stomach or lower chest, one on top of the other. Both hands are moved out and away from the body in unison, describing a small arc. See also BORN.

BIRTHDAY (bûrth′ dā′), *n.* The sign for BIRTH 1 or
BIRTH 2 is made, followed by the sign for DAY:
The left arm, held horizontally, palm down, represents the horizon. The right elbow rests on the back
of the left hand, with the right arm in a perpendicular position. The right "D" hand, palm facing left,
moves in an arc to the left until it is just above the
left elbow.

BITTER (bĭt′ ər), *adj.* (Something sour or bitter.)
The right index finger is brought sharply up against
the lips, while the mouth is puckered up as if tasting
something sour. See also DISAPPOINTED.

BLACK (blăk), *adj.* (The darkest part of the face,
i.e., the brow, is indicated.) The tip of the index
finger moves along the eyebrow.

BLEED (blēd), *v.*, BLED, BLEEDING, *adj.* (Blood trickles down from the hand.) The left "5" hand is held palm facing the body and fingertips pointing right. The right "5" hand touches the back of the left and moves down, with the right fingers wiggling.

_____

BLIND (blīnd), *adj.* (The eyes are blocked.) The tips of the "V" fingers are thrust toward the closed eyes.

_____

BLOOD (blŭd), *n.* See BLEED.

_____

BLUE (blo͞o), *n., adj.* (The letter "B.") The right "B" hand shakes slightly, pivoted at the wrist.

BLUSH (blŭsh), *v.*, BLUSHED, BLUSHING. (The red rises in the cheeks.) The sign for RED is made: The tip of the right index finger of the "D" hand moves down over the lips, which are red. Both hands are then placed palms facing the cheeks, and move up along the face, to indicate the rise of color. See also EMBARRASS, EMBARRASSED.

BOAT (bōt), *n.* (The shape; the bobbing on the waves.) Both hands are cupped together to form the hull of a boat. They move forward in a bobbing motion.

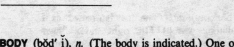

BODY (bŏd' ĭ), *n.* (The body is indicated.) One or both hands are placed against the chest and then are removed and replaced at a point a bit below the first.

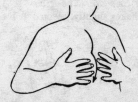

BOOK (bŏŏk), *n.* (Opening a book.) The open hands are held together, fingers pointing away from the body. They open with little fingers remaining in contact, as in the opening of a book.

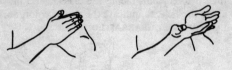

BORE (bōr), *v.,* BORED, BORING, *n.* (A dryness, indicated by a wiping of the lips.) The "X" finger is drawn across the lips, from left to right, as if wiping them. See also DRY.

BORING (bōr' ĭng), *adj.* (The nose is pressed, as if to a grindstone wheel.) The right index finger touches the tip of the nose, as a bored expression is assumed. The right hand is sometimes pivoted back and forth slightly, as the fingertip remains against the nose.

BORN (bôrn), *adj.* (The baby is brought forth from the womb.) Both cupped hands, palms facing the body, are placed at the stomach or lower chest, one on top of the other. Both hands are moved out and away from the body in unison, describing a small arc. See also BIRTH.

BORROW (bŏr′ ō, bôr′ ō), *v.,* -ROWED, -ROWING, (Bring to oneself.) The "K" hands are crossed and moved in toward the body.

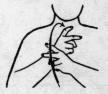

BOTH (bōth), *adj., pron.* (Two fingers are drawn together.) The right "2" hand, palm facing the body, is drawn down through the left "C" hand. As it does, the right index and middle fingers come together.

BOTHER (bŏt͟h' ər), *v.*, -ERED, -ERING, (Obstruct, block.) The left hand, fingers together and palm flat, is held before the body, facing somewhat down. The little finger side of the right hand, held with palm flat, makes one or several up-down chopping motions against the left hand, between its thumb and index finger. See also ANNOY 1, ANNOYANCE, DISTURB, INTERFERE, INTERFERENCE, INTERFERE WITH, INTERRUPT, PREVENT, PREVENTION.

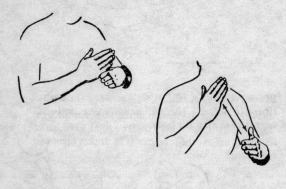

BOX (bŏks), *n.* (The dimensions are indicated.) The open hands, palms facing and fingers pointing out, are dropped an inch or two simultaneously. They then shift their relative positions so that both palms face the body, with one hand in front of the other. In this new position, they again drop an inch or two simultaneously. See also PACKAGE, ROOM 1.

BOY 1 (boi), *n.* (A small male.) The MALE root sign is made: The thumb and extended fingers of the right hand are brought up to grasp an imaginary cap brim, representing the tipping of caps by men in olden days. The downturned right hand then indicates the short height of a small boy.

BOY 2, *n.* (A modification of the MALE root sign; the familiar sign for BOY 1.) The right hand, palm down, is held at the forehead. The fingers open and close once or twice.

BRAG (brăg), *v.*, BRAGGED, BRAGGING. (Indicating the self, repeatedly.) The thumbs of both "A" hands are alternately thrust into the chest a number of times.

BRAVE (brāv), *adj., n., v.,* BRAVED, BRAVING.
(Strength emanating from the body.) Both "5"
hands are placed palms against the chest. They move
out and away, forcefully, closing and assuming the
"S" position. See also HEALTH, HEALTHY, MIGHTY
2, STRENGTH, WELL.

BRAVERY (brā' və rǐ), *n.* See BRAVE.

BREAD (brĕd), *n.* (Act of cutting a loaf of bread.)
The left arm is held against the chest, representing
a loaf of bread. The little finger edge of the right
hand is drawn down over the back of the left hand
several times, to indicate the cutting of slices.

BREAK (brāk), *n., v.*, BROKE, BROKEN, BREAKING.
(The natural sign.) The hands grasp an imaginary
object and break it in two.

BREATH (brĕth), *n.* (The rise and fall of the chest
in respiration.) The hands, folded over the chest,
move forward and back to the chest, to indicate the
breathing.

BREATHE (brĕth), *v.*, BREATHED, BREATHING. See
BREATH.

BRIEF (brēf), *adj.* (To make short; to measure off a
short space.) The index and middle fingers of the
right "H" hand are placed across the top of the index
and middle fingers of the left "H" hand, and move
a short distance back and forth, along the length of
the left index finger. See also SHORT 1, SHORTEN.

BRING (brĭng), *v.*, BROUGHT, BRINGING. (Carrying something over.) Both open hands, palms up, move in an arc from left to right, as if carrying something from one point to another. See also CARRY 2, DELIVER.

BROAD-MINDED (brôd´ mīn´ dĭd), *adj.* (The mind is open, or wide.) The index finger touches the forehead to indicate the MIND. Then the sign for BROAD is made: The open hands, fingers pointing out and palms facing each other, separate from their initial position an inch or two apart.

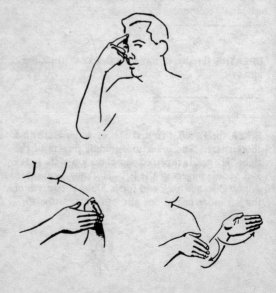

BROKE (brōk), *(sl.)*, *adj.* (The head is chopped off.) The tips of the right fingers are thrust forcefully into the right side of the neck.

BROTHER (brŭth' ər), *n.* (A male who is the same, *i.e.,* from the same family.) The root sign for MALE is made: The thumb and extended fingers of the right hand are brought up to grasp an imaginary cap brim, representing the tipping of caps by men in olden days. Then the sign for SAME 1 is made: The outstretched index fingers are brought together, either once or several times.

BROWN (broun), *adj.* The "B" hand is placed against the face, with the index finger touching the upper cheek. The hand is then drawn straight down the cheek.

BUILD (bĭld), *v.*, BUILT, BUILDING. (Piling bricks one on top of another.) The downturned hands are placed repeatedly atop each other. Each time this is done the arms rise a bit, to indicate the raising of a building. See also CONSTRUCT 1, CONSTRUCTION.

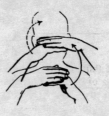

BURN (bûrn), *n.*, *v.*, BURNED or BURNT, BURNING. (The leaping of flames.) The "5" hands are held with palms facing the body. They move up and down alternately, while the fingers wiggle. See also FIRE 1, FLAME.

BUT (bŭt; *unstressed* bət), *conj.* (A divergence or a difference; the opposite of SAME.) The index fingers of both "D" hands, palms facing down, are crossed near their tips. The hands are drawn apart.

BUTTER (bŭt´ ər), *n.*, *v.*, -TERED, -TERING. (The spreading of butter.) The tips of the fingers of the downturned right "U" hand are brushed repeatedly over the upturned left palm.

BUY (bī), *n.*, *v.*, BOUGHT, BUYING. (Giving out money.) The sign for MONEY is made: The up-turned right hand, grasping some imaginary bills, is brought down into the upturned left palm, and then the right hand moves forward and up in a small arc, opening up as it does.

C

CAKE (kāk), *n.* (The rising of the cake.) The fingertips of the right "5" hand are placed in the upturned left palm. The right rises slowly an inch or two above the left.

CALL 1 (kôl), *v.*, CALLED, CALLING. (To tap someone for attention.) The right hand is placed upon the back of the left, held palm down. The right hand then moves up and in toward the body, assuming the "A" position. As an optional addition, the right hand may then assume a beckoning movement.

CALL 2 *n.*, *v.* (The natural sign.) The cupped right hand is held against the right cheek. The mouth is slightly open.

CALLED, *adj.* (NAME, indicating who is named.) The sign for NAME is made: The right "H" hand, palm facing left, is brought down on the left "H" hand, palm facing right. The hands, in this position, move forward a few inches. See also NAMED.

CALM (käm), *adj., v.,* CALMED, CALMING. (Quiet and peace.) The open hands are crossed before the mouth, the right palm facing left, left facing right. Then both hands, held palms down, move down from the mouth, curving outward to either side of the body. See also BE QUIET 2, BE STILL, QUIET 2, SILENCE 2.

CAN (kăn, kən), *v.* (An affirmative movement of the hands, likened to a nodding of the head, to indicate ability or power to accomplish something.) Both "A" hands, held palms down, move down in unison a short distance before the chest. See also CAPABLE, MAY 2, POSSIBLE.

CANCEL (kăn´ səl), *n., v.,* -CELED, -CELING. (A canceling out.) The right index finger makes a cross on the open left palm. See also CORRECT 2.

CANDY 2, *n.* (Wiping the lips; licking the finger.) The right index finger, pointing left, is drawn across the lips from left to right.

CANNOT (kăn´ ŏt), *v.* (One finger encounters an unyielding quality in striking another.) The right index finger strikes the left and continues moving down. The left index finger remains in place.

CAN'T (kănt, känt), *v.* See CANNOT.

CAPABLE (kā´ pǝ bǝl), *adj.* (An affirmative movement of the hands, likened to a nodding of the head, to indicate ability or power to accomplish something.) Both "A" hands, held palm down, move down in unison a short distance before the chest. See also CAN, MAY 2, POSSIBLE.

CAR (kär), *n.* (The steering wheel.) The hands grasp an imaginary steering wheel and manipulate it. See also AUTOMOBILE, DRIVE.

CARE 1 (kâr), *n., v.,* CARED, CARING. (Slow, careful movement.) The "K" hands are crossed, the right above the left, little finger edges down. In this position they describe a small counterclockwise circle in front of the chest.

CARE 2, *n., v.* (A variant of CARE 1) With the hands in the same position as in CARE 1, they are moved up and down a short distance. See also KEEP, MAINTAIN 1, PRESERVE, TAKE CARE OF.

CARE FOR (fôr), *v. phrase.* See CARE 1.

CAREFUL 1 (kâr´ fəl), *adj.* See CARE 1.

CAREFUL 2, *adj.* See CARE 2.

CARELESS (kâr´ lĭs), *adj.* (The vision is side-tracked, causing one to lose sight of the object in view.) The right "V" hand, representing the vision, is held in front of the face, palm facing left. The hand, pivoted at the wrist, moves back and forth a number of times.

CARRY 1 (kăr´ ĭ), *v.*, -RIED, -RYING. (Act of conveying an object from one point to another.) The open hands are held palms up before the chest on the right side of the body. Describing an arc, they move up and forward in unison.

CARRY 2, *v.* (Carrying something over.) Both open hands, palms up, move in an arc from left to right, as if carrying something from one point to another. See also BRING, DELIVER 2.

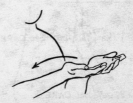

CAT (kăt), *n.* (The whiskers.) The thumbs and index fingers of both hands stroke an imaginary pair of whiskers at either side of the face. The right hand then strokes the back of the left, as if stroking the fur. This latter sign is seldom used today, however. Also one hand may be used in place of two for the stroking of the whiskers.

CATCH 1, (kăch), *v.*, CAUGHT, CATCHING. (Grasping something and holding it down.) Both hands, palms down, quickly close into the "S" position, the right on top of the left. See also GRAB, GRASP.

CATCH 2, *v.* (Catching a ball.) Both hands go through the motions of catching a ball.

CAUTION (kô´ shən), *n.* (Tapping one to draw attention to danger.) The right hand taps the back of the left several times. See also WARN.

CELEBRATE (sĕl´ ə brāt´), *v.*, -BRATED, -BRATING. (Waving of flags.) Both upright hands, grasping imaginary flags, wave them in small circles. See also CHEER, REJOICE, VICTORY 1, WIN 1.

CELEBRATION (sĕl´ ə brā´ shən), *n.* See CELEBRATE.

CENT (sĕnt), *n.* (The Lincoln head.) The right index finger touches the right temple and moves up and away quickly. This is "one cent." For two cents, the "2" hand is used, etc.

CENTER (sĕnt´ ər), *n.*, *v.*, -TERED, -TERING. (The natural sign.) The downturned right fingers describe a small clockwise circle and come to rest in the center of the upturned left palm. See also MIDDLE.

CENTRAL (sĕn´ trəl), *adj.* See CENTER.

CENTS, *n. pl.* See CENT.

CHAIR (châr), *n.* (The act of sitting.) The extended right index and middle fingers are draped across the back of the same two fingers of the downturned left hand. The hands then move straight downward a short distance. See also BE SEATED, SEAT, SIT.

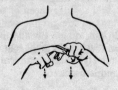

CHANGE (chānj), *n.*, *v.*, CHANGED, CHANGING. (The position of the hands is altered.) Both "A"

hands, thumbs up, are held before the chest, several inches apart. The left hand is pivoted over so that its thumb points to the right. Simultaneously, the right hand is moved up and over the left, describing a small arc, with its thumb pointing to the left.

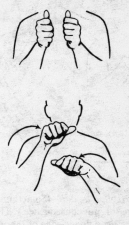

CHASE (chās), *v.*, CHASED, CHASING. (The natural sign.) The "A" hands are held in front of the body, with the thumbs facing forward, the right palm facing left and the left palm facing right. The left hand is held slightly ahead of the right; it then moves forward in a straight line while the right hand follows after, executing a circular motion or swerving back and forth, as if in pursuit.

CHAT (chăt), *n.*, *v.*, CHATTED, CHATTING. (Words tossed back and forth.) The open hands are held side by side with palms up, fingers pointing forward and slightly curved. In this position the hands swing back and forth from side to side before the chest. See also CONVERSATION 2.

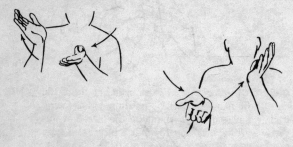

CHEAP (chēp), *(colloq.)*, *adj.* (Something easily moved, therefore of no consequence.) The right fingertips slap the little finger edge of the upturned left hand.

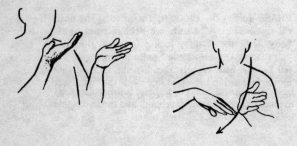

CHEER (chĭr), *n.* (Waving of flags.) Both upright hands, grasping imaginary flags, wave them in small

circles. See also CELEBRATE, CELEBRATION, RE-
JOICE, VICTORY 1, WIN 1.

CHEERFUL (chir´ fəl), *adj.* (A crinkling-up of the
face.) Both hands, in the "5" position, palms facing
back, are placed on either side of the face. The fingers wiggle back and forth, while a pleasant, happy
expression is worn. See also FRIENDLY, PLEASANT.

CHEESE (chēz), *n.* (The pressing of cheese.) The
base of the downturned right hand is pressed against
the base of the upturned left hand, and the two rotate
back and forth against each other.

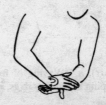

CHICKEN (chĭk´ ən, -ĭn), *n.* (The bill and the scratching.) The right index finger and thumb open and close as they are held pointing out from the mouth. (This is the root sign for any kind of bird.) The right "X" finger then scratches against the up-turned left palm, as if scratching for food. The scratching is sometimes omitted.

CHILD (chīld), *n.* (The child's height.) The down-turned right palm is extended before the body, as if resting on a child's head.

CHILDREN (chĭl´ drən), *n.* (Indicating different heights of children; patting the children on their heads.) The downturned right palm, held before the body, executes a series of movements from left to right, as if patting a number of children on their heads.

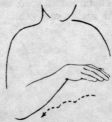

CHOICE (chois), *n.* (Making a choice.) The left "V" hand faces the body. The right thumb and index finger close first over the left index fingertip and then over the left middle fingertip. See also EITHER 2.

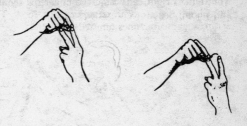

CHOOSE (chōōz), *v.,* CHOSE, CHOSEN, CHOOSING. (Taking unto oneself.) The right hand, palm out, is extended before the chest, index finger and thumb in an open position, the other fingers separated and pointing up. The hand is drawn in toward the chest, and the index and thumb close at the same time, indicating something taken to oneself. See also SE- LECT 2, TAKE.

CITY (sĭt´ ĭ), *n.* (A collection of rooftops.) The fingertips of both hands are joined, the hands and arms forming a pyramid. The fingertips separate and rejoin a number of times. Both arms may move a bit from left to right each time the fingertips separate and rejoin. See also COMMUNITY.

CLASS (klăs, kläs), *n.* (A grouping together.) Both "C" hands, palms facing, are held a few inches apart at chest height. They are swung around in unison, so that the palms now face the body. See also COMPANY, GROUP 1, ORGANIZATION 1.

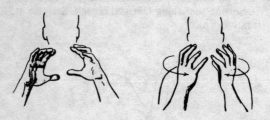

CLASSED *v.* See CLASS.

CLEAN (klēn), *adj.* (Everything is wiped off the hand, to emphasize an uncluttered or clean condition.) The right hand slowly wipes the upturned left palm, from wrist to fingertips. See also NICE, PLAIN 2, PURE, PURITY.

CLEAR (klĭr), *adj.* (Rays of light clearing the way.) Both hands are held at chest height, palms out, all fingertips together. They open into the "5" position in unison, the right hand moving toward the right and the left toward the left. The palms of both hands remain facing out. See also OBVIOUS, PLAIN 1.

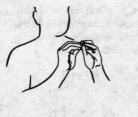 

CLOSE 1 (*adj., adv.* klōs; *v.* klōz), CLOSED, CLOS-ING. (The act of closing.) Both "B" hands, held palms out before the body, come together with some force. See also SHUT.

CLOSE (TO) 2, *adj.* (One hand is near the other.)
The left hand, cupped, fingers together, is held
before the chest, palm facing the body. The right
hand, also cupped, fingers together, moves a very
short distance back and forth, as it is held in front
of the left. See also NEAR.

CLOTHES (klōz, klōthz), *n. pl.* (Draping the clothes
on the body.) With fingertips resting on the chest,
both hands move down simultaneously. The action
is repeated. See also DRESS, SHIRT, WEAR.

CLOTHING (klō′ thĭng), *n.* See CLOTHES.

CLUMSINESS (klŭm′ zĭ nĭs), *n.* (Clumsy in gait; all
thumbs.) The "3" hands, palms down, move alter-

nately up and down before the body. See also AWK-
WARD, AWKWARDNESS.

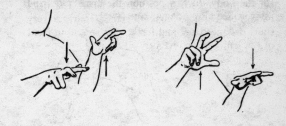

CLUMSY (klŭm´ zĭ), *adj.* See CLUMSINESS.

COAT (kōt), *n.* (The lapels are outlined.) The tips of
the "A" thumbs outline the lapels of the coat.

COFFEE (kôf´ ĭ, kŏf´ ĭ), *n.* (Grinding the coffee
beans.) The right "S" hand, palm facing left, rotates
in a counterclockwise manner, atop the left "S"
hand, palm facing right.

COLD 1 (kōld). *adj.* (The trembling from cold.) Both "S" hands, palms facing, are placed at the sides of the body. In this position the arms and hands shiver. See also SHIVER, WINTER 1.

COLD 2, *n.* (Wiping the nose.) The signer makes the motions of wiping the nose several times with an imaginary handkerchief. This is the common cold.

COLLEGE (kŏl´ ĭj), *n.* (Above ordinary school.) The sign for SCHOOL, *q.v.*, is made, but without the clapping of hands. The upper hand swings up in an arc above the lower. The upper hand may form a "C," instead of assuming a clapping position.

COLLIDE (kə līd´), *v.*, -LIDED, -LIDING. The fists come together with force. See also CRASH.

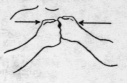

COLLISION (kə lizh´ en), *n.* See COLLIDE.

COLOR (kŭl´ ər), *n.* The fingertips of the right "5" hand, palm facing the body, are placed against the chin and wiggle back and forth.

COMB (kōm) *n., v.,* COMBED, COMBING. (Act of combing the hair.) The downturned curved fingertips of the right hand, representing the teeth of the comb, are drawn through the hair.

COME 1 (kŭm), *v.*, CAME, COME, COMING. (Movement toward the body.) The index fingers, pointing to each other, are rolled in toward the body.

COME 2, *v.* (The natural sign.) The upright hand beckons.

COMFORT (kŭm´ fərt), *n.*, *v.*, -FORTED, -FORTING. (A stroking motion.) Each downturned open hand alternately strokes the back of the other, moving forward from wrist to fingers.

COMFORTABLE (kŭmf´ tə bəl, kŭm´ fər tə bəl), *adj.*
See COMFORT.

COMMUNITY (kə mū´ nə tǐ), *n.* (A collection of
rooftops.) The fingertips of both hands are joined,
the hands and arms forming a pyramid. The fingertips separate and rejoin a number of times. Both
arms may move a bit from left to right each time the
fingertips separate and rejoin. See also CITY.

COMPANY (kŭm´ pə nǐ), *n.,* (A grouping together.)
Both "C" hands, palms facing, are held a few inches
apart at chest height. They are swung around in
unison, so that the palms now face the body. See also
CLASS, CLASSED, GROUP 1, ORGANIZATION 1.

COMPARE (kəm pâr'), *v.*, -PARED, -PARING. (Comparing both palms.) Both open hands are held before the body, with palms facing each other and fingers pointing upward. The hands then turn toward the face while the signer looks from one to the other, as if comparing them.

COMPASSION (kəm păsh' ən), *n.* (Feelings from the heart, conferred on others.) The middle finger of the open right hand moves up the chest over the heart. The same open hand then moves in a small, clockwise circle in front of the right shoulder, with palm facing forward and fingers pointing up. The signer assumes a kindly expression.

COMPETE 1 (kəm pēt'), *v.*, -PETED, -PETING. (Two opponents come together.) Both hands are closed, with thumbs pointing straight up and palms facing the body. From their initial position about a foot apart, the hands are brought together sharply, so that the knuckles strike. The hands, as they are drawn together, also move down a bit, so that they describe a "V."

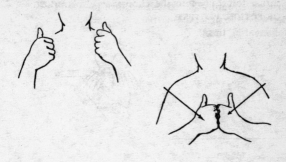

COMPETE 2, *v.* (Opposing objects.) The "A" hands are held side by side before the chest, palms facing each other and thumbs pointing forward. In this position the hands move alternately back and forth, toward and away from the body. See also RACE.

COMPETITION 1 (kŏm´ pə tĭsh´ ən), *n.* See COMPETE 1.

COMPETITION 2, *n.* See COMPETE 2.

COMPLAIN (kəm plān′), *v.*, -PLAINED, -PLAINING. (The hand is thrust into the chest to force a complaint out.) The curved fingers of the right hand are thrust forcefully into the chest. See also OBJECT, OBJECTION, PROTEST.

_____

COMPLAINT (kəm plānt′), *n.* See COMPLAIN.

_____

COMPLETE (kəm plēt′), *v.*, -PLETED, -PLETING. (Wiping off the top of a container, to indicate its condition of fullness.) The downturned open right hand wipes across the index finger edge of the left "S" hand, whose palm faces right. The movement of the right hand is toward the body. See also FILL, FULL.

_____

COMPLICATE (kŏm′ plə kāt′), *v.*, -CATED, -CATING. (Scrambling or mixing up.) The downturned right hand is positioned above the upturned left. The fingers of both are curved. Both hands move in opposite horizontal circles. See also CONFUSE, MIX, MIXED, MIX-UP.

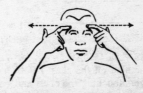

CONCEITED (kən sē´ tĭd), *(colloq.), adj.* (The natural sign.) Both downturned "L" hands are positioned with index fingers at the temples. They move away from the head rather slowly, indicating the size or growth of the head. The head is often moved slightly back and forth as the hands move away. An expression of superiority is assumed.

CONCENTRATE (kŏn´ sən trāt´), *v.,* -TRATED, -TRATING, *n.* (Directing one's attention forward; applying oneself; concentrating.) Both hands, fingers pointing up and together, are held at the sides of the face. They move straight out from the face. See also FOCUS, MIND 2, PAY ATTENTION (TO).

CONCENTRATION (kŏn´ sən tra´ shən), *n.* See CON-CENTRATE.

CONFERENCE (kŏn´ fər əns), *n.* (Assemble all to-gether.) Both "5" hands, palms facing, are held with fingers pointing out from the body. With a sweeping motion they are brought in toward the chest, and all fingertips come together. This is repeated. See also GATHER 2, GATHERING, MEETING.

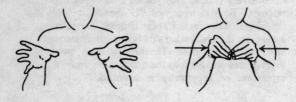

CONFESS (kən fĕs´), *v.,* -FESSED, -FESSING. (Get-ting something off the chest.) Both hands are held with fingers touching the chest and pointing down. They are then swung up and out, ending with both palms facing up before the body.

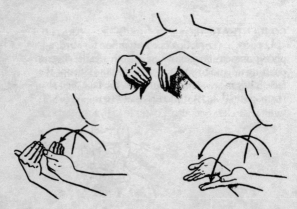

CONFESSION (kən fésh ən), *n.* See CONFESS.

CONFIDENCE (kŏn´ fə dəns), *n.* (Planting a flag-pole, *i.e.,* planting one's trust.) The "S" hands grasp and plant an imaginary flagpole in the ground. This sign may be preceded by BELIEVE, *q.v.*

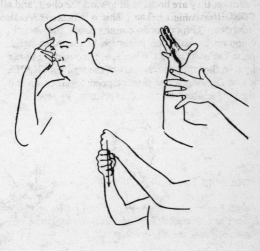

CONFUSE (kən fūz´), *v.,* -FUSED, -FUSING. (Scrambling or mixing up.) The downturned right hand is positioned above the upturned left. The fingers of both are curved. Both hands move in opposite horizontal circles. See also COMPLICATE, MIX, MIXED, MIX-UP.

CONFUSED (kən fūzd´), *adj.* See CONFUSE.

CONFUSION (kən fū´ zhən), *n.* See CONFUSE.

CONGRATULATE 1 (kən grăch´ ə lāt´), *v.*, -LATED, -LATING. (Good words coming from the mouth; clapping hands.) The fingertips of the right hand, palm flat and facing the body, are brought up to the lips, so that they touch (part of the sign for GOOD, *q.v.*). The hands are then clapped together several times. See also APPLAUD, APPLAUSE, PRAISE.

CONGRATULATE 2, *v.* (Shaking the clasped hands in triumph.) The hands are clasped together in front of the face and are shaken vigorously back and forth. The signer smiles.

CONGRATULATIONS 1 (kən grăch′ ə lă′ shənz), *n. pl.* See CONGRATULATE 1.

CONGRATULATIONS 2, *n. pl.* See CONGRATULATE 2.

CONNECT (kə nĕkt′), *v.,* -NECTED, -NECTING. (Joining together.) Both hands, held in the modified "5" position, palms out, move toward each other. The thumbs and index fingers of both hands then connect. See also ATTACH, BELONG, JOIN.

CONSCIENCE (kŏn′ shəns), *n.* (A guilty heart.) The side of the right "G" hand strikes against the heart several times.

CONSENT (kən sĕnt´), *n., v.,* -SENTED, -SENTING. (Agreement; of the same mind; thinking the same way.) The index finger of the right "D" hand, palm back, touches the forehead (the modified sign for THINK), and then the two index fingers, both in the "D" position, palm down, are brought together so they are side by side, pointing away from the body (the sign for SAME).

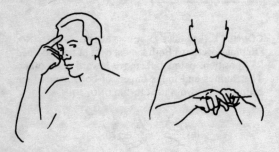

CONSIDER 1 (kən sĭd´ ər), *v.,* -ERED, -ERING. (A thought is turned over in the mind.) The index finger makes a small circle on the forehead. See also SPECU-LATE 1, SPECULATION 1, THINK, THOUGHT, THOUGHTFUL.

CONSIDER 2, *v.* (Turning thoughts over in the mind.) Both index fingers, pointing to the forehead,

describe continuous alternating circles. See also
SPECULATE 2, SPECULATION 2, WONDER.

CONSIDER 3, *v.* (The scales move up and down.)
The two "F" hands, palms facing each other, move
alternately up and down. See also COURT, EVALU-
ATE 1, IF, JUDGE 1, JUDGMENT, JUSTICE.

CONSTRUCT (kən strŭkt´),   *v.*,   -STRUCTED,
-STRUCTING. (Piling bricks one on top of another.)
The downturned hands are placed repeatedly atop
each other. Each time this is done the arms rise a bit,
to indicate the raising of a building. See also BUILD.

CONSTRUCTION (kən strŭk´ shən), *n.* See CON-STRUCT.

CONTACT 1 (kŏn´ tăkt), *n., v.,* -TACTED, -TACTING. (The natural movement of touching.) The tip of the middle finger of the downturned right "5" hand touches the back of the left hand a number of times. See also FEEL 1, TOUCH.

CONTACT 2, *v.* (A pinning down.) The left "D" finger represents the one who is caught. The curved index and middle fingers of the right hand, palm facing down, are thrust against the left "D" finger, impaling it.

CONTENT (kən tĕnt´), *adj.* (The inner feelings settle down.) Both "B" hands (or "5" hands, fingers together) are placed palms down against the chest, the right above the left. Both move down simultaneously a few inches. See also SATISFACTION, SATISFIED, SATISFY 1.

CONTENTED (kən tĕn´ tĭd), *adj.* See CONTENT.

CONTINUE (kən tĭn´ ū), *v.,* -TINUED, -TINUING. (Steady, uninterrupted movement.) The "A" hands are held with palms out, thumbs extended and touching, the right behind the left. In this position the hands move forward in a straight, steady line. See also ENDURE 2, EVER 1, LAST 3, LASTING, PERMANENT, PERSEVERE, PERSIST, REMAIN, STAY 1, STAY STILL.

CONTRAST (*n.* kŏn´ trăst; *v.* kən trăst´), -TRASTED, -TRASTING. (Separateness.) The tips of the extended index fingers touch before the chest, the right finger pointing left and the left finger pointing right. The fingers then draw apart sharply to either side. See also OPPOSITE.

CONTRIBUTE (kən trĭb′ ūt), *v.*, -UTED, -UTING. (A giving of something.) Both "A" hands, with index fingers somewhat draped over the tips of the thumbs, are held palms facing in front of the chest. They are pivoted forward and down, in unison, from the wrists. See also GIFT, PRESENT 2.

CONTROL 1 (kən trōl′), *v.*, -TROLLED, -TROLLING. (Holding the reins over all.) The "A" hands, palms facing, move alternately back and forth, as if grasping and manipulating reins. See also GOVERN, MANAGE, RULE.

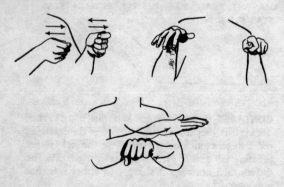

CONTROL 2, *n.*, *v.* (Keeping the feelings down.) The curved fingertips of both hands are placed against the chest. The hands slowly move down as

the fingers close into the "S" position. One hand
only may also be used.

CONVERSATION 1 (kŏn´ vər sā´ shən), *n.* (Movement forward from, and back to, the mouth.) The
tips of both index fingers, held pointing up, move
alternately forward from, and back to, the lips. See
also TALK 3.

CONVERSATION 2, *n.* (Words tossed back and
forth.) The open hands are held side by side with
palms up, fingers pointing forward and slightly
curved. In this position the hands swing back and
forth from side to side before the chest. See also
CHAT.

CONVERSE (kən vûrs′), *v.*, -VERSED, -VERSING. See
CONVERSATION 1.

COOK (kŏŏk), *v.*, COOKED, COOKING. (Turning
over a pancake.) The open right hand rests on the
upturned left palm. The right hand flips over and
comes to rest with its back on the left palm. This is
the action of turning over a pancake.

COOKIE (kŏŏk′ ĭ), *n.* (Act of cutting cookies with a
cookie mold.) The right hand, in the "C" position,
palm down, is placed into the open left palm. It then
rises a bit, swings or twists around a little, and in this
new position is placed again in the open left palm.

COOL (kōōl), *adj., v.,* COOLED, COOLING. (Fanning the face.) Both open hands are held with palms down and fingers spread and pointing toward the face. The hands move up and down as if fanning the face.

COOPERATE (kō ŏp´ ə rāt´), *v.,* -ATED, -ATING. (Joining in movement.) Both "D" hands, thumbs and index fingers interlocked, rotate in a counter-clockwise circle in front of the body.

COP (kŏp), *(colloq.), n.* (The letter "C" for "cop"; the shape and position of the badge.) The right "C" hand, palm facing left, is placed against the heart. See also POLICE.

COPY (kŏp´ ĭ), *n., v.,* COPIED, COPYING. (The natural sign.) The right fingers and thumb close together and move onto the upturned, open left hand, as if taking something from one place to another.

CORRECT 1 (kə rĕkt´), *adj.* The right index finger, held above the left index finger, comes down rather forcefully so that the bottom of the right hand comes to rest on top of the left thumb joint. See also PROPER, RIGHT 3.

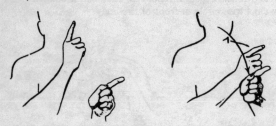

CORRECT 2, *v.,* -RECTED, -RECTING. (A canceling out.) The right index finger makes a cross on the open left palm. See also CANCEL.

COST (kôst, kŏst), *n., v.,* COST, COSTING. (Nicking into one.) The knuckle of the right "X" finger is nicked against the palm of the left hand, held in the "5" position, palm facing right. See also EXPENSE, FINE 2, PENALTY, PRICE, TAX, TAXATION.

COUNT (kount), *v.,* COUNTED, COUNTING. The thumbtip and index fingertip of the right "F" hand move up along the palm of the open left hand, which is held facing right with fingers pointing up.

COUNTRY 1 (kun´trĭ), *n.* (The elbow reinforcement on the jacket of a "country squire" type; also, a place where one commonly "roughs it," *i.e.,* gets rough elbows.) The open right hand describes a continuous counterclockwise circle on the left elbow.

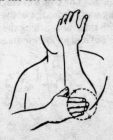

COUNTRY 2, *n*. (An established area.) The right "N" hand, palm down, executes a clockwise circle above the downturned prone left hand. The tips of the "N" fingers then move straight down and come to rest on the back of the left hand. See also LAND 2, NATION.

COURT (kōrt), *n*. (The scales move up and down.) The two "F" hands, palms facing each other, move alternately up and down. See also CONSIDER 3, EVALUATE 1, IF, JUDGE 1, JUDGMENT, JUSTICE.

COW (kou), *n*. (The cow's horns.) The "Y" hands, palms facing away from the body, are placed at the temples, with thumbs touching the head. Both hands are brought out and away simultaneously, in a gentle curve.

CRASH (krăsh), *n., v.,* CRASHED, CRASHING. The fists come together with force. See also COLLIDE, COLLISION.

CRAZY 1 (krā´ zĭ), *adj.* (Turning of wheels in the head.) The open right hand is held palm down before the face, fingers spread, bent, and pointing toward the forehead. The fingers move in circles before the forehead. See also INSANE, INSANITY.

CRAZY 2, *adj.* (Turning of wheels in the head.) The right index finger revolves in a clockwise circle at the right temple.

CREATE (krē āt´), *v.*, CREATED, CREATING. (Fashioning something with the hands.) The right "S" hand, palm facing left, is placed on top of its left counterpart, whose palm faces right. The hands are twisted back and forth, striking each other slightly after each twist. See also MAKE, MEND, PRODUCE.

CROOK (kro͝ok), *n.* (A mustachioed thief.) The fingertips of both "H" hands, palms facing the body, are placed above the lips and are drawn slowly apart, describing a mustache. Sometimes one hand only is used. This is followed by the sign for INDIVIDUAL: Both open hands, palms facing each other, move down the sides of the body, tracing its outline to the hips. See also ROB 3, THEFT 2.

CROSS (krôs), *v.*, CROSSED, CROSSING. (A crossing over.) The left hand is held before the chest, palm down and fingers together. The right hand, fingers together, glides over the left, with the right little finger touching the top of the left hand. See also ACROSS, OVER.

CRUEL (kr$\overline{oo}$´ əl), *adj.* (Striking down against.) Both "A" or "X" hands are held before the chest, the right above the left. The right hand strikes down and out, hitting the left thumb and knuckles with force. See also MEAN 1.

CRY (krī), *v.,* CRIED, CRYING. (Tears streaming down the cheeks.) Both index fingers, in the "D" position, move down the cheeks, either once or several times. Sometimes one finger only is used.

CURIOSITY (kyŏŏr′ ĭ ŏs′ ə tĭ), *n.* See CURIOUS 2.

CURIOUS 1 (kyŏŏr′ ĭ əs), *adj.* (Something which distorts the vision.) The "C" hand describes a small arc in front of the face. See also ODD, STRANGE, WEIRD.

CURIOUS 2, *(colloq.), adj.* (The Adam's apple.) The right thumb and index finger pinch the skin over the Adam's apple, while the hand wiggles up and down.

CURSE 1 (kûrs), *n., v.,* CURSED, CURSING. (Harsh words and a threatening hand.) The right hand appears to claw words out of the mouth. It ends in the

"S" position, above the head, shaking back and forth in a threatening manner. See also SWEAR 2.

CURSE 2, *n., v.* (Harsh words thrown out.) The right hand, as in CURSE 1, appears to claw words out of the mouth. This time, however, it turns and throws them out, ending in the "5" position. See also SCREAM, SHOUT.

CUSTOM (kŭs′ təm), *n.* (Bound down to custom or habit.) Both "S" hands, palms down, are crossed and brought down in unison before the chest. See also HABIT.

CUTE 1 (kūt), *adj.* (Titillating to the taste.) The fingertips of the right "U" hand, palm facing the body, brush against the chin a number of times, beginning at the lips. See also SUGAR, SWEET.

CUTE 2, *adj.* (Tickling.) The open right hand is held with fingers spread and pointing up, palm facing the chest. In this position the fingertips wiggle up and down, tickling the chin several times.

D

DAILY (dā′ lĭ), *adj.* (Tomorrow after tomorrow.)
The sign for TOMORROW, *q.v.*, is made several
times: The right "A" hand moves forward several
times from its initial resting place on the right cheek.
See also EVERYDAY.

DANCE (dăns, däns), *n, v.,* DANCED, DANCING.
(The rhythmic swaying of the feet.) The downturned
index and middle fingers of the right "V" hand
swing rhythmically back and forth over the upturned left palm. See also PARTY 2.

DANGER (dān′ jər), *n.* (An encroachment; parrying
a knife thrust.) The left "A" hand is held palm toward the body, knuckles facing right. The extended
thumb of the right "A" hand is brought sharply over
the back of the left.

DANGEROUS *adj.* See DANGER.

DAUGHTER (dô′ tər), *n.* (Female baby.) The FE-MALE prefix sign is made: The thumb of the right "A" hand traces a line on the right jaw from just below the ear to the chin. The sign for BABY is then made: The right arm is folded on the left arm. Both palms face up.

DAY (dā), *n., adj.* (The letter "D"; the course of the sun across the sky.) The left arm, held horizontally, palm down, represents the horizon. The right elbow rests on the back of the left hand, with the right arm in a perpendicular position. The right "D" hand, palm facing left, moves in an arc to the left until it is just above the left elbow.

DEAD (dĕd), *adj.* (Turning over on one's side.) The open hands, fingers pointing ahead, are held side by side, with the right palm down and the left palm up. The two hands reverse their relative positions as they move from the left to the right. See also DIE.

DEAF 1 (dĕf), *adj.* (Deaf and mute.) The tip of the extended right index finger touches first the right ear and then the closed lips.

DEAF 2 (dĕf), *adj.* (The ear is shut.) The right index finger touches the right ear. Both "B" hands, palms out, then draw together until their index finger edges touch.

DEATH (dĕth), *n.* See DEAD.

DECIDE (dĭ sīd′), *v.*, -CIDED, -CIDING. (The mind stops wavering, and the pros and cons are resolved.) The right index finger touches the forehead, the sign for THINK, *q.v.* Both "F" hands, palms facing each other and fingers pointing straight out, then drop down simultaneously. The sign for JUDGE, *q.v.*, explains the rationale behind the movement of the two hands here.

DECISION (dĭ sĭzh′ ən), *n.* See DECIDE.

DECLINE (dĭ klīn′), *v.*, -CLINED, -CLINING. (Going down step by step.) The little finger edge of the open right hand is placed on the upper side of the extended left arm, which is held with the open left hand palm down. The right hand moves down along the left arm in a series of short movements. This is the opposite of IMPROVE, *q.v.*

DECREASE (*n.* dē′ krēs; *v.* dǐ krēs′), -CREASED, -CREASING. (The diminishing size or amount.) With palms facing, the right hand is held above the left. The right hand moves slowly down toward the left, but does not touch it. See also LESS, REDUCE.

DEDUCT (dǐ dŭkt′), *v.*, -DUCTED, -DUCTING. (Removing.) The right "A" hand, resting in the palm of the left "5" hand, moves slightly up and away, describing a small arc. It is then cast downward, opening into the "5" position, palm down, as if removing something from the left hand and casting it down. See also REMOVE.

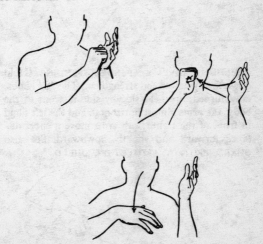

DEFEAT (dĭ fēt′), v., -FEATED, -FEATING. (Forcing the head into a bowed position.) The right "S" hand, placed across the left "S" hand, moves over and down a bit. See also BEAT 2, OVERCOME.

DEFEATED, adj. (Overpowered by great strength.) The right "S" hand (a fist) is held with palm facing the right shoulder. In this position it moves back toward the shoulder, pivoting from the elbow. The left "S" hand, at the same time, is held palm down with knuckles facing right, and is positioned below the right hand and over the right biceps.

DEFEND (dĭ fĕnd′), v., -FENDED, -FENDING. (Hold down firmly; cover and strengthen.) The "S" hands, downturned, are held side by side in front of the body, the arms almost horizontal, and the left hand in front of the right. Both arms move a short distance forward and slightly downward. See also GUARD, PROTECT, PROTECTION, SHIELD.

DEFENSE (dĭ fĕns′), *n.* See DEFEND.

DEFINE 1 (dĭ fīn′), *v.,* -FINED, -FINING. (Unraveling something to get at its parts.) The "F" hands, palms facing and fingers pointing straight out, are held about an inch apart. They move alternately back and forth a few inches. See also DESCRIBE, DESCRIPTION, EXPLAIN.

DEFINE 2, *v.* This is the same sign as for DEFINE 1, except that the "D" hands are used.

DELAY (dĭ lā′), *n., v.,* -LAYED, -LAYING. (Putting off; moving things forward repeatedly.) The "F" hands, palms facing and fingers pointing out from the body, are moved forward simultaneously in a series of short movements. See also POSTPONE, PROCRASTINATE, PUT OFF.

DELICIOUS (dĭ lĭsh′ əs), *adj.* (Smooth to the taste.) The right middle finger is placed on the lips, and then the hand moves down and out a bit. As it does, the thumb rubs over the middle finger. Both hands may be used.

DELIVER (dĭ lĭv′ ər), *v.*, -ERED, -ERING. (Carrying something over.) Both open hands, palms up, move in an arc from left to right, as if carrying something from one point to another. See also BRING, CARRY 2.

DEMAND (dĭ mănd′, -mänd´), *v.*, -MANDED, -MANDING. (Something specific is moved in toward oneself.) The palm of the left "5" hand faces right.

The right index finger is thrust into the left palm, and both hands are drawn sharply in toward the chest. See also REQUIRE.

DEMONSTRATE (dĕm′ ən strāt′), *v.*, -STRATED, -STRATING. (Directing the attention to something, and bringing it forward.) The right index finger points into the left palm, held facing out before the body. The left palm moves straight out. For the passive form of this verb, *i.e.,* BE SHOWN or DEMONSTRATED, the movement is reversed: The left hand, palm facing in, is moved in toward the body, while the right index finger remains pointing into the left palm. See also DISPLAY, EXAMPLE, EXHIBIT, EXHIBITION, REPRESENT, SHOW.

DENY 1 (dǐ nī'), *v.*, -NIED, -NYING. (An emphatic NOT 2, *q.v.*) The thumbs of both "A" hands, positioned under the chin, move out simultaneously, each toward their respective sides of the body. The head may be shaken slightly as the hands move out.

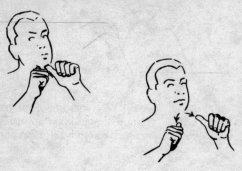

DENY 2, *v.* (Turning down.) The right "A" hand swings down sharply, its thumb pointing down. Both hands are sometimes used here.

DEPART (dǐ part'), *v.*, -PARTED, -PARTING. (Pulling away.) The downturned open hands are held in a line, with fingers pointing to the left, the right hand behind the left. Both hands move in unison toward the right. As they do so, they assume the "A" position. See also LEAVE, WITHDRAW 1.

DEPEND (dǐ pĕnd'), v., -PENDED, -PENDING. (Hanging onto.) With the right index finger resting across its left counterpart, both hands drop down a bit. See also RELY.

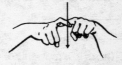

DEPENDABLE (dǐ pĕn' də bəl), adj. See DEPEND.

DEPTH (dĕpth), n. (The "D" hand, movement downward.) The right "D" hand is held with index finger pointing down. In this position it moves down along the left palm, which is held facing right with fingertips pointing forward.

DESCRIBE (dĭ skrīb'), *v.,* -SCRIBED, -SCRIBING. (Unraveling something to get at its parts.) The "F" hands, palms facing and fingers pointing straight out, are held about an inch apart. They move alternately back and forth a few inches. See also DEFINE 1, EXPLAIN.

DESCRIPTION (dĭ skrĭp' shən), *n.* See DESCRIBE.

DESIRE (dĭ zīr'), *n., v.,* -SIRED, -SIRING. (Grasping something and pulling it in.) The upturned "5" hands, held side by side before the chest, close slightly into a grasping position as they move in toward the body. See also NEED 2, WANT, WISH 1.

DESTROY (dĭ stroi'), *v.,* -STROYED, -STROYING. (Wiping off.) The left "5" hand, palm up, is held slightly above the right "5" hand, held palm down.

The right hand swings up, just brushing over the left palm. Both hands close into the "S" position, and the right is brought back with force to its initial position, striking a glancing blow against the left knuckles as it returns. See also RUIN.

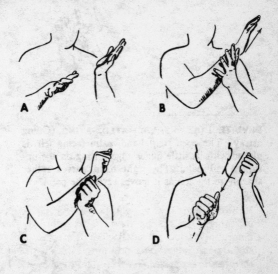

DETACH (dĭ tăch′), *v.*, -TACHED, -TACHING. (An unlocking.) With thumbs and index fingers interlocked initially (the links of a chain), the hands draw apart, showing the break in the chain. See also DIS-CONNECT.

DEVELOP (dǐ věl′ əp), *v.*, -OPED, -OPING. (The letter "D"; moving upward, as if in growth.) The right "D" hand is placed against the left palm, which is facing right with fingers pointing up. The "D" hand moves straight up to the left fingertips.

DEVIATE 1 (dē′ vǐ āt′), *v.*, -ATED, -ATING. (Going astray.) The open right hand, palm facing left, is placed with its little finger edge resting on the up-turned left palm. The right hand curves rather sharply to the left as it moves across the palm.

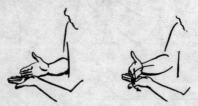

DEVIATE 2, *v.* (The natural motion.) The "G" hands are held side by side and touching, palms down, index fingers pointing forward. Then the right hand moves forward, curving toward the right side as it does.

DEVIATION (dē´ vĭ ā´ shən), *n.* See DEVIATE 1 and 2.

DIE (dī), *v.,* DIED, DYING. (Turning over on one's side.) The open hands, fingers pointing ahead, are held side by side, with the right palm down and the left palm up. The two hands reverse their relative positions as they move from the left to the right. See also DEAD, DEATH.

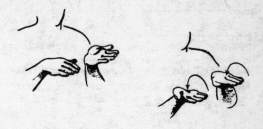

DIFFER (dĭf´ ər), *v.,* -FERED, -FERING. (To think in opposite terms.) The sign for THINK is made: The right index finger touches the forehead. The sign for OPPOSITE is then made: The "D" hands, palms facing the body and index fingers touching, draw apart sharply. See also DISAGREE.

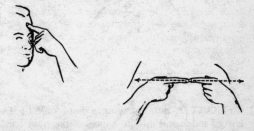

DIFFERENCE (dĭf' ər əns, dĭf' rəns,), *n.* (Separated many times; different.) The "D" hands, palms down, are crossed at the index fingers or are held side by side. They separate and return to their initial position a number of times. See also DIVERSE 1, DIVERSITY 1, VARIED.

DIFFERENT (dĭf' ər ənt, dĭf' rənt), *adj.* See DIFFERENCE.

DIFFICULT 1 (dĭf' ə kŭlt´), *adj.* (The knuckles are rubbed, to indicate a condition of being worn down.) The knuckles of the curved index and middle fingers of both hands are rubbed up and down against each other. Instead of the up-down rubbing, they may rub against each other in an alternate clockwise-counterclockwise manner. See also HARD 1, HARDSHIP, POVERTY, PROBLEM 2.

DIFFICULT 2, *adj.* (Striking a hard object.) The curved index and middle fingers of the right hand, whose palm faces the body or the left, are brought down sharply against the back of the downturned left "S" hand. See also HARD 2.

DIFFICULTY (dĭf′ ə kŭl′ tĭ, -kəl tĭ), *n*. See DIF-FICULT 1.

DIRT (dûrt), *n*. (Fingering the soil.) Both hands, held upright before the body, finger imaginary pinches of soil. See also GROUND.

DIRTY (dûr′ tĭ), *adj*. (A modification of the pig's snout groveling in a trough.) The downturned right hand is placed under the chin. Its fingers, pointing left, wiggle repeatedly. See also FILTHY.

DISAGREE (dĭs′ ə grē′), v., -GREED, -GREEING. (To think in opposite terms.) The sign for THINK is made: The right index finger touches the forehead. The sign for OPPOSITE is then made: The "D" hands, palms facing the body and index fingers touching, draw apart sharply. See also DIFFER.

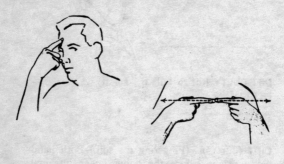

DISAPPEAR (dĭs′ ə pir′). v., -PEARED, -PEARING. (A disappearance.) The right open hand, palm facing the body, is held by the left hand and is drawn down and out, ending in a position with fingers drawn together. The left hand, meanwhile, may close into a position with fingers also drawn together. See also GONE 1.

DISAPPOINT (dĭs´ ə point´), *v.*, -POINTED, -POINT-
ING. (The feelings sink.) The middle fingers of both
"5" hands, one above the other, rest on the heart.
They both move down a few inches.

DISAPPOINTED *adj.* (Something sour or bitter.)
The right index finger is brought sharply up against
the lips, while the mouth is puckered up as if tasting
something sour. See also BITTER.

DISAPPOINTMENT (dĭs´ ə point´ mənt), *n.* See
DISAPPOINTED.

DISBELIEF (dĭs bĭ lēf'), *n.* (The nose is wrinkled in disbelief.) The right "V" hand faces the nose. The index and middle fingers bend as a cynical expression is assumed. See also DON'T BELIEVE, DOUBT 1.

DISCONNECT (dĭs' kə nĕkt'), *v.,* -NECTED, -NECT-ING. (An unlocking.) With thumbs and index fingers interlocked initially (the links of a chain), the hands draw apart, showing the break in the chain. See also DETACH.

DISCUSS (dĭs kŭs'), *v.,* -CUSSED, -CUSSING. (Expounding one's points.) The right "D" hand is held with the palm facing the body. It moves down repeatedly so that the side of the index finger strikes the upturned left palm.

DISCUSSION (dĭs kŭsh′ ən), *n.* See DISCUSS.

DISOBEDIENCE (dĭs′ ə bē′ dĭ əns), *n.* See DISOBEY.

DISOBEY (dĭs′ ə bā′), *v.*, -BEYED, -BEYING. (Turning the head.) The right "S" hand, held up with its palm facing the body, swings sharply around to the palm-out position. The head meanwhile moves slightly toward the left.

DISPLAY (dĭs plā′), *v.*, -PLAYED, -PLAYING. (Directing the attention to something, and bringing it forward.) The right index finger points into the left palm, held facing out before the body. The left palm moves straight out. For the passive form of this verb, *i.e.,* BE SHOWN or DISPLAYED, the movement is reversed: The left hand, palm facing in, is moved in toward the body, while the right index finger remains pointing into the left palm. See also DEMONSTRATE, EVIDENCE, EXAMPLE, EXHIBIT, EXHIBITION, REPRESENT, SHOW.

DISREGARD (dĭs´ rĭ gärd´), v., -GARDED, -GARD-
ING. (Thumbing the nose.) The index finger of the
right "B" hand is placed under the tip of the nose.
From this position the right hand moves straight
forward, away from the face. See also IGNORE.

DISSATISFACTION (dĭs´ săt ĭs făk´ shən), n. (NOT,
SATISFIED.) The sign for NOT 1 is made: The
crossed downturned open hands draw apart. The
sign for SATISFIED then follows: The downturned
"B" hands, the right above the left, are positioned on
the chest. They move straight down simultaneously.

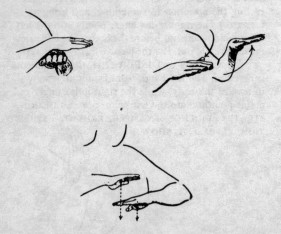

DISSATISFIED (dĭs săt′ ĭs fĭd′), *adj.* See DISSATIS-
FACTION.

DISSOLVE (dĭ zŏlv′), *v.*, -SOLVED, -SOLVING. (Fingering the small pieces resulting from the breaking
up of something.) The thumbs rub slowly across the
fingertips of the upturned hands, from the little fingers to the index fingers, and then continue to the
"A" position, palms up. See also MELT.

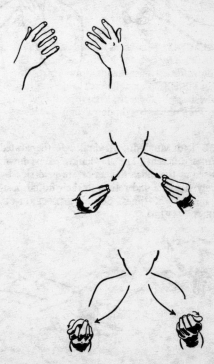

DISTURB (dĭs tûrb′), *v.*, -TURBED, -TURBING. (Obstruct, bother.) The left hand, fingers together and palm flat, is held before the body, facing somewhat down. The little finger side of the right hand, held with palm flat, makes one or several up-down chopping motions against the left hand, between its thumb and index finger. See also ANNOY, ANNOYANCE, BOTHER, INTERFERE, INTERFERENCE, INTERFERE WITH, INTERRUPT, PREVENT, PREVENTION.

DIVERSE 1 (dĭ vûrs′, dī-, dī′ vûrs), *adj.* (Separated many times; different.) The "D" hands, palms down, are crossed at the index fingers or are held side by side. They separate and return to their initial position a number of times. See also DIFFERENCE, DIFFERENT, VARIED.

DIVERSE 2, *adj.* (The fingertips indicate many things.) Both hands, in the "D" position, palms out and index fingertips touching, are drawn apart. As they move apart, the index fingers wiggle up and down. See also VARIOUS, VARY.

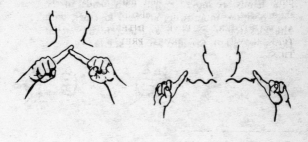

DIVERSITY 1 (dĭ vûr′ sə tĭ, dī-), *n.* See DIVERSE 1.

DIVERSITY 2, *n.* See DIVERSE 2.

DIVIDE (dĭ vīd′), *v.*, -VIDED, -VIDING. (A splitting apart or dividing.) The two hands are crossed, with the right little finger resting on the left index finger. Both hands are dropped down and separated simultaneously, so that the palms face down.

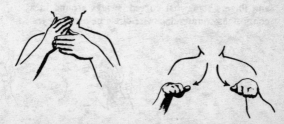

DIVISION (dǐ vǐzh′ ən), *n.* See DIVIDE.

DIVORCE 1 (dǐ vōrs′), *n., v.,* -VORCED, -VORCING. (The hands are moved apart.) Both hands, in the "A" position, thumbs up, are held together, with knuckles touching. With a deliberate movement they come apart. See also APART, SEPARATE 1.

DIVORCE 2, *n., v.* (The letter "D"; a separating.) The "D" hands, palms facing and fingertips touching, draw apart.

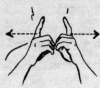

DIZZY (dǐz′ ǐ), *adj.* (Images swinging around before the eyes.) The right "5" hand, palm facing the body and fingers somewhat curved, swings around in a continuous counterclockwise circle before the eyes.

DO (dōō), *v.*, DOES, DID, DONE, DOING. (An activity.) Both open hands, palms down, are swung right and left before the chest. See also PERFORM 1, PERFORMANCE 1.

DOCTOR (dŏk′ tər), *n.* (The letter "M," from "M.D."; feeling the pulse.) The fingertips of the right "M" hand lightly tap the left pulse a number of times. The right "D" hand may also be used, in which case the thumb and fingertips tap the left pulse.

DOG (dôg), *n.* (Patting the knee and snapping the fingers to beckon the dog.) The right hand pats the right knee, and then the fingers are snapped.

DOLLAR(S) (dŏl' ər), *n.* (The natural sign; drawing a bill from a billfold.) The right thumb and index finger trace the outlines of a bill on the upturned left palm. Or, the right thumb and fingers may grasp the base of the open left hand, which is held palm facing right and fingers pointing forward; the right hand, in this position, then slides forward along and off the left hand, as if drawing bills from a billfold.

DONE (dŭn), *v.* (Shaking the hands to rid them of something.) The upright "5" hands, palms facing each other, are suddenly and quickly swung around to a palm-out position. See also END 3, FINISH.

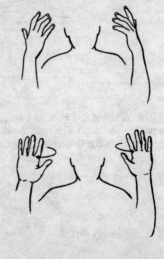

DO NOT 1, *v. phrase.* (The natural sign.) The crossed "5" hands, palms facing out (or down), separate and recross quickly and repeatedly. The head is usually shaken simultaneously. This sign is from NOT 1, *q.v.*

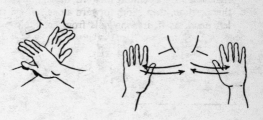

DO NOT 2, *v. phrase.* The thumb of the right "A" hand is placed under the chin. From this position it is flicked outward in an arc. This sign is a variant of DO NOT 1.

DON'T 1 (dōnt) *v.* See DO NOT 1.

DON'T 2, *v.* See DO NOT 2.

DON'T BELIEVE, *v. phrase.* (The nose is wrinkled in disbelief.) The right "V" hand faces the nose. The index and middle fingers bend as a cynical expression is assumed. See also DISBELIEF 1, DOUBT 1.

DON'T CARE 1, *(colloq.),* *v. phrase,* (Wiping the nose, *i.e.,* "Keeping the nose clean" or not becoming involved.) The downturned right "D" hand, index finger touching the nose, is suddenly flung down and to the right.

DON'T CARE 2, *(colloq.),* *v. phrase.* The thumb of the right "Y" hand touches the right ear. The right "Y" hand is then flung down and to the right.

DON'T CARE FOR *(colloq.), v. phrase.* See DON'T CARE 2.

_____

DON'T KNOW, *v. phrase.* (Knowledge is lacking.) The sign for KNOW is made: The right fingertips tap the forehead several times. The right hand is then flung over to the right, ending in the "5" position, palm out.

_____

DON'T LIKE *(colloq.), v. phrase.* See DON'T CARE 3.

_____

DON'T WANT, *v. phrase.* (The hands are shaken, indicating a wish to rid them of something.) The "5" hands, palms facing the body, suddenly swing around to the palms-down position.

DOOR (dōr), *n.* (The opening and closing of the door.) The "B" hands, palms out and edges touching, are drawn apart and then come together again. See also OPEN THE DOOR.

DOORWAY (dōr′ wā´), *n.* See DOOR.

DOUBT 1 (dout), *n., v.,* DOUBTED, DOUBTING. (The nose is wrinkled in disbelief.) The right "V" hand faces the nose. The index and middle fingers bend as a cynical expression is assumed. See also DISBELIEF 1, DON'T BELIEVE.

DOUBT 2, *n., v.* (The wavering.) The downturned "S" hands swing alternately up and down.

DOUBTFUL (dout' fəl), *adj.* See DOUBT 2.

DOWN (doun), *prep.* (The natural sign.) The right hand, pointing down, moves down an inch or two.

DREAM (drēm), *n., v.,* DREAMED, DREAMT, DREAMING. (A thought wanders off into space.) The right curved index finger opens and closes quickly as it leaves its initial position on the forehead and moves up into the air.

DRESS (drĕs), *n., v.,* DRESSED, DRESSING. (Draping the clothes on the body.) With fingertips resting on the chest, both hands move down simultaneously. The action is repeated. See also CLOTHES, CLOTHING, GOWN, SHIRT, WEAR.

DRINK (drĭngk), *n., v.,* DRANK, DRUNK, DRINK-ING. (The natural sign.) An imaginary glass is tipped at the open lips.

DRIVE (drīv), *v.,* DROVE, DRIVEN, DRIVING, *n.* (The steering wheel.) The hands grasp an imaginary steering wheel and manipulate it. See also AUTOMO-BILE, CAR.

DRUNK (drŭngk), *adj.* (The act of drinking.) The thumbtip of the right "Y" hand is tilted toward the mouth, as if it were a drinking glass or bottle. The signer tilts his head back slightly, as if drinking. See also INTOXICATE, INTOXICATION, LIQUOR.

DRUNKARD (drŭngk' ərd), *n.* See DRUNK.

DRUNKENNESS (drŭngk′ ən nĭs), *n.* See DRUNK.

DRY (drī), *adj., v.,* DRIED, DRYING. (A dryness, indicated by a wiping of the lips.) The "X" finger is drawn across the lips, from left to right, as if wiping them. See also BORE.

DUE (dū, dōō), *adj.* (Pointing to the palm, where the money should be placed.) The index finger of one hand is thrust into the upturned palm of the other several times. See also OWE.

DURING (dyŏŏr′ ĭng, dŏŏr′-), *prep.* (Parallel time.) Both "D" hands, palms down, move forward in unison, away from the body. They may move straight forward or may follow a slight upward arc. See also MEANTIME, WHILE.

E

EACH (ēch), *adj.* (Peeling off, one by one.) The left "A" hand is held palm facing the right. The knuckles of the right "A" hand are drawn repeatedly down the left thumb, from its tip to its base. See also EVERY.

EACH OTHER, *pron. phrase.* (Mingling with.) Both hands are held in modified "A" positions, thumbs out. The left hand is positioned with its thumb pointing straight up, and the right hand, with its thumb pointing down, revolves above the left thumb in a counterclockwise direction. See also MINGLE, ONE ANOTHER.

EAGER (ē′ gər), *adj.* (Rubbing the hands together in zeal or ambition.) The open hands are rubbed vigorously back and forth against each other. See also AMBITIOUS, ENTHUSIASM, ENTHUSIASTIC.

EAGERNESS, *n.* See EAGER.

EAR (ĭr), *n.* (The natural sign.) The right index finger touches the right ear.

EARTH (ûrth), *n.* (The earth and its axes are indicated.) The downturned left "S" hand indicates the earth. The thumb and index finger of the downturned right "5" hand are placed at each edge of the left. In this position the right hand swings back and forth, while maintaining contact with the left.

EASY 1 (ē′ zǐ), *adj.* (The fingertips are easily moved.) The right fingertips brush repeatedly over their upturned left counterparts, causing them to move. See also SIMPLE.

EASY 2, *(loc., colloq.), adj.* (Rationale obscure.) The thumb and index finger of the right "F" hand are placed on the chin.

EAT (ēt), *v.*, ATE, EATEN, EATING. (The natural sign.) The closed right hand goes through the natural motion of placing food in the mouth. This movement is repeated. See also FEED 1, FOOD 1, MEAL.

EDUCATE (ĕj' ŏo kāt´), *v.*, -CATED, -CATING. (Giving forth from the mind.) The fingertips of each hand are placed on the temples. They then swing out and open into the "5" position. See also CONSTRUCT, TEACH.

EFFORT 1 (ĕf' ərt), *n.* (Trying to push through.)
The "A" hands, palms facing before the body, are
swung around and a bit down, so that the palms now
face out. The movement indicates an attempt to
push through a barrier. See also ATTEMPT 1, TRY 1.

EFFORT 2, *n.* (Trying to push through, using the
"T" hands, for "try.") This is the same sign as EF-
FORT 1, except that the "T" hands are employed.
See also ATTEMPT 2, TRY 2.

EFFORT 3, *n.* (The letter "E"; attempting to break
through.) Both "E" hands move forward simultaneously, describing a small, downturned arc.

EGG (ĕg), *n.* (Act of breaking an egg into a bowl.) The right "H" hand is brought down on the left "H" hand, and then both hands are pivoted down and slightly apart.

EITHER 1 (ē′ thər *or. esp. Brit.,* ī′ thər), *conj.* (Selection between two or among multiple choices.) The left "L" hand is held palm facing the body and thumb pointing straight up. The right index finger touches the left thumbtip and then the left index fingertip.

EITHER 2, *adj.* (Making a choice.) The left "V" hand faces the body. The right thumb and index finger close first over the left index fingertip and then over the left middle fingertip. See also CHOICE.

EITHER 3, *conj.* (Considering one thing against another.) The "A" hands, palms facing and thumbs pointing straight up, move alternately up and down before the chest. See also OR, WHETHER, WHICH.

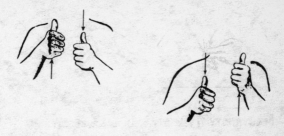

ELECT (ĭ lĕkt′), *n., v.,* -LECTED, -LECTING (Placing a ballot in a box.) The right hand, holding an imaginary ballot between the thumb and index finger, places it into an imaginary box formed by the left "O" hand, palm facing right. See also VOTE.

ELECTION (ĭ lĕk′ shən), *n.* See ELECT.

ELECTRIC (ĭ lĕk′ trĭk), *adj.* (The points of the electrodes.) The "X" hands are held palms facing the body, thumb edges up. The knuckles of the index fingers touch each other repeatedly.

ELECTRICITY (ĭ lĕk′ trĭs′ ə tĭ), *n.* See ELECTRIC.

ELEGANT (el′ ə gənt), *adj.* (The feelings are titillated.) With the thumb resting on the upper part of the chest, the fingers are wiggled back and forth. See also FINE 1, WONDERFUL 2.

ELEVATOR (ĕl′ ə vā′ tər), *n.* (The letter "E"; the rising.) The right "E" hand, palm facing left and thumb edge up, rises straight up.

ELIMINATE (ĭ lĭm ə nāt′), *v.*, -NATED, -NATING.
(Scratching something out and throwing it away.)
The fingertips of the open right hand scratch downward across the palm of the upright left hand. In one
continuous motion, the right hand then closes as if
holding something, and finally opens again forcefully and motions as if throwing something away.

EMBARRASS (ĕm băr′ əs), *v.*, -RASSED, -RASSING.
(The red rises in the cheeks.) The sign for RED is
made: The tip of the right index finger of the "D"
hand moves down over the lips, which are red. Both
hands are then placed palms facing the cheeks, and
move up along the face, to indicate the rise of color.
See also BLUSH.

EMBARRASSED *adj.*, See EMBARRASS.

EMOTION 1 (ĭ mō′ shən), *n.* (The welling up of feelings or emotions in the heart.) The right middle finger, touching the heart, moves up an inch or two a number of times. See also FEEL 2, FEELING.

EMOTION 2, *n.* (The letter "E"; that which moves about in the chest, *i.e.* the heart.) The "E" hands, palms facing in, are positioned close to the chest. Both hands describe alternate circles, the left hand clockwise and the right hand counterclockwise. The right hand alone may be used.

EMPHASIS (ĕm′ fə sĭs), *n.* (Pressing down to emphasize.) The right thumb is pressed down deliberately against the upturned left palm. Both hands move forward a bit.

EMPHASIZE (ĕm′ fə sīz′), *v.*, -SIZED, -SIZING. See
EMPHASIS.

EMPHATIC (ĕm făt′ ĭk), *adj.* See EMPHASIS.

ENCOURAGE (ĕn kûr′ ĭj), *v.*, -AGED, -AGING.
(Pushing forward.) Both "5" hands are held, palms
out, the right fingers facing right and the left fingers
left. The hands move straight forward in a series of
short movements. See also MOTIVATE, MOTIVA-
TION, URGE 1.

END 1 (ĕnd), *n., v.*, ENDED, ENDING. (The little,
i.e., LAST, fingers are indicated.) With the hands in
the "I" position, the tip of the right little finger
strikes the tip of its left counterpart. The right index
finger may be used instead of the right little finger.
See also FINAL 1, FINALLY 1, LAST 1.

END 2, *n., v.,* (A single little, *i.e.,* LAST, finger is indicated.) The tip of the index finger of the right "D" hand strikes the tip of the little finger of the left "I" hand. See also FINAL 2, FINALLY 2, LAST 2.

END 3, *n., v.* (Shaking the hands to rid them of something.) The upright "5" hands, palms facing each other, are suddenly and quickly swung around to a palm-out position. See also DONE, FINISH.

ENDORSE 1 (ĕn dôrs′), *v.,* -DORSED, -DORSING. (Holding up.) The right "S" hand pushes up the left "S" hand. See also SUPPORT, SUSTAIN, SUSTE-NANCE.

ENDORSE 2, *v.* (One hand upholds the other.) Both hands, in the "S" position, are held palms facing the body, the right under the left. The right hand pushes up the left in a gesture of support.

ENDURE 1 (ĕn dyŏŏr', -dŏŏr'), *v.,* -DURED, -DUR-ING. (A clenching of the fists; the rise and fall of pain.) Both "S" hands, tightly clenched, revolve about each other, slowly and deliberately, while a pained expression is worn. See also SUFFER.

ENDURE 2, *v.* (Steady, uninterrupted movement.) The "A" hands are held with palms out, thumbs extended and touching, the right behind the left. In this position the hands move forward in a straight, steady line. See also CONTINUE, EVER 1, LAST 3, LASTING, PERMANENT, PERSEVERE, PERSIST, RE-MAIN, STAY 1, STAY STILL.

ENEMY (ĕn' ə mĭ), *n.* (At sword's point.) The two index fingers, after pointing to each other, are drawn sharply apart. This is followed by the sign for INDIVIDUAL: Both open hands, palms facing each other, move down the sides of the body, tracing its outline to the hips. See also OPPONENT.

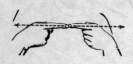

ENGAGED (ĕn gājd'), *adj.* (The letter "E"; the ring finger.) The right "E" hand moves in a clockwise circle over the downturned left hand, and then comes to rest on the left ring finger.

ENGINE (ĕn' jən), *n.* (The meshing gears.) With the knuckles of both hands interlocked, the hands pivot up and down, imitating the meshing of gear teeth. See also MACHINE, MOTOR.

ENJOY (ĕn joi′), *v.*, -JOYED, -JOYING. (A pleasurable feeling on the heart.) The open right hand is circled on the chest, over the heart. See also LIKE 3, PLEASE, PLEASURE.

ENJOYMENT (ĕn joi′ mənt), *n.* See ENJOY.

ENOUGH (ĭ nŭf′), *adj.* (A full cup.) The left hand, in the "S" position, is held palm facing right. The right "5" hand, palm down, is brushed outward several times over the top of the left, indicating a wiping off of the top of a cup. See also PLENTY.

ENTER (ĕn′ tər), *v.*, -TERED, -TERING. (Going in.) The downturned open right hand sweeps under its downturned left counterpart.

ENTHUSIASM (ĕn thōō′ zĭ ăz′ əm), *n.* (Rubbing the hands together in zeal or ambition.) The open hands are rubbed vigorously back and forth against each other. See also AMBITIOUS, EAGER, EAGERNESS.

ENTHUSIASTIC (ĕn thōō′ zĭ ăs′ tĭk), *adj.* See ENTHUSIASM.

ENTIRE (ĕn tīr′), *adj.* (Encompassing; a gathering together.) Both hands are held in the right angle position, palms facing the body, and the right hand in front of the left. The right hand makes a sweeping outward movement around the left, and comes to rest with the back of the right hand resting in the left palm. See also ALL.

ENTRANCE (ĕn trəns′), *n.* See ENTER.

ENVIOUS (ĕn′ vĭ əs), *adj.* (Biting the finger to suppress the feelings.) The tip of the index finger is bitten. The tip of the little finger is sometimes used. See also JEALOUS, JEALOUSY.

ENVY (en' vǐ), *n.* See ENVIOUS.

EQUAL (ē' kwəl), *adj., n., v.,* -QUALED, -QUALING. (Sameness is stressed.) The downturned "B" hands, held at chest height, are brought together repeatedly, so that the index finger edges or fingertips come into contact. See also EVEN, FAIR, LEVEL.

EQUIVALENT (ǐ kwǐv' ə lənt), *adj.* See EQUAL.

ERROR (ĕr' ər), *n.* (Rationale obscure; the thumb and little finger are said to represent, respectively, right and wrong, with the head poised between the two.) The right "Y" hand, palm facing the body, is brought up to the chin. See also MISTAKE, WRONG.

ESCAPE (ĕs kāp'), v., -CAPED, -CAPING. (Emerging from a hiding place.) The downturned right "D" hand is positioned under the downturned open left hand. The right "D" hand suddenly emerges and moves off quickly to the right.

ESTABLISH (ĕs tăb' lǐsh), v., -LISHED, -LISHING. (To set up.) The right "A" hand, thumb up and palm facing left, comes down to rest on the back of the downturned left "S" hand. Before doing so, the right "A" hand may describe a clockwise circle above the left hand, but this is optional. See also FOUND, FOUNDED.

ETERNITY (ĭ tûr' nə tĭ), n. (Around the clock and ahead into the future.) The right index finger, pointing forward, traces a clockwise circle in the air. The downturned right "Y" hand then moves forward, either in a straight line or in a slight downward curve. See also EVER 2, EVERLASTING, FOREVER.

EVADE (ĭ vād′), *v.*, -VADED, -VADING. (Ducking back and forth, away from something.) Both "A" hands, thumbs pointing straight up, are held some distance before the chest, with the left hand in front of the right. The right hand, swinging back and forth, moves away from the left and toward the chest. See also AVOID 1.

EVALUATE 1 (ĭ văl′ yōō āt′), *v.*, -ATED, -ATING. (The scales move up and down.) The two "F" hands, palms facing each other, move alternately up and down. See also CONSIDER 3, COURT, IF, JUDGE 1, JUDGMENT, JUSTICE.

EVALUATE 2, *v.* (The letter "E"; weighing up and down.) The "E" hands, palms facing out from the body, move alternately up and down.

EVASION (ĭ vā′ zhən), *n.* See EVADE.

EVEN (ē′ vən), *adj.* (Sameness is stressed.) The downturned "B" hands, held at chest height, are brought together repeatedly, so that the index finger edges or fingertips come into contact. See also EQUAL, EQUIVALENT, FAIR, LEVEL.

EVENT (ĭ vĕnt′), *n.* (A befalling.) Both "D" hands, index fingers pointing away from the body, are simultaneously pivoted over so that the palms face down. See also HAPPEN 1, INCIDENT.

EVER 1 (ĕv′ ər), *adv.* (Steady, uninterrupted movement.) The "A" hands are held with palms out, thumbs extended and touching, the right behind the left. In this position the hands move forward in a straight, steady line. See also CONTINUE, ENDURE 2, LAST 3, LASTING, PERMANENT, PERSERVERE, PERSIST, REMAIN, STAY 1, STAY STILL.

EVER 2, *adv.* (Around the clock and ahead into the future.) The right index finger, pointing forward, traces a clockwise circle in the air. The downturned right "Y" hand then moves forward, either in a straight line or in a slight downward curve. See also ETERNITY, FOREVER.

EVERLASTING (ĕv´ ər lăs´ tĭng, -läs´-), *adj.* See EVER 2.

EVER SINCE (ĕv´ ər sĭns), *phrase.* (From a point up and over.) In the "D" position, palms down, both index fingers touch the right shoulder and then are brought up and over, ending in a palm-up position, pointing straight ahead of the body. See also ALL ALONG, ALL THE TIME, SINCE, SO FAR, THUS FAR.

EVERY (ĕv′ rĭ), *adj.* (Peeling off, one by one.) The left "A" hand is held palm facing the right. The knuckles of the right "A" hand are drawn repeatedly down the left thumb, from its tip to its base. See also EACH.

EVERYDAY (ĕv′ rĭ dā′), *adj.* (Tomorrow after tomorrow.) The sign for TOMORROW, *q.v.,* is made several times: The right "A" hand moves forward several times from its initial resting place on the right cheek. See also DAILY.

EXACT (ĭg zăkt′), *adj.* (The fingers come together precisely.) The thumb and index finger of each hand, palms facing, the right above the left, form circles. They are brought together with a deliberate movement, so that the fingers and thumbs now touch. Sometimes the right hand, before coming together with the left, executes a slow clockwise circle above the left. See also PRECISE, SPECIFIC.

EXACTLY (ĭg zăkt′ lĭ), *adv.* See EXACT.

EXAGGERATE (ĭg zăj′ ə rāt′), *(sl.)*, *v.*, -ATED, -ATING. (Stretching out one's words.) The left "S" hand, palm facing right, is held before the mouth. Its right counterpart, palm facing left, is moved forward in a series of short up-and-down arcs.

EXAMINATION 1 (ĭg zăm′ ə nā′ shən), *n.* (A series of questions spread out on a page.) Both "D" hands, palms down, simultaneously execute a single circle, the right hand moving in a clockwise direction and the left in a counterclockwise direction. Upon completion of the circle, both hands open into the "5" position and move straight down a short distance. (The hands actually draw question marks in the air.) See also TEST.

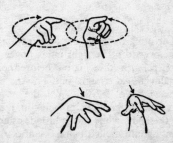

EXAMINATION 2, *n.* (Firing questions.) The index fingers of both "D" hands repeatedly curve and straighten out as the hands are alternately flung forward and back, as if firing questions. See also QUERY, QUESTION 2, QUIZ.

EXAMINE (ĭg zăm′ ĭn), *v.*, -INED, -INING. (Directing the vision from place to place.) The right "C" hand, palm facing left, moves from right to left across the line of vision, in a series of counterclockwise circles. The signer's gaze remains concentrated and his head turns slowly from right to left. See also LOOK FOR, SEARCH, SEEK.

EXAMPLE (ĭg zăm′ pəl, -zăm′ -), *n., v.,* -PLED, -PLING. (Directing the attention to something, and bringing it forward.) The right index finger points into the left palm, held facing out before the body. The left palm moves straight out. For the passive form of this verb, *i.e.,* BE SHOWN, the movement is reversed: The left hand, palm facing in, is moved in toward the body, while the right index finger remains pointing into the left palm. See also DEMON-

STRATE, DISPLAY, EXHIBIT, EXHIBITION, REPRE-
SENT, SHOW 1.

EXCELLENT (ĕk′ sə lənt), *adj.* (The hands gesture toward the heavens.) The "5" hands, palms out and arms raised rather high, are positioned somewhat above the line of vision. The arms move abruptly forward and up once or twice. An expression of pleasure or surprise is usually assumed. See also GREAT 2.

EXCEPT (ĭk sĕpt′), *prep., conj.* (Selecting a particular item from among several.) The index finger and thumb of the right hand grasp and pull up the left index finger. See also SPECIAL.

EXCEPTION (ĭk sĕp′ shən), *n.* See EXCEPT.

EXCHANGE (ĭks chānj′), *v.*, -CHANGED, -CHANG-ING. (Exchanging places.) The right "A" hand, positioned above the left "A" hand, swings down and under the left, coming up a bit in front of it. See also REPLACE, SUBSTITUTE, TRADE.

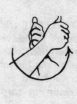

EXCITE (ĭk sīt′), *v.*, -CITED, -CITING. (The heart beats violently.) Both middle fingers move up alternately to strike the heart sharply.

EXCITEMENT (ĭk sīt′ mənt), *n.* See EXCITE.

EXCITING (ĭk sī′ tĭng), *adj*. See EXCITE.

EXCUSE (*n.* ĭk skūs′; *v.* ĭk skūz′), -CUSED, -CUSING. (A wiped-off and cleaned slate.) The right hand wipes off the left palm several times. See also APOLOGIZE 2, APOLOGY 2, FORGIVE, PARDON.

EXHIBIT (ĭg zĭb′ ĭt), *v.*, -ITED, -ITING. (Directing the attention to something, and bringing it forward.) The right index finger points into the left palm, held facing out before the body. The left palm moves straight out. For the passive form of this verb, *i.e.*, BE SHOWN, the movement is reversed: The left hand, palm facing in, is moved in toward the body, while the right index finger remains pointing into the left palm. See also DEMONSTRATE, DISPLAY, EXAMPLE, REPRESENT, SHOW 1.

EXHIBITION (ĕk′ sə bĭsh′ ən), *n*. See EXHIBIT.

EXPAND (ĭk spănd′), v., -PANDED, -PANDING. (A large amount.) The "5" hands face each other, fingers curved and touching. They move apart rather quickly. See also GREAT 1, MUCH.

EXPECT (ĭk spĕkt′), v., -PECTED, -PECTING. (A thought awaited.) The tip of the right index finger, held in the "D" position, palm facing the body, is placed on the forehead (modified THINK, q.v.). Both hands then assume right angle positions, fingers facing, with the left hand held above left shoulder level and the right before the right breast. Both hands, held thus, wave to each other several times. See also HOPE.

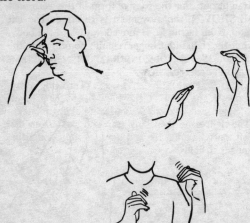

EXPEL (ĭk spĕl′), *v.*, -PELLED, -PELLING. ("Getting
the axe"; the head is chopped off.) The upturned
open right hand is swung sharply over the index
finger edge of the left "S" hand, whose palm faces
right. See also FIRE 2.

EXPENSE (ĭk spĕns′), *n.* (Nicking into one.) The
knuckle of the right "X" finger is nicked against the
palm of the left hand, held in the "5" position, palm
facing right. See also COST, FINE 2, PENALTY, PRICE,
TAX, TAXATION.

EXPENSIVE (ĭk spĕn′ sĭv), *adj.* (Throwing away
money.) The right "AND" hand lies in the palm of
the upturned, open left hand (as if holding money).
The right hand then moves up and away from the
left, opening abruptly as it does (as if dropping the
money it holds).

EXPERIENCE 1 (ĭk spĭr′ ĭ əns), *n.* (A sharp-edged hand.) The right hand grasps the little finger edge of the left firmly. As it leaves this position, moving down and out, it assumes the "A" position, palm facing left. See also SKILL, SKILLFUL.

EXPERIENCE 2, *n.* (White hair.) The right fingertips gently pull the hair of the right temple. The movement is repeated.

EXPERT (*n.* ĕks′ pûrt; *adj.* ĭk spûrt′). See EXPERIENCE 1.

EXPLAIN (ĭk splān′), *v.*, -PLAINED, -PLAINING. (Unraveling something to get at its parts.) The "F" hands, palms facing and fingers pointing straight out, are held about an inch apart. They move alternately back and forth a few inches. See also DEFINE 1, DESCRIBE, DESCRIPTION.

EYE (ī), *n.*, *v.*, EYED, EYING or EYEING. (The natural sign.) The right index finger touches the lower lid of the right eye.

EYEGLASSES (ī′ glăs′ əs), *n. pl.* (The shape.) The thumb and index finger of the right hand, placed flat against the right temple, move back toward the right ear, tracing the line formed by the eyeglass frame. See also GLASSES.

F

FACE (fās), *v.*, FACED, FACING. (Face to face.) The left hand, fingers together, palm flat and facing the eyes, is held a bit above eye level. The right hand, fingers also together, is held in front of the mouth, with palm facing the left hand. With a sweeping upward movement the right hand moves toward the left, which moves straight up an inch or two at the same time.

FACE TO FACE, *phrase.* See FACE.

FAIL (fāl), *v.*, FAILED, FAILING. (A sliding.) The right "V" hand, palm up, slides along the upturned left palm, from its base to its fingertips.

FAIR (fâr), *adj.* (Sameness is stressed.) The down-turned "B" hands, held at chest height, are brought

172

together repeatedly, so that the index finger edges or fingertips come into contact. See also EQUAL, EQUIVALENT, EVEN, LEVEL.

FALL 1 (fôl), *n.* (The falling of leaves.) The left arm, held upright with palm facing back, represents a tree trunk. The right hand, fingers together and palm down, moves down along the left arm, from the back of the wrist to the elbow, either once or several times. This represents the falling of leaves from the tree branches, indicated by the left fingers.

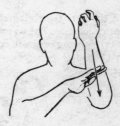

FALL 2, *n., v.,* FELL, FALLEN, FALLING, (Falling on one's side.) The downturned index and middle fingers of the right "V" hand are placed in a standing position on the upturned left palm. The right "V" hand flips over, coming to rest palm up on the up-turned left palm.

FALSE (fôls), *adj.* (Words diverted instead of coming straight, or truthfully, out.) The index finger of the right "D" hand, pointing to the left, moves along the lips from right to left. See also LIAR, LIE 1.

FALSEHOOD (fôls' hŏŏd), *n.* See FALSE.

FAME (fām), *n.* (One's fame radiates far and wide.) The extended index fingers rest on the lips (or on the temples). Moving in small, continuous spirals, they move up and to either side of the head. See also PROMINENT.

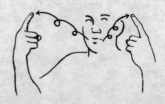

FAMILY (făm' ə lǐ), *n.* (The letter "F;" a circle or group.) The thumb and index fingers of both "F" hands are in contact, palms facing. The hands swing open and around, coming together again at their little finger edges, palms now facing the body.

FAMOUS (fā' məs), *adj.* See FAME.

FAR (fär), *adj.* (Moving beyond, *i.e.*; the concept of distance or "farness.") The "A" hands are held together, thumbs pointing away from the body. The right hand moves straight ahead in a slight arc. The left hand does not move.

FASCINATE (făs′ ə nāt′), *v.*, -NATED, -NATING. (Drawing one out.) The index and middle fingers of both hands, one above the other, are placed on the middle part of the chest. Both hands move forward simultaneously. As they do, the index and middle fingers of each hand come together. See also INTEREST 1, INTERESTED 1, INTERESTING 1.

FAST (făst), *adj.* (A quick movement.) The thumb-tip of the upright right hand is flicked quickly off the tip of the curved right index finger, as if shooting marbles. See also IMMEDIATELY, QUICK, QUICKNESS, SPEED, SPEEDY.

FAT (făt), *adj.* (The swollen cheeks.) The cheeks are puffed out and the open "C" hands, positioned at either cheek, move away to their respective sides.

FATHER 1 (fä' *th*ər), *n.* (Male who holds the baby.) The sign for MALE, *q.v.,* is made: The thumb and extended fingers of the right hand are brought up to grasp an imaginary cap brim, representing the tipping of caps by men in olden days. Both hands are then held open with palms facing up, as if holding a baby. This is the formal sign.

FATHER 2, *(informal), n.* (Derived from the formal sign for FATHER 1, *q.v.*) The thumbtip of the right "5" hand touches the right temple a number of times. The other fingers may also wiggle.

FEAR 1 (fĭr), *n., v.,* FEARED, FEARING. (The heart is suddenly covered with fear.) Both hands, fingers together, are placed side by side, palms facing the chest. They quickly open and come together over the heart, one on top of the other. See also AFRAID, FRIGHT, FRIGHTEN, SCARE(D), TERROR 1.

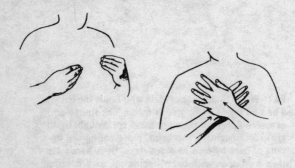

FEAR 2, *n., v.* (The hands attempt to ward off something which causes fear.) The "5" hands, right behind left, move downward before the body, in a wavy motion. See also TERROR 2.

FEED 1 (fēd), *v.,* FED, FEEDING. (The natural sign.) The closed right hand goes through the natural motion of placing food in the mouth. This movement is repeated. See also EAT, FOOD 1, MEAL.

FEED 2, *v.* (Placing food before someone; the action of placing food in someone's mouth.) The upturned hands, holding imaginary pieces of food, the right behind the left, move forward simultaneously, in a gesture of placing food in someone's mouth.

FEEL 1 (fēl), *v.*, FELT, FEELING. (The natural movement of touching.) The tip of the middle finger of the downturned right "5" hand touches the back of the left hand a number of times. See also CONTACT 1, TOUCH.

FEEL 2, *v.* (The welling up of feelings or emotions in the heart.) The right middle finger, touching the heart, moves up an inch or two a number of times. See also EMOTION 1.

FEELING (fē' lĭng), *n.* See FEEL 2.

FEEL TOUCHED (tŭcht), *v. phrase.* (A piercing of the heart.) The tip of the middle finger of the right "5" hand is thrust against the heart. The head, at the same time, moves abruptly back a very slight distance. See also TOUCHED, TOUCHING.

FEMALE (fē' māl), *n., adj.* (The bonnet string used by women of old.) The right "A" hand's thumb moves down along the line of the right jaw, from ear

almost to chin. This outlines the string used to tie
ladies' bonnets in olden days. This is a root sign to
modify many others. *Viz:* FEMALE plus BABY;
DAUGHTER, FEMALE plus SAME; SISTER,
etc.

FEW (fū), *adj.* (The fingers are presented in order,
to convey the concept of "several.") The right "A"
hand is held palm facing up. One by one the fingers
open, beginning with the index finger and ending
with the little finger. Some use only the index and
middle fingers. See also SEVERAL.

FEW SECONDS AGO, A, *adv. phrase.* (Time moved
backward a bit.) The right "D" hand, palm facing
the body, is placed in the palm of the left hand,
which is facing right. The right hand swings back a
bit toward the body, with the index finger describing
an arc. See also JUST A MOMENT AGO, WHILE AGO
2.

FIGHT 1 (fĭt), *n., v.,* FOUGHT, FIGHTING. (The fists in combat.) The "S" hands, palms facing, swing down simultaneously toward each other. They do not touch, however.

FIGHT 2, *n., v.* (The natural sign.) Both clenched fists go through the motions of boxing.

FIGURE 1 (fĭg′ yər), *n., v.,* -URED, -URING. (A multiplying.) The "V" hands, palms facing the body, alternately cross and separate, several times. See also MULTIPLY.

FIGURE 2, *n., v.* (Contours are indicated or outlined.) Both "A" hands, held about a foot apart before the face, with palms facing each other, move

down simultaneously in a wavy, undulating motion.
See also FORM, SHAPE, STATUE.

FILL (fĭl), *v.* FILLED, FILLING. (Wiping off the top
of a container, to indicate its condition of fullness.)
The downturned open right hand wipes across the
index finger edge of the left "S" hand, whose palm
faces right. The movement of the right hand is toward the body. See also COMPLETE, FULL.

FILM (fĭlm), *n.* (The frames of the film speeding
through the projector.) The left "5" hand, palm facing right and thumb pointing up, is the projector.
The right "5" hand is placed against the left, and
moves back and forth quickly. See also MOVIE(s),
MOVING PICTURE.

FILTHY (fĭl′ thĭ), *adj.* (A modification of the pig's snout groveling in a trough.) The downturned right hand is placed under the chin. Its fingers, pointing left, wiggle repeatedly. See also DIRTY.

FINAL 1 (fī′ nəl), *adj.* (The little, *i.e.,* LAST, fingers are indicated.) With the hands in the "I" position, the tip of the right little finger strikes the tip of its left counterpart. The right index finger may be used instead of the right little finger. See also END 1, LAST 1.

FINAL 2, *adj.* (A single little, *i.e.,* LAST, finger is indicated.) The tip of the index finger of the right "D" hand strikes the tip of the little finger of the left "I" hand. See also END 2, LAST 2.

FINALLY 1 (fī′ nə lǐ), *adv.* See FINAL 1.

FINALLY 2, *adv.* See FINAL 2.

FIND (find), *n., v.,* FOUND, FINDING, (The natural motion of selecting something from the hand.) The thumb and index fingers of the outstretched right hand grasp an imaginary object on the upturned left palm. The right hand then moves straight up. See also PICK 1, SELECT 1.

FINE 1 (fin), *adj., interj.* (The feelings are titillated.) With the thumb resting on the upper part of the chest, the fingers are wiggled back and forth. See also ELEGANT, WONDERFUL.

FINE 2, *n., v.,* FINED, FINING. (Nicking into one.) The knuckle of the right "X" finger is nicked against the palm of the left hand, held in the "5" position, palm facing right. See also COST, EXPENSE, PENALTY, PRICE, TAX, TAXATION.

FINISH (fĭn′ ĭsh), *(colloq.), n., v,* -ISHED, -ISHING. (Shaking the hands to rid them of something.) The upright "5" hands, palms facing each other, are suddenly and quickly swung around to a palm-out position. See also DONE, END 3.

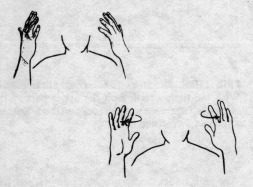

FIRE 1 (fīr), *n., v.,* FIRED, FIRING. (The leaping of flames.) The "5" hands are held with palms facing the body. They move up and down alternately, while the fingers wiggle. See also BURN, FLAME.

FIRE 2, *v.* ("Getting the axe"; the head is chopped off.) The upturned open right hand is swung sharply over the index finger edge of the left "S" hand, whose palm faces right. See also EXPEL.

FIRST (fûrst), *adj.* (The first finger is indicated.) The right index finger touches the upturned left thumb.

FLAME (flām), *n.*, *v.*, FLAMED, FLAMING. (The leaping of flames.) The "5" hands are held with palms facing the body. They move up and down alternately, while the fingers wiggle. See also BURN, FIRE 1.

FLIRT (flûrt), *v.*, FLIRTED, FLIRTING. (Dazzling one with scintillating looks.) The "5" hands, thumbs touching, swing alternately up and down. The fingers sometimes wiggle.

FLOWER (flou' ər), *n.* (The natural motion of smelling a flower.) The right hand, grasping an imaginary flower, holds it first against the right nostril and then against the left.

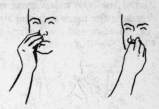

FLUNK (flŭngk), *v.*, FLUNKED, FLUNKING. The right "F" hand strikes forcefully against the open left palm, which faces right with fingers pointing forward.

FLY 1 (flī), *v.*, FLEW, FLOWN, FLYING. (The wings of the airplane.) The "Y" hand, palm down and drawn up near the shoulder, moves forward, up and away from the body. Either hand may be used. See also AIRPLANE, PLANE 1.

FLY 2, *v., n.* (The wings and fuselage of the airplane.) The hand assumes the same position as in FLY 1, but the index finger is also extended, to represent the fuselage of the airplane. Either hand may be used, and the movement is the same as in FLY 1. See also PLANE 2.

FOCUS (fō′ kəs), *n., v.,* -CUSED, -CUSING. (Directing one's attention forward; applying oneself; concentrating.) Both hands, fingers pointing up and together, are held at the sides of the face. They move straight out from the face. See also CONCENTRATE, CONCENTRATION, MIND 2, PAY ATTENTION (TO).

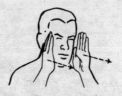

FOLLOW (fŏl′ ō), *v.,* -LOWED, -LOWING. (One hand follows the other.) The "A" hands are used, thumbs pointing up. The right is positioned a few inches behind the left. The left hand moves straight for-

ward, while the right follows behind in a series of
wavy, movements.

FOLLOWING (fŏl' ō ĭng), *adj.* See FOLLOW.

FOOD (fōōd), *n.* (The natural sign.) The closed
right hand goes through the natural motion of placing food in the mouth. This movement is repeated.
See also EAT, FEED 1, MEAL.

FOOLISH (fōō' lĭsh), *adj.* (Thoughts flickering back
and forth.) The right "Y" hand, thumb almost
touching the forehead, is shaken back and forth
across the forehead several times. See also NON-
SENSE, RIDICULOUS, SILLY.

FOOTBALL (fŏŏt' bôl´), *n.* (The teams lock in combat.) The "5" hands, facing each other, are interlocked suddenly. They are drawn apart and the action is repeated.

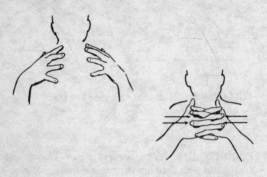

FOR 1 (fôr), *prep.* (The thoughts are directed outward, toward a specific goal or purpose.) The right index finger, resting on the right temple, leaves its position and moves straight out in front of the face.

FOR 2, *prep.* (A thought or knowledge uppermost in the mind.) The fingers of the right hand or the index finger are placed on the center of the forehead, and then the hand is brought strongly up above the

head, assuming the "A" position, with thumb pointing up. See also BECAUSE.

FORBID 1 (fər bĭd′), *v.*, -BADE *or* -BAD, -BIDDEN *or*
-BID, -BIDDING. (A modification of LAW, *q.v.*;
"against the law.") The downturned right "D" or
"L" hand is thrust forcefully into the left palm. See
also PROHIBIT.

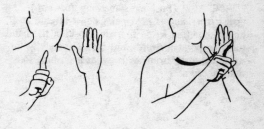

FORBID 2, *v.* (The letter "F"; the same sign as
above.) The right "F" hand makes the same sign as
in FORBID 1.

FORBIDDEN 1 (fər bĭd′ ən), *v.* See FORBID 1.

FORBIDDEN 2, *adj.* See FORBID 2.

FORCE 1 (fōrs), *v.*, FORCED, FORCING. (Forcing the head to bow.) The right "C" hand pushes down on an imaginary neck.

FORCE 2, *v.* (Pushing something forward.) The open right hand is held palm down at chin level, fingers pointing left. From this position the hand turns to point forward, and moves forcefully forward and away from the body, as if pushing something ahead of it.

FOREVER (fôr ĕv′ ər), *adv.* (Around the clock and ahead into the future.) The right index finger, pointing forward, traces a clockwise circle in the air. The downturned right "Y" hand then moves forward, either in a straight line or in a slight downward curve. See also ETERNITY, EVER 2, EVERLASTING.

FORGET 1 (fər gĕt'), *v.*, -GOT, -GOTTEN, -GETTING. (Wiping knowledge from the mind.) The right hand, fingers pointing left, rests on the forehead. It moves off to the right, assuming the "A" position, thumb up and palm facing the signer's rear.

FORGET 2, *v.* (The thought is gone.) The sign for THINK is made: The index finger makes a small circle on the forehead. This is followed by the sign for GONE 1: The right open hand, palm facing the body, is held by the left hand and is drawn down and out, ending in a position with fingers drawn together. The left hand, meanwhile, has closed into a position with fingers also drawn together.

FORGIVE (fər gǐv′), *v.*, -GAVE, -GIVEN, -GIVING. (A wiped-off and cleaned slate.) The right hand wipes off the left palm several times. See also APOLOGIZE 2, APOLOGY 2, EXCUSE, PARDON.

FORM (fôrm), *n.* (Contours are indicated or outlined.) Both "A" hands, held about a foot apart before the face, with palms facing each other, move down simultaneously in a wavy, undulating motion. See also FIGURE 2, SHAPE, STATUE.

FOUND (found), *v.*, FOUNDED, FOUNDING. (To set up.) The right "A" hand, thumb up and palm facing left, comes down to rest on the back of the down-turned left "S" hand. Before doing so, the right "A" hand may describe a clockwise circle above the left hand, but this is optional. See also ESTABLISH.

FOUNDATION (foun dā′ shən), *n.* (The area below.) Both hands, in the "5" position, palms down, are held before the chest, the right under the left. The right hand moves under the left in a counterclockwise fashion. See also BELOW 1.

FOUNDED, *v.* See FOUND.

FREE 1 (frē), *adj., v.,* FREED, FREEING. (Breaking the bonds.) The "S" hands, crossed in front of the body, swing apart and face out. See also INDEPENDENCE, INDEPENDENT, RESCUE, SAFE, SAVE 1.

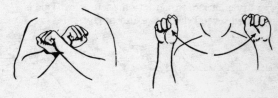

FREE 2, *adj., v.* (The letter "F.") The "F" hands make the same sign as in FREE 1.

FREEDOM (frē' dəm), *n.* See FREE 1.

FREEZE (frēz), *v.,* FROZE, FROZEN, FREEZING. (The stiff fingers.) The fingers of the "5" hands, held palms down, stiffen and contract. See also FROZEN, ICE.

FREQUENT (*adj.* frē' kwənt; *v.* frĭ kwĕnt'), -QUENTED, -QUENTING. The left hand, open in the "5" position, palm up, is held before the chest. The right hand, in the right-angle position, fingers pointing up, arches over and into the left palm. This is repeated several times. See also OFTEN.

FRIEND (frĕnd), *n.* (Locked together in friendship.) The right and left hands are interlocked at the index fingers. The hands separate, change their relative positions, and come together again as before.

FRIENDLY (frĕnd′ lĭ), *adj.* (A crinkling-up of the face.) Both hands, in the "5" position, palms facing back, are placed on either side of the face. The fingers wiggle back and forth, while a pleasant, happy expression is worn. See also CHEERFUL, PLEASANT.

FRIENDSHIP (frĕnd′ shĭp), *n.* See FRIEND.

FRIGHT (frīt), *n.* (The heart is suddenly covered with fear.) Both hands, fingers together, are placed side by side, palms facing the chest. They quickly open and come together over the heart, one on top of the other. See also AFRAID, FEAR 1, SCARE(D), TERROR 1.

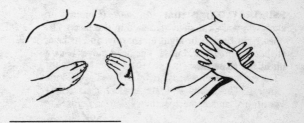

FRIGHTEN (frī′ tən), *v.,* -TENED, -TENING. See FRIGHT.

FROM (frŏm), *prep.* (The "away from" action is indicated.) The knuckle of the right "X" finger is placed against the base of the left "D" or "X" finger, and then moved away in a slight curve toward the body.

FROZEN (frō′ zən), *adj.* (The stiff fingers.) The fingers of the "5" hands, held palms down, stiffen and contract. See also FREEZE, ICE.

FRUSTRATED (frŭs′ trāt ĭd), *adj.* (Coming up against a wall; a door is slammed in the face.) The open right hand is brought up sharply, and its back strikes the mouth and nose. The head moves back a bit at the same time.

FULL (fo͝ol), *adj.* (Wiping off the top of a container, to indicate its condition of fullness.) The down-turned open right hand wipes across the index finger edge of the left "S" hand, whose palm faces right. The movement of the right hand is toward the body. See also COMPLETE, FILL.

FUN (fŭn), *n.* (The wrinkled nose—indicative of laughter or fun.) The index and middle fingers of the right "U" hand, whose palm faces the body, are placed on the nose. The right hand swings down in an arc and, palm down, the "U" fingers strike their left counterparts on the downturned left "U" hand, and either stop at that point or continue on.

FUNNY (fŭn' ĭ), *adj.* (The nose wrinkles in laugh-ter.) The tips of the right index and middle fingers brush repeatedly off the tip of the nose. See also HUMOR, HUMOROUS.

FURY (fyŏŏr′ ĭ), *n.* (A violent welling-up of the emotions.) The curved fingers of the right hand are placed in the center of the chest, and fly up suddenly and violently. An expression of anger is worn. See also ANGER, ANGRY 2, MAD, RAGE.

FUTURE (fū′ chər), *n.* (Something ahead or in the future.) The upright, open right hand, palm facing left, moves straight out and slightly up from a position beside the right temple. See also IN THE FUTURE, LATER 2, LATER ON, WILL 1, WOULD.

G

GAIN (gān), *v.*, GAINED, GAINING. (Adding on.) The index and middle fingers of the right "H" hand, palm up, are swung up and over until they come to rest on the index and middle fingers of the left "H" hand, held palm down. See also ADD 2, ADDITION, INCREASE, RAISE.

GAME (gām), *n., v.*, GAMED, GAMING. (Two individuals pitted against each other.) The hands are held in the "A" position, thumbs pointing straight up, palms facing the body. They come together forcefully, moving down a bit as they do, and the knuckles of one hand strike those of the other.

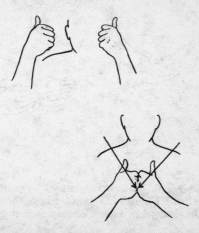

GAS (găs), *n.* (The act of pouring gasoline into an automobile tank.) The thumb of the right "A" hand is placed into the hole formed by the left "O" hand.

GASOLINE (găs′ ə lēn′, găs ə lēn′), *n.* See GAS.

GATE (gāt), *n.* (The natural sign.) The fingertips of both open hands touch each other before the body, palms toward the chest, thumbs pointing upward. Then the right fingers swing forward and back to their original position several times, imitating the movement of a gate opening and closing.

GATHER 1 (găth′ ər), *v.*, -ERED, -ERING. (A gathering together.) The right "5" hand, fingers curved and palm facing left, sweeps across and over the upturned left palm, several times, in a circular movement.

GATHER 2, *v.* (Assemble all together.) Both "5" hands, palms facing, are held with fingers pointing out from the body. With a sweeping motion they are brought in toward the chest, and all fingertips come together. This is repeated. See also CONFERENCE, MEETING.

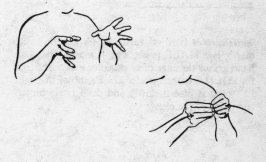

GATHERING (găth′ ər ĭng), *n.* See GATHER 2.

GATHERING TOGETHER, *phrase.* See GATHER 1.

GENEROUS (jěn′ ər əs), *adj.* (The heart rolls out.) Both right-angle hands roll over each other as they move down and away from their initial position at the heart. See also KIND 1.

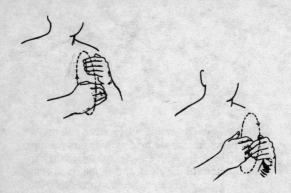

GENTLEMAN (jěn′ təl mən), *n.* (A fine or polite man.) The MALE prefix sign is made: The right hand grasps the edge of an imaginary cap. The sign for POLITE is then made: The thumb of the right "5" hand is placed slowly and deliberately on the right side of the chest.

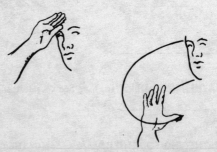

GET (gĕt), *v.*, GOT, GOTTEN, GETTING. (A grasping and bringing forward to oneself.) Both hands, in the "5" position, fingers curved, are crossed at the wrists, with the left palm facing right and the right palm facing left. They are brought in toward the chest, while closing into a grasping "S" position. See also RECEIVE.

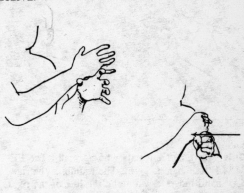

GET UP (ŭp), *v. phrase.* (Getting onto one's feet.) The upturned index and middle fingers of the right hand, representing the legs, are swung up and over in an arc, coming to rest in the upturned left palm. See also STAND 2, STAND UP.

GIFT (gĭft), *n.* (A giving of something.) Both "A" hands, with index fingers somewhat draped over the tips of the thumbs, are held palms facing in front of the chest. They are pivoted forward and down, in unison, from the wrists. See also CONTRIBUTE, PRESENT 2.

GIRL (gûrl), *n.* (A female who is small.) The FEMALE root sign is given: The thumb of the right "A" hand moves down along the line of the right jaw, from ear almost to chin. This outlines the string used to tie ladies' bonnets in olden days. The downturned open right hand is then held at waist level, indicating the short height of the female.

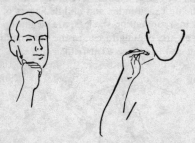

GIVE (gĭv), *v.*, GAVE, GIVEN, GIVING. (Holding something and extending it toward someone.) The

right "O" hand is held before the right shoulder and
then moved outward in an arc, away from the body.

GIVE ME (mē), *v. phrase.* (Extending the hand toward oneself.) This sign is a reversal of GIVE.

GIVE UP (gĭv ŭp'), *v. phrase.* (Throwing up the
hands in a gesture of surrender.) Both "A" hands are
held palms down before the chest and then thrown
up in unison, ending in the "5" position. See also
SURRENDER.

GLAD (glăd), *adj.* (The heart is stirred; the spirits bubble up.) The open right hand, palm facing the body, strikes the heart repeatedly, moving up and off the heart after each strike. See also HAPPY, JOY, MERRY.

GLASS 1 (glăs, gläs), *n.* (The finger touches a brittle substance.) The index finger is brought up to touch the exposed front teeth.

GLASS 2, *n.* (The shape of a drinking glass.) The little finger edge of the right "C" hand rests in the upturned left palm. The right hand moves straight up a few inches, tracing the shape of a drinking glass.

GLASSES (glăs' əs), *n. pl.* (The shape.) The thumb and index finger of the right hand, placed flat against the right temple, move back toward the right ear, tracing the line formed by the eyeglass frame. See also EYEGLASSES.

GLOOM (glo͞om), *n.* (The facial features drop.) Both "5" hands, palms facing the eyes and fingers slightly curved, drop simultaneously to a level with the mouth. The head drops slightly as the hands move down, and an expression of sadness is assumed. See also GRIEF, SAD, SORROWFUL 1.

GLOOMY (glo͞o' mĭ), *adj.* See GLOOM.

GO 1 (gō), *v.*, WENT, GONE, GOING. (Continuous motion forward.) With palms facing each other, the index fingers of the "D" hands revolve around each other as both hands move forward.

GO 2, *interj., v.* (The natural sign.) The right index finger is flung out, as a command to go. A stern expression is usually assumed.

GO AHEAD (ə hĕd′), *v. phrase.* (Moving forward.) Both right-angle hands, palms facing each other and knuckles facing forward, move forward simultaneously. See also PROCEED.

GOAL (gōl), *n.* (A thought directed upward, toward a goal.) The left "D" hand, palm facing the body, is held above the head, to represent the goal. The index finger of the right "D" hand, after touching the forehead (modified sign for THINK, *q.v.*), moves slowly and deliberately up to the tip of the left index finger. See also AIM.

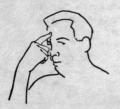 

GOLD (gōld), *n.* (Yellow earrings, *i.e.,* gold, which was discovered in California.) The earlobe is pinched, and then the sign for YELLOW is made: The "Y" hand, pivoted at the wrist, is shaken back and forth repeatedly.

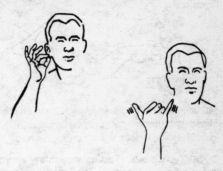

GONE 1 (gôn, gŏn), *adj.* (A disappearance.) The right open hand, palm facing the body, is held by the left hand and is drawn down and out, ending in a position with fingers drawn together. The left hand, meanwhile, may close into a position with fingers also drawn together. See also DISAPPEAR.

GONE 2, *(sl.)*, *adj.* (A disappearance into the distance. The narrowing perspective is the main feature here.) The right "L" hand, resting on the back of the downturned left hand, moves straight forward suddenly. As it does, the index finger and thumb come together.

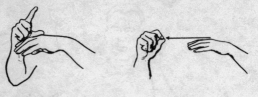

GOOD (go͝od), *adj.* (Tasting something, approving it, and offering it forward.) The fingertips of the right "5" hand are placed at the lips. The right hand then moves out and into a palm-up position on the upturned left palm.

GOODBYE (go͝od′ bī′), *interj.* (A wave of the hand.) The right open hand waves back and forth several times. See also HELLO.

GO TO BED *v. phrase.* (Laying the head on the pillow.) The head is placed on its side, in the open palm, and the eyes are closed.

GOVERN (gŭv' ərn), *v.,* -ERNED, -ERNING. (Holding the reins over all.) The "A" hands, palms facing, move alternately back and forth, as if grasping and manipulating reins. See also CONTROL 1, MANAGE, RULE.

GOVERNMENT (gŭv' ərn mənt, -ər-), *n.* (The head indicates the head or seat of government.) The right index finger, pointing toward the right temple, describes a small clockwise circle and comes to rest on the right temple.

GRAB (grăb), *v.*, GRABBED, GRABBING, *n.* (Grasping something and holding it down.) Both hands, palms down, quickly close into the "S" position, the right on top of the left. See also CATCH.

GRADUATE (*n.* grăj′ o͝o ĭt; *v.* grăj′ o͝o āt′), -ATED, -ATING. (The letter "G"; the ribbon around the diploma.) The right "G" hand makes a single clockwise circle, and drops down into the upturned left palm.

GRANDFATHER 1 (grănd′ fä′ t͡hər), *n.* (A male baby-holder; a predecessor.) The sign for FATHER 2 is made: The thumbtip of the right "5" hand touches the right temple a number of times. Then both open hands, palms up, are extended in front of the chest, as if supporting a baby. From this position they sweep over the left shoulder. The whole sign is smooth and continuous.

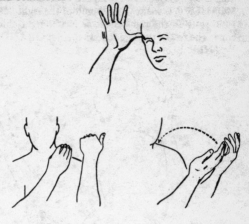

GRANDFATHER 2, *n.* (A variation of GRANDFA-THER 1. The "A" hands are held with the left in front of the right, and the right thumb positioned against the forehead. Both hands open into the "5" position, so that the right little finger touches or almost touches the left thumb. Both hands may, as they open, move forward an inch or two.

GRANDMOTHER 1 (grănd′ mŭ*t*h′ ər), *n.* (Same rationale as for GRANDFATHER 1.) The sign for MOTHER 2 is made: The thumb of the right "5" hand rests on the right cheek or on the right chin bone. The rest of the sign follows that for **GRANDFATHER** 1.

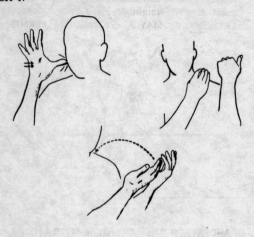

GRANDMOTHER 2, *n.* (A variation of GRANDMOTHER 1.) The "A" hands are positioned as in GRANDFATHER 2 but with the right thumb on the right cheek. They open in the same manner as in GRANDFATHER 2.

GRANT 1 (grănt, gränt), *v.*, GRANTED, GRANTING. (A permissive upswinging of the hands, as if giving in.) Both hands, palms facing and fingers pointing away from the body, are held at chest level, almost a foot apart. With an upward movement, using their wrists as pivots, the hands sweep up until the fingers point almost straight up. See also ALLOW, LET, LET'S, LET US, MAY 3, PERMISSION 1, PERMIT 1.

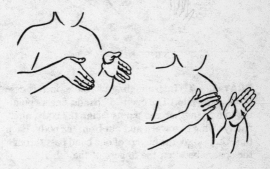

GRANT 2, *v.* The modified "O" hand, little finger edge down, moves forward and down in an arc before the body, as if giving something to someone.

GRASP (grăsp, gräsp), *v.*, GRASPED, GRASPING. See GRAB.

GRAY 1 (grā), *(loc.)*, *adj.* The right "O" hand traces an S-curve in the air as it moves down before the body.

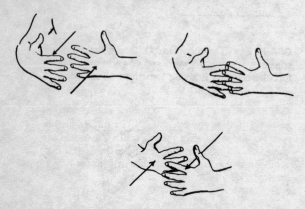

GRAY 2, *adj.* (Intermingling of colors, in this case black and white.) The open "5" hands, fingers pointing to one another and palms facing the body, alternately swing in toward and out from the body. Each time they do so, the fingers of one hand pass through the spaces between the fingers of the other.

GREAT 1 (grāt), *adj.* (A large amount.) The "5" hands face each other, fingers curved and touching.

They move apart rather quickly. See also EXPAND,
MUCH.

GREAT 2, *adj.* (The hands gesture toward the heavens.) The "5" hands, palms out and arms raised
rather high, are positioned somewhat above the line
of vision. The arms move abruptly forward and up
once or twice. An expression of pleasure or surprise
is usually assumed. See also EXCELLENT.

GREEDY 1 (grē′ dĭ), *adj.* (Pulling things toward
oneself.) Both prone open or "V" hands are held in
front of the body with fingers bent. The hands are
then drawn quickly and forcefully inward, as if raking things toward oneself. See also SELFISH 1,
STINGY 1.

GREEDY 2, *adj.* (Scratching the palm in greed.) The right fingers scratch the upturned left palm several times. A frowning expression is often used. See also SELFISH 2, STINGY 2.

GREY (grā), *adj.* See GRAY 1, 2.

GRIEF (grēf), *n.* (The facial features drop.) Both "5" hands, palms facing the eyes and fingers slightly curved, drop simultaneously to a level with the mouth. The head drops slightly as the hands move down, and an expression of sadness is assumed. See also GLOOM, GLOOMY, SAD, SORROWFUL 1.

GROUND (ground), *n.* (Fingering the soil.) Both hands, held upright before the body, finger imaginary pinches of soil. See also DIRT.

GROUP 1 (grōōp), *n.* (A grouping together.) Both "C" hands, palms facing, are held a few inches apart at chest height. They are swung around in unison, so that the palms now face the body. See also CLASS, CLASSED, COMPANY, ORGANIZATION 1.

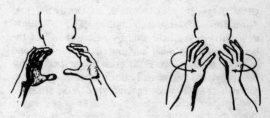

GROUP 2, *n.* (The letter "G.") The sign for GROUP 1 is made, using the "G" hands.

 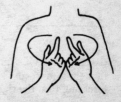

GROW (grō), *v.*, GREW, GROWN, GROWING. (Flowers or plants emerge from the ground.) The right fingers, pointing up, emerge from the closed left hand, and they spread open as they do. See also SPRING.

GROWN (grōn), *adj.* See GROW.

GUARD (gärd), *v.*, GUARDED, GUARDING. (Hold down firmly; cover and strengthen.) The "S" hands, downturned, are held side by side in front of the body, the arms almost horizontal, and the left hand in front of the right. Both arms move a short distance forward and slightly downward. See also DEFEND, DEFENSE, PROTECT, PROTECTION, SHIELD.

GUESS (gĕs), *n.*, *v.*, GUESSED, GUESSING. (A thought is grasped.) The right fingertip touches the forehead; then the right hand makes a quick grasping movement in front of the head, ending in the "S" position.

_____

GUIDE (gīd), *n., v.,* GUIDED, GUIDING. (One hand leads the other.) The right hand grasps the tips of the left fingers and pulls the left hand forward. See also LEAD.

GUILTY (gĭl′ tĭ), *adj.* (The "G" hand; a guilty heart.) The index finger edge of the right "G" hand taps the chest over the heart.

H

HABIT (hăb' ĭt), *n.* (Bound down to custom or habit.) Both "S" hands, palms down, are crossed and brought down in unison before the chest. See also CUSTOM, LOCKED.

HAIR (hâr), *n.* (The natural sign.) A lock of hair is grasped by the right index finger and thumb.

HAND (hănd), *n.* (The natural sign.) The prone right hand is drawn over the back of the prone left hand. For the plural, the action is repeated with the hands switched. The little finger edge of the right hand may instead be drawn across the back of the left wrist, as if cutting off the left hand; and for the plural the action is repeated with the hands switched.

HANG (hăng), *v.*, HUNG, HANGED, HANGING. (Hanging by the throat.) The thumb of the "Y" hand is placed at the right side of the neck, and the head hangs toward the left, as if it were caught in a noose.

HAPPEN 1 (hăp′ ən), *v.*, -ENED, -ENING. (A befalling.) Both "D" hands, index fingers pointing away from the body, are simultaneously pivoted over so that the palms face down. See also EVENT, INCIDENT.

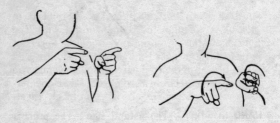

HAPPEN 2, *v.* The same sign as for HAPPEN 1 but the "H" hands are used.

HAPPY (hăp′ ĭ), *adj.* (The heart is stirred; the spirits bubble up.) The open right hand, palm facing the body, strikes the heart repeatedly, moving up and off the heart after each strike. See also GLAD, JOY, MERRY.

HARD 1 (härd), *adj.* (The knuckles are rubbed, to indicate a condition of being worn down.) The knuckles of the curved index and middle fingers of both hands are rubbed up and down against each other. Instead of the up-down rubbing, they may rub against each other in an alternate clockwise-counterclockwise manner. See also DIFFICULT 1, DIFFICULTY, POVERTY, PROBLEM 2.

HARD 2, *adj.* (Striking a hard object.) The curved index and middle fingers of the right hand, whose palm faces the body or the left, are brought down sharply against the back of the downturned left "S" hand. See also DIFFICULT 2.

HARD OF HEARING, *adj. phrase.* (The "H" is indicated twice.) The right "H" hand drops down an inch or so, rises, moves in a short arc to the right, and drops down an inch or so again.

HARDSHIP (härd' shĭp), *n.* See HARD 1.

HARM (härm), *n.* (A stabbing pain.) The "D" hands, index fingers pointing to each other, are rotated in elliptical fashion before the chest—simultaneously but in opposite directions. See also HURT, INJURE, INJURY, PAIN.

HATE (hāt), *n., v.,* HATED, HATING. (To push away and recoil from; avoid.) The two open hands, palms facing left, are pushed deliberately to the left, as if pushing something away. An expression of disdain or disgust is worn. See also AVOID 2.

HAVE (hăv), *v.,* HAS, HAD, HAVING. (The act of bringing something over to oneself.) The right-angle hands, palms facing and thumbs pointing up, are swept toward the body until the fingertips come to rest against the middle of the chest.

HAVE TO, *v. phrase.* (Being pinned down.) The right hand, in the "X" position, palm down, moves forcefully up and down once or twice. An expression of determination is frequently assumed. See also MUST, NECESSARY, NECESSITY, NEED 1, OUGHT TO, SHOULD.

HE (hē), *pron.* (Pointing at a male.) The MALE prefix sign is made: The right hand grasps an imaginary cap brim. The right index finger then points at an imaginary male. If in context the gender is clear, the prefix sign is usually omitted. See also HIM.

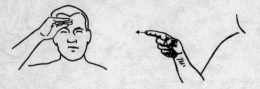

HEAD (hĕd), *n.* (The head is indicated.) The tips of the fingers of the right right-angle hand are placed at the right temple, and then move down in an arc to the right jaw.

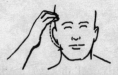

HEADACHE (hĕd′ āk′), *n.* (A stabbing pain in the head.) The index fingers, pointing to each other, move back and forth on the forehead.

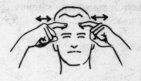

HEALTH (hĕlth), *n.* (Strength emanating from the body.) Both "5" hands are placed palms against the chest. They move out and away, forcefully, closing and assuming the "S" position. See also BRAVE, BRAVERY, MIGHTY 2, STRENGTH.

HEALTHY (hĕl′ thĭ), *adj.* See HEALTH.

HEARING (hĭr′ ĭng), *n., adj.* (Words tumbling from the mouth, indicating the old association of being able to hear with being able to speak.) The right index finger, pointing left, describes a continuous small circle in front of the mouth. See also MENTION, SAID, SAY, SPEAK, SPEECH 1, TALK 1, TELL.

HEAVY (hĕv′ ĭ), *adj.* (The hands drop under a weight.) The upturned "5" hands, held before the chest, suddenly drop a short distance.

HEIGHT 1 (hīt), *n.* (The height is indicated.) The index finger of the right "D" hand moves straight up against the palm of the left "5" hand. See also TALL 1.

HEIGHT 2, *n.* (The height is indicated.) The right right-angle hand, palm facing the left, is held at the height the signer wishes to indicate. See also BIG 2, HIGH 2, TALL 2.

HELLO (hĕ lō'), *interj.* (A wave of the hand.) The right open hand waves back and forth several times. See also GOODBYE.

HELP (hĕlp), *n., v.,* HELPED, HELPING. (Helping up; supporting.) The left "S" hand, thumb side up, rests in the open right palm. In this position the left hand is pushed up a short distance by the right. See also ASSIST, ASSISTANCE.

HER (hûr), *pron.* (Pointing at a female.) The FE-MALE prefix sign is made: The right "A" hand's thumb moves down along the line of the right jaw, from ear almost to chin. The right index finger then points at an imaginary female. If in context the gender is clear, the prefix sign is usually omitted. See also SHE. For the possessive sense of this pronoun, see HERS.

HERE (hĭr), *adv.* The open "5" hands, palms up and fingers slightly curved, move back and forth in front of the body, the right hand to the right and the left hand to the left. See also WHERE 2.

HERS (hûrz), *pron.* (Belonging to a female.) The FEMALE prefix sign is made. The open right hand, palm facing out, then moves straight forward a few inches. If in context the gender is clear, the prefix sign is usually omitted.

HERSELF (hər sĕlf'), *pron.* (The thumb indicates an individual who is stressed above others.) The FEMALE prefix sign is made. The right "A" hand, thumb upturned, then moves forward an inch or two, either once or twice. If in context the gender is clear, the prefix sign is usually omitted.

HIDE (hīd), *v.*, HID, HIDDEN, HIDING. (One hand is hidden under the other.) The thumb of the right "A" hand, whose palm faces left, is placed against the lips. The hand then swings down and under the downturned left hand. The initial contact with the lips is sometimes omitted.

HIGH 1 (hī), *adj.* (Something high up.) Both hands, in the right angle position, are held before the face, about a foot apart, palms facing. They are raised abruptly about a foot, in a slight outward curving movement. See also PROMOTE, PROMOTION.

HIGH 2, *adj.* (The height is indicated.) The right right-angle hand, palm facing the left, is held at the

height the signer wishes to indicate. See also BIG 2,
HEIGHT 2, TALL 2.

HIM (hĭm), *pron.* (Pointing at a male.) The MALE
prefix sign is made: The right hand grasps an imaginary cap brim. The right index finger then points at
an imaginary male. If in context the gender is clear,
the prefix sign is usually omitted. See also HE.

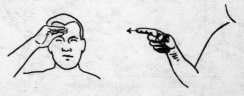

HIMSELF (hĭm sĕlf'), *pron.* (The thumb indicates an
individual who is stressed above others.) The MALE
prefix sign is made. The right "A" hand, thumb
upturned, then moves forward an inch or two, either
once or twice. If in context the gender is clear, the
prefix sign is usually omitted.

HIS (hĭz), *poss. pron.* (Belonging to a male.) The MALE prefix sign is made. The open right hand, palm facing out, then moves straight forward a few inches. If in context the gender is clear, the prefix sign is usually omitted.

HIT (hĭt), *n., v.*, HIT, HITTING. (The natural sign.) The right "S" hand strikes its knuckles forcefully against the open left palm, which is held facing right. See also PUNCH 1, STRIKE.

HOME (hōm), *n.* (A place where one eats and sleeps.) The closed fingers of the right hand are placed against the lips (the sign for EAT), and then, opening into a flat palm, against the right cheek (resting the head on a pillow, as in SLEEP). The head leans slightly to the right, as if going to sleep in the right palm, during this latter movement.

HONEST (ŏn′ ĭst), *adj*. (The letter "H," for HON-
EST; a straight and true path.) The index and middle
fingers of the right "H" hand, whose palm faces left,
move straight forward along the upturned left palm.
See also SINCERE.

HONESTY (ŏn′ ĭs tĭ), *n*. See HONEST.

HONOR (ŏn′ ər), *n., v.,* -ORED, -ORING. (The letter
"H"; a gesture of respect.) The right "H" hand,
palm facing left, swings down in an arc from its
initial position in front of the forehead. The head
bows slightly during this movement of the hand.

HONORARY (ŏn′ ə rĕr′ ĭ), *adj*. See HONOR.

HOPE (hōp), *n., v.,* HOPED, HOPING. (A thought awaited.) The tip of the right index finger, held in the "D" position, palm facing the body, is placed on the forehead (modified THINK, *q.v.*). Both hands then assume right angle positions, fingers facing, with the left hand held above left shoulder level and the right before the right breast. Both hands, held thus, wave to each other several times. See also EXPECT.

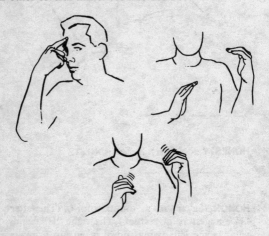

HORSE (hôrs), *n.* (The ears.) The "U" hands are placed palms out at either side of the head. The index and middle fingers move forward and back repeatedly, imitating the movement of a horse's ears. One hand may be omitted.

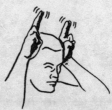

HOSPITAL (hŏs' pĭ təl), *n.* (The letter "H"; the red cross on the sleeve.) The index and middle fingers of the right "H" hand trace a cross on the upper part of the left arm.

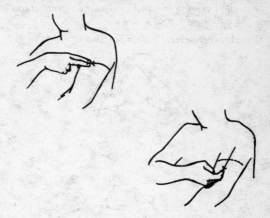

HOT (hŏt), *adj.* (Removing hot food from the mouth.) The cupped hand, palm facing the body, moves up in front of the slightly open mouth. It is then flung down to the palm-down position.

HOUSE (hous), *n.* (The shape of the house.) The open hands are held with fingertips touching, so that they form a pyramid a bit above eye level. From this position, the hands separate and move diagonally downward for a short distance; then they continue straight down a few inches. This movement traces the outline of a roof and walls.

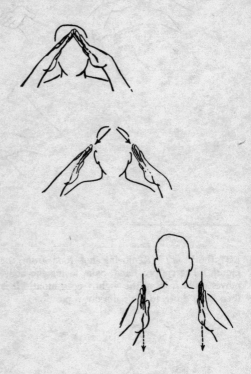

HOW (hou), *adv.* (The hands come into view, to reveal something.) The right-angle hands, palms

down and knuckles touching, swing up and open to
the palms-up position.

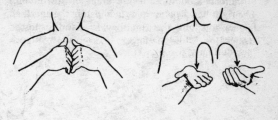

HOWEVER (hou ĕv′ ər), *conj.* Both hands, in the
"5" position are held before the chest, fingertips facing each other. With an alternate back-forth movement the fingertips are made to strike each other. See
also NEVERTHELESS.

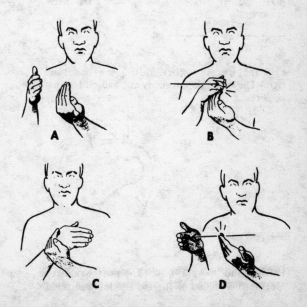

HOW MANY?, *interrogative phrase.* (Throwing up a number of things before the eyes; a display of fingers to indicate a question of how many or how much.) The right hand, palm up, is held before the chest, all fingers touching the thumb. The hand is tossed straight up, while the fingers open to the "5" position. See also AMOUNT.

HOW MUCH?, *interrogative phrase.* See HOW MANY?

HUG (hŭg), *v.*, HUGGED, HUGGING, *n.* (The natural sign.) The arms clasp the body in a natural hugging position.

HUMOR (hū′ mər, ū′-), *n.* (The nose wrinkles in laughter.) The tips of the right index and middle fingers brush repeatedly off the tip of the nose. See also FUNNY.

HUMOROUS (hū′ mər əs, ŭ′-), *adj.* See HUMOR.

HUNDRED (hŭn′ drəd), *n., adj.* (The Roman "C," *centum,* for "hundred.") The letter "C" is formed. This is preceded by a "1" for a simple hundred, or by whatever number of hundreds one wishes to indicate.

HURRY (hûr′ ĭ), *v.,* -RIED, -RYING. (Letter "H"; quick movements.) The "H" hands, palms facing each other and held about six inches apart, shake alternately up and down. One hand alone may be used.

HURT (hûrt), *v.*, HURT, HURTING, *n.* (A stabbing pain.) The "D" hands, index fingers pointing to each other, are rotated in elliptical fashion before the chest—simultaneously but in opposite directions. See also HARM, INJURE, INJURY, PAIN.

HUSBAND (hŭz' bənd), *n.* (A male joined in marriage.) The MALE prefix sign is formed: The right hand grasps the brim of an imaginary cap. The hands are then clasped together.

I

I 1 (ī), *pron.* (The letter "I," held to the chest.) The right "I" hand is held with its thumb edge to the chest and little finger pointing up.

I 2, *pron.* (The natural sign.) The signer points to himself. See also ME.

ICE (īs), *n., v.,* ICED, ICING. (The stiff fingers.) The fingers of the "5" hands, held palms down, stiffen and contract. See also FREEZE, FROZEN.

ICE CREAM (crēm), *n.* (The eating action.) The upturned left palm represents a dish or plate. The
curved index and middle fingers of the right hand
represent the spoon. They are drawn up repeatedly
from the left palm to the lips.

IF (ĭf), *conj.* (The scales move up and down.) The
two "F" hands, palms facing each other, move alternately up and down. See also CONSIDER 3, COURT,
EVALUATE 1, JUDGE 1, JUDGMENT, JUSTICE.

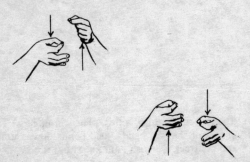

IGNORANT (ĭg′ nə rənt), *adj.* (The head is struck to
emphasize its emptiness or lack of knowledge.) The
back of the right "V" hand strikes the forehead once

or twice. Two fingers represent prison bars across the mind—the mind is imprisoned.

IGNORE (ĭg nôr'), *v.,* -NORED, -NORING. (Thumbing the nose.) The index finger of the right "B" hand is placed under the tip of the nose. From this position the right hand moves straight forward, away from the face. See also DISREGARD.

ILL (ĭl), *adj., n., adv.* (The sick parts of the anatomy are indicated.) The right middle finger rests on the forehead, and its left counterpart is placed against the stomach. The signer assumes an expression of sadness or physical distress. See also SICK.

IMAGINATION (ĭ măj´ ə nā´ shən), *n.* (A thought coming forward from the mind, modified by the letter "I" for "idea.") With the "I" position on the right hand, palm facing the body, touch the little finger to the forehead, and then move the hand up and away in a circular, clockwise motion. The hand may also be moved up and away without this circular motion.

IMAGINE (ĭ măj´ ĭn), *v.*, -INED, -INING. See IMAGINATION.

IMMEDIATELY (ĭ mē´ dĭ ĭt lĭ), *adv.* (A quick movement.) The thumbtip of the upright right hand is flicked quickly off the tip of the curved right index finger, as if shooting marbles. See also FAST, QUICK, QUICKNESS, SPEED, SPEEDY.

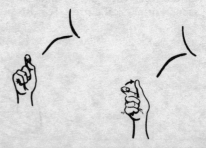

IMPORTANT (ĭm pôr′ tənt), *adj.* Both "F" hands, palms facing each other, move apart, up, and together in a smooth elliptical fashion, coming together at the tips of the thumbs and index fingers of both hands. See also SIGNIFICANCE 1, SIGNIFICANT, VALUABLE, VALUE, WORTH, WORTHWHILE, WORTHY.

IMPOSSIBLE (ĭm pŏs′ ə bəl), *(loc.)*, *adj.* The downturned right "Y" hand is placed in the upturned left palm a number of times. The up-down movement is very slight.

IMPROVE (ĭm prōōv′), *v.*, -PROVED, -PROVING. (Moving up.) The little finger edge of the right hand rests on the back of the downturned left hand. It moves up the left arm in successive stages, indicating improvement or upward movement.

IN (ĭn), *prep., adv., adj.* (The natural sign.) The fingers of the right hand are thrust into the left. See also INSIDE, INTO, WITHIN.

IN A FEW DAYS, *adv. phrase.* (Several TOMORROWS ahead.) The thumb of the right "A" hand is positioned on the right cheek. One by one, the remaining fingers appear, starting with the index finger. Usually, when all five fingers have been presented, the hand moves forward a few inches, to signify the concept of the future.

IN A WEEK, *adv. phrase.* (A week around the corner.) The upright, right "D" hand is placed palm-to-palm against the left "5" hand, whose palm faces right. The right "D" hand moves along the left palm from base to fingertips and then curves to the left, around the left fingertips.

INCIDENT (ĭn′ sə dənt), *n.* (A befalling.) Both "D" hands, index fingers pointing away from the body, are simultaneously pivoted over so that the palms face down. See also EVENT, HAPPEN 1.

INCLUDE (ĭn klōōd′), *v.,* -CLUDED, -CLUDING. (All; the whole.) The left hand is held in the "C" position, fingers pointing right. The right hand, in the "5" position, fingers facing out from the body, palm down, is held above the left. With a horizontal swing to the right, the right hand describes an arc, as the fingers close and are thrust into the left "C" hand, which closes over it.

INCLUSIVE (ĭn klōō′ sĭv), *adj.* See INCLUDE.

INCOME (ĭn′ kŭm), *n.* (A regular taking in.) The outstretched open left hand, held palm facing right, moves in toward the body, assuming the "A" position, palm still facing right. This is repeated several times.

INCREASE (*n.* ĭn′ krēs; *v.* ĭn krēs′) -CREASED, -CREASING. (Adding on.) The index and middle fingers of the right "H" hand, palm up, are swung up and over until they come to rest on the index and middle fingers of the left "H" hand, held palm down. See also ADD 2, ADDITION, GAIN, RAISE.

INDEPENDENCE (ĭn′ dĭ pĕn′ dəns), *n.* (Breaking the bonds.) The "S" hands, crossed in front of the body, swing apart and face out. See also FREE 1, RESCUE, SAFE, SAVE 1.

INDEPENDENT (ĭn´ dĭ pĕn´ dənt), *adj.* See INDE-PENDENCE.

———————

INDIVIDUAL 1 (ĭn´ də vĭj´ ŏo əl), *n.* (The shape of an individual.) Both open hands, palms facing each other, move down the sides of the body, tracing its outline to the hips. This is an important suffix sign, that changes a verb to a noun. *E.g.,* TEACH, *v.,* becomes TEACHER, *n.,* by the addition of this sign.

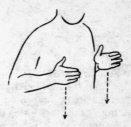

INDIVIDUAL 2, *n.* (The "I" hands; the outline of a person.) The "I" hands, palms facing and little fingers pointing out, are held before the body. They are drawn down a few inches, outlining the shape of an imaginary person standing before the signer.

INFLUENCE (ĭn′ floŏ əns), *n., v.* (Take something, *influence,* and disseminate it.) The left hand, held limp in front of the body, has its fingers pointing down. The fingers of the right hand, held all together, are placed on the top of the left hand, and then move forward, off the left hand, assuming a "5" position, palm down. See also ADVICE, ADVISE.

INFORM (ĭn fôrm′), *v.,* -FORMED, -FORMING. (Taking knowledge from the mind and giving it out to all.) The fingertips are positioned on either side of the forehead. Both hands then swing down and out, opening into the upturned "5" position. See also LET KNOW, NOTIFY.

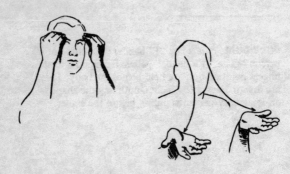

INFORMATION (ĭn fər mā′ shən), *n.* See INFORM.

INJURE (ĭn′ jər), *v.*, -JURED, -JURING. (A stabbing pain.) The "D" hands, index fingers pointing to each other, are rotated in elliptical fashion before the chest—simultaneously but in opposite directions. See also HARM, HURT, PAIN.

INJURY (ĭn′ jə rĭ), *n.* See INJURE.

INQUIRE (ĭn kwīr′), *(colloq.)*, *v.* -QUIRED, -QUIR- ING. (Fire a question.) The right hand, held in a modified "S" position with palm facing out, assumes a position with the thumb resting on the fingernail of the index finger. The index finger is flicked out and forward, usually directed at the person being asked a question. See also ASK 2.

INSANE (ĭn sān′), *adj.* (Turning of wheels in the head.) The open right hand is held palm down before the face, fingers spread, bent, and pointing toward the forehead. The fingers move in circles before the forehead. See also CRAZY 1.

INSANITY (ĭn săn′ ə tĭ), *n.* See INSANE.

INSECT (ĭn′ sĕkt), *(sl.), n.* (The quivering antennae.) The thumb of the "3" hand rests against the nose, and the index and middle fingers bend slightly and straighten again a number of times.

INSIDE (*prep., adv.* ĭn′ sīd′; *adj.* ĭn′ sīd′). (The natural sign.) The fingers of the right hand are thrust into the left. See also IN, INTO, WITHIN.

INSTRUCT (ĭn strŭkt′), *v.*, -STRUCTED, -STRUCT-ING. (Giving forth from the mind.) The fingertips of each hand are placed on the temples. They then swing out and open into the "5" position. See also EDUCATE, TEACH.

INTELLIGENT (ĭn tĕl′ ə jənt), *adj.* (The mind is bright.) The middle finger is placed at the forehead, and then the hand, with an outward flick, turns around so that the palm faces outward. This indicates a brightness flowing from the mind. See also SMART.

INTEND (ĭn tĕnd'), *v.*, -TENDED, -TENDING. (Relative standing of one's thoughts.) A modified sign for **THINK** is made: The right index finger touches the middle of the forehead. The tips of the right "V" hand, palm down, are then thrust into the upturned left palm (as in STAND, *q.v.*). The right "V" hand is then re-thrust into the upturned left palm, with right palm now facing the body. See also MEAN 2, MEANING, PURPOSE, SIGNIFICANCE 2, SIGNIFY.

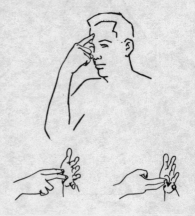

INTENT (ĭn tĕnt'), *n.* See INTEND.

INTENTION (ĭn tĕn' shən), *n.* See INTEND.

INTEREST 1 (ĭn' tər ĭst, -trĭst), *n.*, *v.*, -ESTED, -ESTING. (Drawing one out.) The index and middle fingers of both hands, one above the other, are placed on the middle part of the chest. Both hands move forward simultaneously. As they do, the index

and middle fingers of each hand come together. See
also FASCINATE.

INTEREST 2, *n., v.* (The tongue is pulled out, causing the mouth to gape.) The curved open right hand
is placed at the mouth, with index finger and thumb
poised as if to grasp the tongue. The hand moves
straight out, assuming the "A" position.

INTERESTED 1 (ĭn′ tər ĭs tĭd, -trĭs tĭd, -tə rĕs′ tĭd),
adj. See INTEREST 1.

INTERESTED 2, *adj.* See INTEREST 2.

INTERESTING 1 (ĭn′ tər ĭs tĭng, -trĭs tĭng, -tə rĕs′
tĭng), *adj.* See INTEREST 1.

INTERESTING 2, *adj.* See INTEREST 2.

INTERFERE (ĭn´ tər fîr´), *v.,* -FERED, -FERING. (Obstruct, block.) The left hand, fingers together and palm flat, is held before the body, facing somewhat down. The little finger side of the right hand, held with palm flat, makes one or several up-down chopping motions against the left hand, between its thumb and index finger. See also ANNOY, ANNOYANCE, BOTHER, DISTURB, INTERRUPT, PREVENT, PREVENTION.

INTERFERENCE (ĭn´ tər fîr´ əns), *n.* See INTERFERE.

INTERFERE WITH *v. phrase.* See INTERFERE.

INTERPRET (ĭn tûr´ prĭt), *v.,* -PRETED, -PRETING. (Changing one language to another.) The "F" hands

are held palms facing and thumbs and index fingers
in contact with each other. The hands swing around
each other, reversing their relative positions.

INTERROGATION 2, *(colloq.), n.* See INTERROGATE
2.

INTERRUPT (ĭn´ tə rŭpt´), *v.*, -RUPTED, -RUPTING.
(Obstruct, block.) The left hand, fingers together
and palm flat, is held before the body, facing somewhat down. The little finger side of the right hand,
held with palm flat, makes one or several up-down
chopping motions against the left hand, between its
thumb and index finger. See also ANNOY, ANNOY-
ANCE, BOTHER, DISTURB, INTERFERE, INTERFER-
ENCE, INTERFERE WITH, PREVENT, PREVENTION.

INTERSECT (ĭn′ tər sĕkt′), *v.,* -SECTED, -SECTING. (Intersecting lines.) The extended index fingers move toward each other at right angles and cross.

INTERSECTION (ĭn′ tər sĕk shən), *n.* See INTERSECT.

IN THE FUTURE, *adv. phrase.* (Something ahead or in the future.) The upright, open right hand, palm facing left, moves straight out and slightly up from a position beside the right temple. See also FUTURE, LATER 2, LATER ON, WILL 1, WOULD.

INTO (ĭn′ tōō), *prep.* (The natural sign.) The fingers of the right hand are thrust into the left. See also IN, INSIDE, WITHIN.

INTOXICATE (ĭn tŏk′ sə kāt′), *v.*, -CATED, -CATING.
(The act of drinking.) The thumbtip of the right "Y"
hand is tilted toward the mouth, as if it were a
drinking glass or bottle. The signer tilts his head
back slightly, as if drinking. See also DRUNK,
DRUNKARD, DRUNKENNESS, LIQUOR.

INTOXICATION (ĭn tŏk′ sə ka′ shən), *n.* See INTOXI-
CATE.

INVITE (ĭn vīt′), *v.*, -VITED, -VITING. (Opening or
leading the way toward something.) The open right
hand, held up before the body, sweeps down in an
arc and over toward the left side of the chest, ending
in the palm-up position. Reversing the movement
gives the passive form of the verb, except that the
hand does not arc upward but rather simply moves
outward in a small arc from the body. See also IN-
VITED, WELCOME.

INVITED, *passive voice of the verb* INVITE. The upturned right hand, touching the chest, moves
straight forward and away from the body.

J

JEALOUS (jĕl′ əs), *adj.* (Biting the finger to suppress the feelings.) The tip of the index finger is bitten. The tip of the little finger is sometimes used. See also ENVIOUS, ENVY.

JEALOUSY (jĕl′ ə sĭ), *n.* See JEALOUS.

JOB (jŏb), *n.* (Striking an anvil.) Both "S" hands are held palms down. The right hand strikes against the back of the left a number of times. See also WORK.

JOIN (join), *v.*, JOINED, JOINING. (Joining together.) Both hands, held in the modified "5" position, palms out, move toward each other. The thumbs and index fingers of both hands then connect. See also ATTACH, BELONG, CONNECT.

JOY (joi), *n.* (The heart is stirred; the spirits bubble up.) The open right hand, palm facing the body, strikes the heart repeatedly, moving up and off the heart after each strike. See also GLAD, HAPPY, MERRY.

JUDGE (jŭj), *n., v.,* JUDGED, JUDGING. (The scales move up and down.) The two "F" hands, palms facing each other, move alternately up and down. See also CONSIDER 3, COURT, EVALUATE 1, IF, JUSTICE.

JUDGMENT (jŭj′ mənt), *n.* See JUDGE.

JUST A MOMENT AGO, *adv. phrase.* (Time moved backward a bit.) The right "D" hand, palm facing the body, is placed in the palm of the left hand, which is facing right. The right hand swings back a bit toward the body, with the index finger describing an arc. See also FEW SECONDS AGO, A; WHILE AGO, A 2.

JUSTICE (jŭs′ tĭs), *n.* (The scales move up and down.) The two "F" hands, palms facing each other, move alternately up and down. See also CONSIDER 3, COURT, EVALUATE 1, IF, JUDGE 1.

KEEP (kēp), *v.*, KEPT, KEEPING. (Slow, careful movement.) The "K" hands are crossed, the right above the left, little finger edges down. In this position the hands are moved up and down a short distance. See also CARE 2, CAREFUL 2, MAINTAIN 1, PRESERVE, TAKE CARE OF.

KEEP QUIET 1, *v. phrase.* (The natural sign.) The index finger is placed forcefully against the closed lips. The signer frowns or looks stern.

KEEP QUIET 2, *v. phrase.* (The mouth is sealed; the sign for QUIET.) The downturned open hands are crossed at the lips with the left in front of the right. Both hands are drawn apart and down rather forcefully, while the signer frowns or looks stern.

KEEP STILL 1, *v. phrase.* See KEEP QUIET 1.

KEEP STILL 2, *v. phrase.* See KEEP QUIET 2.

KEY (kē), *n.* (The turning of the key.) The right hand, holding an imaginary key, twists it in the open left palm, which is facing right. See also LOCK 1.

KID (kĭd), *(colloq.), n.* (The running nose.) The index and little fingers of the right hand, held palm

down, are extended, pointing to the left. The index
finger is placed under the nose and the hand trembles
somewhat.

KILL (kĭl), *v.*, KILLED, KILLING. (Thrusting a dagger and twisting it.) The outstretched right index
finger is passed under the downturned left hand. As
it moves under the left hand, the right wrist twists
in a clockwise direction. See also MURDER.

KIND 1 (kīnd), *adj.* (The heart rolls out.) Both right-
angle hands roll over each other as they move down
and away from their initial position at the heart. See
also GENEROUS.

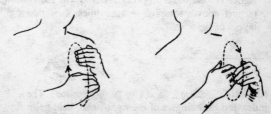

KIND 2, *n*. (The letter "K"; the wholeness or global characteristic.) The right "K" hand revolves once around the left "K" hand. This is used to describe a class or group.

KISS (kĭs), *n., v.,* KISSED, KISSING. (Lips touch lips.) With fingers touching their thumbs, both hands are brought together. They tremble slightly, indicating the degree of intensity of the kiss.

KNIFE (nīf), *n*. (Shaving or paring.) The edge of the right "H" hand, resting on the edge of its left counterpart, moves forward several times, as if shaving layers of flesh.

KNOW (nō), *v.*, KNEW, KNOWN, KNOWING. (Patting the head to indicate something of value inside.) The right fingers pat the forehead several times.

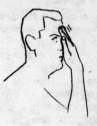

KNOWING (nō′ ĭng), *adj.* See KNOW.

KNOWLEDGE (nŏl′ ĭj), *n.* See KNOW.

L

LADY (lā' dĭ), *n.* (A female with a ruffled bodice; *i.e.,* an elegantly dressed woman, a lady.) The FE-MALE root sign is made: The thumb of the right "A" hand moves down along the right jaw, from ear almost to chin. The thumbtip of the right "5" hand, palm facing left, is then placed on the chest, with the other fingers pointing up. Pivoted at the thumb, the hand swings down a bit, so that the other fingers are now pointing out somewhat.

LAND 1 (lănd), *n.* (An expanse of ground.) The sign for SOIL 1 is made: Both hands, held upright before the body, finger imaginary pinches of soil. The downturned open right "5" hand then sweeps in an arc from right to left.

LAND 2, *n.* (An established area.) The right "N" hand, palm down, executes a clockwise circle above the downturned prone left hand. The tips of the "N" fingers then move straight down and come to rest on the back of the left hand. See also COUNTRY 2, NATION.

LANGUAGE 1 (lăng′ gwĭj), *n.* (A series of letters spelled out on the printed page.) The downturned "F" hands are positioned with thumbs and index fingertips touching. The hands move straight apart to either side in a wavy motion. See also SENTENCE.

LANGUAGE 2, *n.* (The letter "L.") The sign for LANGUAGE 1 is made, but with the "L" hands.

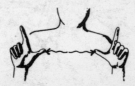

LANGUAGE OF SIGNS, *n.* (LANGUAGE 1 and hand/arm movements.) The "D" hands, palms facing and index fingers pointing back toward the face, describe a series of continuous counterclockwise circles toward and away from the face, imitating the foot motions in bicycling. This is followed by the sign for LANGUAGE 1. See also SIGN LANGUAGE, SIGNS.

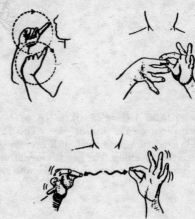

LARGE (lärj), *adj.* (A delineation of something big, modified by the letter "L," which stands for LARGE.) Both "L" hands, palms facing out, are placed before the face, and separate rather widely. See also BIG 1.

LAST 1 (lăst), *adj.* (The little, *i.e.*, LAST, fingers are indicated.) With the hands in the "I" position, the tip of the right little finger strikes the tip of its left counterpart. The right index finger may be used instead of the right little finger. See also END 1, FINAL 1, FINALLY 1.

LAST 2, *adj.* (A single little, *i.e.*, LAST, finger is indicated.) The tip of the index finger of the right "D" hand strikes the tip of the little finger of the left "I" hand. See also END 2, FINAL 2, FINALLY 2.

LAST 3, *v.* (Steady, uninterrupted movement.) The "A" hands are held with palms out, thumbs extended and touching, the right behind the left. In this position the hands move forward in a straight, steady line. See also CONTINUE, ENDURE 2, EVER 1, PERMANENT, PERSEVERE, PERSIST, REMAIN, STAY 1, STAY STILL.

LASTING (lăs′ tĭng), *adj.* See LAST 3.

LASTLY (lăst′ lĭ), *adv.* See LAST 1 or 2.

LATE (lāt), *adj.* (Hanging back.) The "5" hand and forearm, hanging loosely and straight down from the elbow, move back and forth under the armpit. See also NOT YET.

LATER 1, *adj.* (A moving on of the minute hand of the clock.) The right "L" hand, its thumb thrust into the palm of the left and acting as a pivot, moves forward a short distance. See also AFTER A WHILE, AFTERWARD.

LATER 2, *adj., adv.* (Something ahead or in the future.) The upright, open right hand, palm facing left, moves straight out and slightly up from a position beside the right temple. See also FUTURE, IN THE FUTURE, WILL 1, WOULD.

————————

LATER ON, *adv. phrase.* See LATER 2.

————————

LAUGH (lăf), *n., v.,* LAUGHED, LAUGHING. (The natural sign.) The fingers of both "D" hands move repeatedly up along the jawline, or up from the corners of the mouth. The signer meanwhile laughs.

————————

LAUGHTER 1 (lăf′ tər), *n.* See LAUGH.

LAUGHTER 2, *(colloq.)*, *n.* (The shaking of the stomach.) The cupped hands, held at stomach level, palms facing the body, move alternately up and down, describing short arcs. The signer meanwhile laughs.

LAUGHTER 3, *(colloq.)*, *n.* (Literally, rolling in the aisles; the legs are doubled up and the body rolls on the floor.) With index and middle fingers crooked, and its little finger edge or back resting on the up-turned left palm, the right hand moves in a continuous counterclockwise circle in the left palm. The signer meanwhile laughs.

LAW (lô), *n.* (A series of LAWS as they appear on the printed page.) The upright right "L" hand, resting palm against palm on the upright left "5" hand, moves down in an arc a short distance, coming to rest on the base of the left palm.

LAZINESS (lā' zǐ nǐs), *n.* (The initial "L" rests against the body; the concept of inactivity.) The right "L" hand is placed against the left shoulder once or a number of times. The palm faces the body.

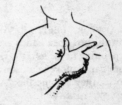

LAZY (lā' zǐ), *adj.* See LAZINESS.

LEAD (lēd), *v.,* LED, LEADING, *n.* (One hand leads the other.) The right hand grasps the tips of the left fingers and pulls the left hand forward. See also GUIDE.

LEARN (lûrn), *v.*, LEARNED, LEARNING. (Taking knowledge from a book and placing it in the head.) The downturned fingers of the right hand are placed on the upturned left palm. They close, and then the hand rises and the right fingertips are placed on the forehead.

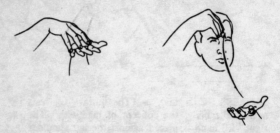

LEAVE (lēv), *v.*, LEFT, LEAVING. (Pulling away.) The downturned open hands are held in a line, with fingers pointing to the left, the right hand behind the left. Both hands move in unison toward the right. As they do so, they assume the "A" position. See also DEPART, WITHDRAW 1.

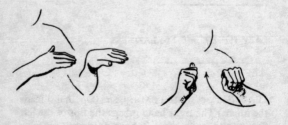

LECTURE (lek' chər), *n.*, *v.*, -TURED, -TURING. (A gesture of an orator.) The right open hand, palm facing left, is held above and to the right of the head.

It pivots on the wrist, forward and backward, several times. See also SPEECH 2, TALK 2.

LEFT 1 (lĕft), *adj.* (The remainder is left behind.) The "5" hands, palms facing each other and fingers pointing forward, are dropped simultaneously a few inches, as if dropping something on the table. See also REMAINDER.

LEFT 2, *adj., adv.* (The letter "L"; to the left side.) The left "L" hand, palm out, moves to the left.

LEND 1 (lĕnd), *v.*, LENT, LENDING. (Something kept, *i.e.,* in one's custody, is moved forward to other, temporary, ownership.) The crossed "K" hands, for KEEP, *q.v.,* are moved forward simultaneously, in a short arc. See also LOAN 1.

LEND 2, *v.* The side of the right index finger is brought up against the right side of the nose. See also LOAN 2.

LESS (lĕs), *adj.* (The diminishing size or amount.) With palms facing, the right hand is held above the left. The right hand moves slowly down toward the left, but does not touch it. See also DECREASE, REDUCE.

LESSON (lĕs′ ən), *n.* (A section of a page.) The upturned open left hand represents the page. The little finger edge of the right-angle hand is placed on the left palm near the fingertips. It moves up and over, in an arc, to the base of the left palm.

LET (lĕt), *v.*, LET, LETTING, *n.* (A permissive up-swinging of the hands, as if giving in.) Both hands, palms facing and fingers pointing away from the body, are held at chest level, almost a foot apart. With an upward movement, using their wrists as pivots, the hands sweep up until the fingers point almost straight up. See also ALLOW, GRANT 1, MAY 3, PERMISSION 1, PERMIT 1.

LET KNOW *v. phrase.* (Taking knowledge from the mind and giving it out to all.) The fingertips are positioned on either side of the forehead. Both hands then swing down and out, opening into the upturned "5" position. See also INFORM, INFORMATION 1, NOTIFY.

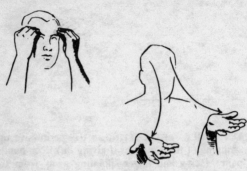

LET'S (lĕts); **LET US,** *v. phrase.* See LET.

LETTER (lĕt′ ər), *n.* (The stamp is affixed.) The right thumb is placed on the tongue, and is then pressed into the open left palm. See also MAIL 1.

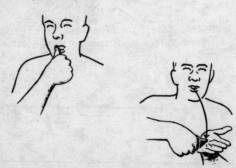

LEVEL (lĕv′ əl), *adj., n., v.,* -ELED, -ELING. (Sameness is stressed.) The downturned "B" hands, held at chest height, are brought together repeatedly, so that the index finger edges or fingertips come into contact. See also EQUAL, EQUIVALENT, EVEN, FAIR.

LIAR (lī′ ər), *n.* (Words diverted instead of coming straight, or truthfully, out.) The index finger of the right "D" hand, pointing to the left, moves along the lips from the right to left. See also FALSE, FALSEHOOD, LIE 1.

LIBRARY (lī′ brĕr′ ĭ), *n.* (The initial "L.") The right "L" hand, palm out, describes a small clockwise circle.

LICENSE (lī səns), *(loc.)*, *n.*, -CENSED, -CENSING. (The "L" hands outline the dimensions of the license form.) The "L" hands, palms out, touch at the thumbtips several times.

LIE 1 (lī), *n.*, *v.*, LIED, LYING. (Words diverted instead of coming straight, or truthfully, out.) The index finger of the right "D" hand, pointing to the left, moves along the lips from right to left. See also FALSE, FALSEHOOD, LIAR.

LIE 2, *n.*, *v.* (Same rationale as in LIE 1 but more emphatic, as indicated by several fingers.) The index finger edge of the downturned "B" hand moves along the lips (or under the chin) from right to left.

LIFE 1 (līf), *n.* (The fountain [of LIFE] wells up from within the body.) The upturned thumbs of the "A" hands move in unison up the chest. See also AD-DRESS, ALIVE, LIVE 1, LIVING.

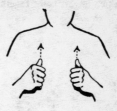

LIFE 2, *n.* (Same rationale as for LIFE 1 with the initials "L.") The upturned thumbs of the "L" hands move in unison up the chest.

LIGHT (līt), *adj.* (Easily lifted.) The open hands, palms up, move up and down together in front of the body, as if lifting something very light.

LIKE 1 (līk), *v.*, LIKED, LIKING. (Drawing out the feelings.) The thumb and index finger of the right open hand, held an inch or two apart, are placed at mid-chest. As the hand moves straight out from the chest the two fingers come together.

LIKE 2, *adj., n.* (Matching fingers are brought together.) The outstretched index fingers are brought together, either once or several times. See also ALIKE, SAME 1, SIMILAR.

LIKE 3, *v.* (A pleasurable feeling on the heart.) The open right hand is circled on the chest, over the heart. See also ENJOY, ENJOYMENT, PLEASE, PLEASURE.

LIMIT (lǐm′ ǐt), *n.*, *v.*, LIMITED, LIMITING. (The upper and lower limits are defined.) The right-angle hands, palms facing, are held before the body, the right above the left. They swing out 45 degrees simultaneously, pivoted from their wrists. See also RESTRICT.

LIQUOR (lǐk′ ər), *n.*, (The act of drinking.) The thumbtip of the right "Y" hand is tilted toward the mouth, as if it were a drinking glass or bottle. The signer tilts his head back slightly, as if drinking. See also DRUNK, DRUNKARD, DRUNKENNESS, INTOXI-CATE, INTOXICATION.

LISTEN (lĭs' ən), *v.*, -TENED, -TENING. (Cupping the hand at the ear.) The right hand is placed, usually slightly cupped, behind the right ear.

LITTLE (lĭt əl), *adj., adv., n.* (A small or tiny movement.) The right thumbtip is flicked off the index finger several times, as if shooting marbles, although the movement is not so pronounced.

LIVE 1 (lĭv), *v.*, LIVED, LIVING. (The fountain [of LIFE] wells up from within the body.) The upturned thumbs of the "A" hands move in unison up the chest. See also ADDRESS, ALIVE, LIFE 1.

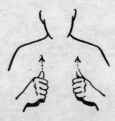

LIVE 2, *v.* See LIFE 2.

_____

LIVING (lĭv′ ĭng), *adj.* See LIVE 1.

_____

LOAN 1 (lōn), *n.* (Something kept, *i.e.,* in one's custody, is moved forward to other, temporary, ownership.) The crossed "K" hands, for KEEP, *q.v.,* are moved forward simultaneously, in a short arc. See also LEND 1.

_____

LOAN 2, *(loc.), (colloq.), n., v.,* LOANED, LOANING. The side of the right index finger is brought up against the right side of the nose. See also LEND 2.

LOCATION (lō kā′ shən), *n.* (The letter "P"; a circle or square is indicated, to show the locale or place.) The "P" hands are held side by side before the body, with middle fingertips touching. From this position, the hands separate and outline a circle (or a square), before coming together again closer to the body. See also PLACE, POSITION.

LOCK 1 (lŏk), *n., v.,* LOCKED, LOCKING. (The turning of the key.) The right hand, holding an imaginary key, twists it in the open left palm, which is facing right. See also KEY.

LOCK 2, *(loc.), v.* (Bind down.) The right "S" hand, palm down, makes a clockwise circle and comes down on the back of the left "S" hand, also held palm down.

LOCKED, *(loc.), adj.* (Bound down to custom or habit.) Both "S" hands, palms down, are crossed and brought down in unison before the chest. See also CUSTOM, HABIT.

LONE (lōn), *adj.* (One, wandering around in a circle.) The index finger, pointing straight up, palm facing the body (the number *one*), is rotated before the face in a counterclockwise direction. See also ALONE, ONLY.

LONELY 1 (lōn′ lĭ), *adj.* ("Oneness"; quietness.) The index finger of the right "1" hand moves straight down across the lips once or twice.

LONELY 2, *(colloq.), adj.* ("I" signs; *i.e.,* alone with oneself.) Both "I" hands are held facing the body, the little fingers upright and held an inch or two apart. The little fingers come together and separate repeatedly.

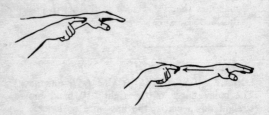

LONESOME (lōn′ səm), *adj.* See LONELY 1.

LONG 1 (lông, lŏng), *adj. n., adv.* (The distance is traced.) The right index finger traces a long line along the upturned left arm from wrist almost to shoulder.

LOOK 1 (loŏk), *v.,* LOOKED, LOOKING. (The eyesight is directed forward.) The right "V" hand, palm facing the body, is placed so that the fingertips are just under the eyes. The hand swings around and out, so that the fingertips are now pointing forward.

See also PERCEIVE, PERCEPTION, SEE, SIGHT, WATCH 1.

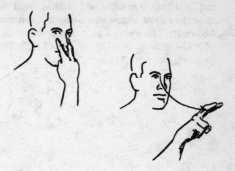

LOOK 2 (lo͝ok), *v.* (Something presented before the eyes.) The open right hand, palm flat and facing out, with fingers together and pointing up, is positioned at shoulder level. Pivoting from the wrist, the hand is swung around so that the palm now faces the eyes. Sometimes the eyes glance at the newly presented palm. See also SEEM.

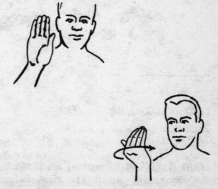

LOOK FOR *v. phrase.* (Directing the vision from place to place; the French *chercher*.) The right "C" hand, palm facing left, moves from right to left across the line of vision, in a series of counterclockwise circles. The signer's gaze remains concentrated and his head turns slowly from right to left. See also EXAMINE, SEARCH, SEEK.

LOSE (lo͞oz), *v.,* LOST, LOSING. (Dropping something.) Both hands, with fingers touching their respective thumbs, are held palms up and with the backs of the fingers almost touching or in contact with one another. The hands drop into an open position, with fingers pointing down.

LOST (lôst, lŏst), *adj.* See LOSE.

LOUD (loud), *adj.* (Something heard which shakes the surrounding area.) The right index finger touches the ear. The "5" hands, palms down, then move sharply in front of the body, in quick alternate motions, first away from and then back to the body.

LOUDLY (loud' lĭ), *adv.* See LOUD.

LOUD NOISE, *n. phrase.* See LOUD.

LOUSY (lou' zĭ), *(sl.), adj.* (A modification of the sign for spitting or thumbing the nose.) The right "3" hand is held with thumbtip against the nose. Then it is thrown sharply forward, and an expression of contempt is assumed.

LOVE (lŭv), *n., v.,* LOVED, LOVING. (Clasping the heart.) The "5" hands are held one atop the other over the heart. Sometimes the "S" hands are used, in which case they are crossed at the wrists.

LOVER (lŭv' ər), *(colloq.), n.* (Heads nodding toward each other.) The "A" hands are placed together before the body with thumbs up. The thumbs wiggle up and down. See also SWEETHEART.

LUGGAGE (lŭg' ĭj), *n.* (The natural sign.) The downturned right "S" hand grasps an imaginary piece of luggage and shakes it up and down slightly, as if testing its weight.

M

MACHINE (mə shēn′), *n.* (The meshing gears.) With the knuckles of both hands interlocked, the hands pivot up and dōwn, imitating the meshing of gear teeth. See also ENGINE, MOTOR.

MAD (măd), *adj.* (A violent welling-up of the emotions.) The curved fingers of the right hand are placed in the center of the chest, and fly up suddenly and violently. An expression of anger is worn. See also ANGER, ANGRY 2, FURY, RAGE.

MAIL 1 (māl), *n.* (The stamp is affixed.) The right thumb is placed on the tongue, and is then pressed into the open left palm. See also LETTER.

MAIL 2, *v.*, MAILED, MAILING. (Sending a letter.) The sign for LETTER is made: The right thumbtip is licked and placed against the upturned left palm. The right hand, palm out and fingers touching thumb, is then thrown forward, opening into the "5" position, palm out.

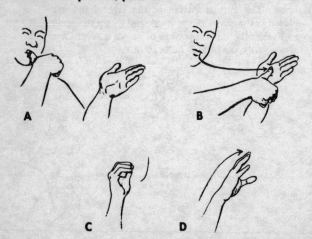

MAINTAIN 1 (mān tān′), *v.*, -TAINED, -TAINING. (Slow, careful movement.) The "K" hands are crossed, the right above the left, little finger edges down. In this position the hands are moved up and down a short distance. See also CARE 2, CAREFUL 2, KEEP, PRESERVE, TAKE CARE OF.

MAKE (māk), *v.*, MADE, MAKING, *n.* (Fashioning something with the hands.) The right "S" hand, palm facing left, is placed on top of its left counterpart, whose palm faces right. The hands are twisted back and forth, striking each other slightly after each twist. See also CREATE, MEND, PRODUCE.

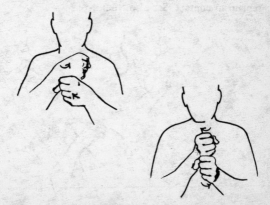

MAKE BRIEF, *v. phrase.* (To squeeze or condense into a small space.) The "C" hands face each other, with the right hand nearer to the body than the left. Both hands draw together and close deliberately, squeezing an imaginary object. See also SUMMARIZE 1, SUMMARY 1.

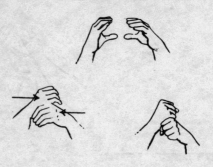

MAKE LOVE *(sl.),* *v. phrase.* (Necks interlocked.) The "S" hands, palms facing, are crossed at the wrists. They swing up and down while the wrists remain in contact. See also NECKING.

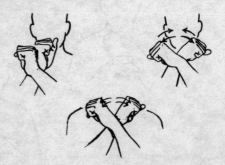

MALE (māl), *n., adj.* (The man's cap.) The thumb and extended fingers of the right hand are brought up to grasp an imaginary cap brim, representing the tipping of caps by men in olden days. This is a root sign used to modify many others. *Viz.* MALE plus BABY: SON; MALE plus SAME: BROTHER; etc.

MAN (măn), *n.* See MALE.

MANAGE (măn′ ĭj), *v.,* -AGED, -AGING. (Holding the reins over all.) The "A" hands, palms facing, move alternately back and forth, as if grasping and manipulating reins. See also CONTROL 1, GOVERN, RULE.

MANKIND (măn′ kīnd′), *n.* See MALE.

MANY (mĕn' ĭ), *adj.* (*Many* fingers are indicated.)
The upturned "S" hands are thrown up, opening
into the "5" position, palms up. This may be repeated. See also NUMEROUS, QUANTITY.

MARRIAGE (măr' ĭj), *n.* (A clasping of hands, as
during the wedding ceremony.) The hands are
clasped together, the right on top of the left.

MARRY (măr' ĭ), *v.*, -RIED, -RYING. See MARRIAGE.

MAY 1 (mā), *v.* (Weighing one thing against another.) The upturned open hands move alternately
up and down. See also MIGHT 2, PERHAPS, POSSIBIL-
ITY, POSSIBLY, PROBABLE, PROBABLY.

MAY 2, *v.* (An affirmative movement of the hands, likened to a nodding of the head, to indicate ability or power to accomplish something.) Both "A" hands, held palms down, move down in unison a short distance before the chest. See also CAN, CAPABLE, POSSIBLE.

MAY 3, *v.* (A permissive upswinging of the hands, as if giving in.) Both hands, palms facing and fingers pointing away from the body, are held at chest level, almost a foot apart. With an upward movement, using their wrists as pivots, the hands sweep up until the fingers point almost straight up. See also ALLOW, GRANT 1, LET, LET'S, LET US, PERMISSION 1, PERMIT 1.

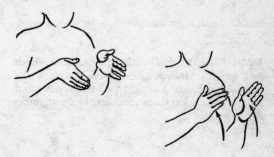

MAYBE (mā' bĭ, -bē), *adv.* See MAY 1.

ME (mē; *unstressed* mĭ), *pron.* (The natural sign.)
The signer points to himself. See also I 2.

MEAL (mēl), *n.* (The natural sign.) The closed right
hand goes through the natural motion of placing
food in the mouth. This movement is repeated. See
also EAT, FEED 1, FOOD.

MEAN 1 (mēn), *adj.* (Striking down against.) Both
"A" or "X" hands are held before the chest, the
right above the left. The right hand strikes down and
out, hitting the left thumb and knuckles with force.
See also CRUEL.

MEAN 2, *v.*, MEANT, MEANING. (Relative standing of one's thoughts.) A modified sign for THINK is made: The right index finger touches the middle of the forehead. The tips of the right "V" hand, palm down, are then thrust into the upturned left palm (as in STAND, *q.v.*). The right "V" hand is then re-thrust into the upturned left palm, with right palm now facing the body. See also INTEND, INTENT, INTENTION, PURPOSE, SIGNIFICANCE 2, SIGNIFY.

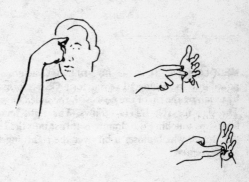

MEANING (mē′ nĭng), *n.* See MEAN 2.

MEANTIME (mēn′ tīm′), *n., adv.* (Parallel time.) Both "D" hands, palms down, move forward in unison, away from the body. They may move straight forward or may follow a slight upward arc. *Cf.* DURING, WHILE.

MEAT (mēt), *n*. (The fleshy part of the hand.) The right index finger and thumb squeeze the fleshy part of the open left hand, between thumb and index finger.

MEDDLE (med' 'l), *v.*, -DLED, -DLING. (The nose is poked into something.) The sign for NOSE is formed by touching the tip of the nose with the index finger. The sign for IN, INTO follows: The right hand, fingertips touching the thumb, is thrust into the left "C" hand, which closes a bit over the right fingers as they enter.

MEDICINE (mĕd' ə sən), *n*. (Mixing of medicine; rolling a pill.) The ball of the middle fingertip of the right "5" hand describes a small counterclockwise circle in the upturned left palm.

MEET (mēt), *v.*, MET, MEETING. (A coming together of two persons.) Both "D" hands, palms facing each other, are brought together.

MEETING (mē′ tǐng), *n.* (Assemble all together.) Both "5" hands, palms facing, are held with fingers pointing out from the body. With a sweeping motion they are brought in toward the chest, and all fingertips come together. This is repeated. See also CONFERENCE, GATHER 2, GATHERING.

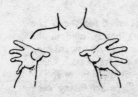 

MELT (mĕlt), *v.*, MELTED, MELTING. (Fingering the small pieces resulting from the breaking up of something.) The thumbs rub slowly across the fingertips of the upturned hands, from the little fingers to the index fingers, and then continue to the "A" position, palms up. See also DISSOLVE.

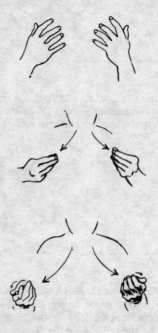

MEMBER 1 (mĕm′ bər), *n.* (Linked together.) The sign for JOIN is made: Both hands, held in the modified "5" position, palms out, move toward each other. The thumbs and index fingers of both hands then connect. This is followed by the sign for INDIVIDUAL: Both open hands, palms facing each

other, move down the sides of the body, tracing its
outline to the hips.

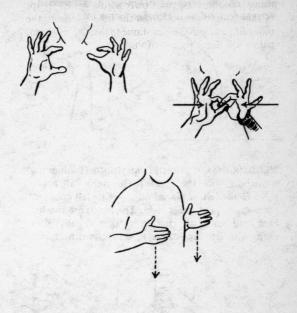

MEMBER 2, *n.* The right "M" hand, palm facing the
body and fingers pointing left, moves from the left
shoulder to the right.

MEMORIZE (mĕm' ə rīz´), *v.*, -RIZED, -RIZING. (Holding on to knowledge.) The open right hand is placed on the forehead. Then as it is removed straight forward, it is clenched into a fist.

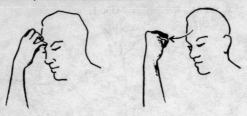

MEND (mĕnd), *v.*, MENDED, MENDING. (Fashioning something with the hands.) The right "S" hand, palm facing left, is placed on top of its left counterpart, whose palm faces right. The hands are twisted back and forth, striking each other slightly after each twist. See also CREATE, MAKE, PRODUCE.

MENTAL (mĕn' təl), *adj.* (Patting the head to indicate something of value inside.) The right fingers pat the forehead several times. See also MIND 1.

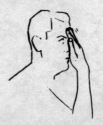

MENTION (měn′ shən), *v.*, -TIONED, -TIONING. (Words tumbling from the mouth.) The right index finger, pointing left, describes a continuous small circle in front of the mouth. See also HEARING, SAID, SAY, SPEAK, SPEECH 1, TALK 1, TELL.

MERCY (mûr′ sĭ), *n.* (Feelings from the heart, conferred on others.) The middle fingertip of the open right hand touches the chest over the heart. The same open hand then moves in a small, clockwise circle before the right shoulder, with palm facing forward and fingers pointing up. See also PITY, SYMPATHY.

MERRY (mĕr′ ĭ), *adj.* (The heart is stirred; the spirits bubble up.) The open right hand, palm facing the body, strikes the heart repeatedly, moving up and off the heart after each strike. See also GLAD, HAPPY, JOY.

ME TOO, *(colloq.).* (Two figures are compared, back and forth.) The right "Y" hand, palm facing left, is moved alternately toward and away from the body. See also SAME 2.

MIDDAY (mĭd′ dā′), *n.* (The sun is directly overhead.) The right "B" hand, palm facing left, is held upright in a vertical position, its elbow resting on the back of the open left hand. See also NOON.

MIDDLE (mĭd′ əl), *adj.* (The natural sign.) The downturned right fingers describe a small clockwise circle and come to rest in the center of the upturned left palm. See also CENTER, CENTRAL.

MIDNIGHT (mĭd′ nīt′), *n.* (The sun is directly opposite the NOON position, *q. v.*) The right "B" hand is held fingers pointing straight down and palm facing left. The left hand, representing the horizon, is held open and fingers together, palm down, its little finger edge resting against the right arm near the crook of the elbow.

MIGHT 1 (mīt), *n.* (Flexing the muscles.) With fists clenched, palms facing back, the signer raises both arms and shakes them once, with force. See also POWER 1, POWERFUL 1, STRONG.

MIGHT 2, *v.* (Weighing one thing against another.) The upturned open hands move alternately up and down. See also MAY 1, MAYBE, PERHAPS, POSSIBILITY, POSSIBLY, PROBABLE, PROBABLY.

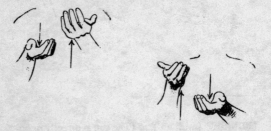

MIGHTY 1 (mī′ tĭ), *adj.* See MIGHT 1.

MIGHTY 2, *adj.* (Strength emanating from the body.) Both "5" hands are placed palms against the chest. They move out and away, forcefully, closing and assuming the "S" position. See also BRAVE, BRAVERY, HEALTH, HEALTHY, STRENGTH.

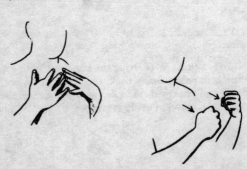

MILK (mĭlk), *n., v.,* MILKED, MILKING. (The act of milking a cow.) Both hands, alternately grasping and releasing imaginary teats, move alternately up and down before the body.

MILLION (mĭl' yən), *n., adj.* (A thousand thousands.) The fingertips of the right "M" hand, palm down, are thrust twice into the upturned left palm, first at the base of the palm and then near the base of the left fingers. (The "M" stands for *mille,* the Latin word for *thousand.*)

MIND 1 (mīnd), *n.* (Patting the head to indicate something of value inside.) The right fingers pat the forehead several times. See also MENTAL.

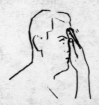

MIND 2, *n.* (Directing one's attention forward; applying oneself; concentrating.) Both hands, fingers pointing up and together, are held at the sides of the face. They move straight out from the face. See also CONCENTRATE, CONCENTRATION, FOCUS, PAY ATTENTION (TO).

MINE (mīn), *pron.* (Pressing something to one's bosom.) The "5" hand is brought up against the chest. See also MY.

MINGLE (mĭng′ gəl), *v.* (Mingling with.) Both hands are held in modified "A" positions, thumbs out. The left hand is positioned with its thumb pointing straight up, and the right hand, with its thumb pointing down, revolves above the left thumb in a counterclockwise direction. See also EACH OTHER, FELLOWSHIP, ONE ANOTHER.

MINUTE (mǐn′ ĭt), *n.* (The minute hand of a clock.) The right "D" hand is held with its index finger edge against the palm of the left "5" hand, which faces right. The right index finger moves forward in a short arc. See also MOMENT.

MISSING (mǐs′ ĭng), *adj.* The extended right index finger strikes against the downturned middle finger of the left hand, which is held with palm down and other fingers pointing right.

MISTAKE (mǐs tāk′), *n.* (Rationale obscure; the thumb and little finger are said to represent, respectively, right and wrong, with the head poised between the two.) The right "Y" hand, palm facing the body, is brought up to the chin. See also ERROR, WRONG.

MISUNDERSTAND (mĭs′ ŭn dər stănd′), *v.*, -STOOD, -STANDING. (The thought is twisted around.) The right "V" hand is positioned with index and middle fingers touching the right side of the forehead. The hand swings around so that the palm now faces out, with the two fingers still on the forehead.

MIX (mĭks), *n.*, *v.*, MIXED, MIXING. (Scrambling or mixing up.) The downturned right hand is positioned above the upturned left. The fingers of both are curved. Both hands move in opposite horizontal circles. See also COMPLICATE, CONFUSE, CONFUSED, CONFUSION.

MIXED (mĭkst), *adj.* See MIX.

MIXED UP, *adj. phrase*. See MIX.

MIX-UP (mĭks' ŭp'), *n.* See MIX.

MOMENT (mō' mənt), *n.* (The minute hand of a clock.) The right "D" hand is held with its index finger edge against the palm of the left "5" hand, which faces right. The right index finger moves forward in a short arc. See also MINUTE.

MONEY 1 (mŭn' ĭ), *n.* (Slapping of paper money in the palm.) The upturned right hand, grasping some imaginary bills, is brought down into the upturned left palm a number of times.

MONEY 2, *n.* (Fingering the money.) The thumb rubs over the index and middle fingers of the upturned hand, as if fingering money.

MONTH (mŭnth), *n.* (The tip and three joints represent the four weeks of a month.) The extended right index finger moves down along the upturned, extended left index finger.

_____

MONTHLY (mŭnth′ lĭ), *adj., adv.* (Month after month.) The sign for MONTH is made several times.

_____

MOON (mōōn), *n.* (The face only.) The right "C" hand indicates the face of the moon.

_____

MORE (mōr), *adj., n., adv.* (One hand is added to the other; an addition.) Both hands, palms facing, are held fingers together, the left a bit above the right. The right hand is brought up to the left until their fingertips touch.

MORNING (môr′ nĭng), *n.* (The sun comes over the horizon.) The little finger edge of the left hand rests in the crook of the right elbow. The left arm, held horizontally, represents the horizon. The open right hand, fingers together and pointing up, with palm facing the body, rises slowly to an almost upright angle.

MOTHER 1 (mŭth′ ər), *n.* (A female who carries a baby.) The FEMALE root sign is made: The thumb of the right "A" hand moves down along the line of the right jaw, from ear almost to chin. Both hands are then held open and palms facing up, as if holding a baby. This is the formal sign.

MOTHER 2, *(colloq.)*, *n.* (Derived from the FE-MALE root sign.) The thumb of the right "5" hand rests on the right cheek or on the right chin bone. The other fingers wiggle slightly. Or the thumb is thrust repeatedly into the right side of the face, and the rest of the hand remains open and in the "5" position, palm facing out. This latter modification is used for MAMA.

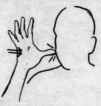

MOTIVATE (mō′ tə vāt´), *v.*, -VATED, -VATING. (Pushing forward.) Both "5" hands are held, palms out, the right fingers facing right and the left fingers left. The hands move straight forward in a series of short movements. See also ENCOURAGE, URGE 1.

MOTIVATION (mō′ tə vā′ shən), *n.* See MOTIVATE.

MOTOR (mō′ tər), *n.* (The meshing gears.) With the knuckles of both hands interlocked, the hands pivot up and down, imitating the meshing of gear teeth. See also ENGINE, MACHINE.

MOVE (mo͞ov), *n., v.,* MOVED, MOVING. (Moving from one place to another.) The downturned hands, fingers touching their respective thumbs, move in unison from left to right. See also PUT.

MOVIE(S) (mo͞o′ vĭ), *n.* (The frames of the film speeding through the projector.) The left "5" hand, palm facing right and thumb pointing up, is the projector. The right "5" hand is placed against the left, and moves back and forth quickly. See also FILM.

MOVING PICTURE. See MOVIE(S).

MUCH (mŭch), *adj., adv.* (A large amount.) The "5" hands face each other, fingers curved and touching. They move apart rather quickly. See also EXPAND, GREAT 1.

MULTIPLY (mŭl′ tə plī′), *v.*, -PLIED, -PLYING. (A multiplying.) The "V" hands, palms facing the body, alternately cross and separate, several times. See also FIGURE 1.

MURDER (mûr′ dər), *n.* (Thrusting a dagger and twisting it.) The outstretched right index finger is passed under the downturned left hand. As it moves under the left hand, the right wrist twists in a clock-wise direction. See also KILL.

MUSIC (mū′ zĭk), *n.* (A rhythmic, wavy movement of the hand, to indicate a melody; the movement of a conductor's hand in directing a musical perform-ance.) The right "5" hand, palm facing left, is waved back and forth over the downturned left hand, in a series of elongated figure-eights. See also SING, SONG.

MUST (mŭst), *aux. v.* (Being pinned down.) The right hand, in the "X" position, palm down, moves forcefully up and down once or twice. An expression of determination is frequently assumed. See also HAVE TO, NECESSARY, NECESSITY, NEED 1, OUGHT TO, SHOULD.

MY (mī), *pron.* (Pressing something to one's bosom.) The "5" hand is brought up against the chest. See also MINE.

MYSELF (mī sĕlf'), *pron.* (The thumb represents the self.) The upturned thumb of the right "A" hand is brought up against the chest.

N

NAG (năg), *v.*, NAGGED, NAGGING. (The hen's beak pecks.) The index finger and thumb of the right hand, held together, are brought against the index finger of the left "D" hand a number of times. See also PICK ON.

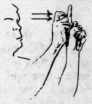

NAKED (nā′ kĭd), *adj.* (Devoid of everything on the surface.) The middle finger of the downturned right "5" hand sweeps over the back of the downturned left "A" or "S" hand, from wrist to knuckles, and continues beyond a bit. See also NUDE.

NAME (nām), *n.*, *v.*, NAMED, NAMING. (The "X" used by illiterates in writing their names. This sign is indicative of widespread illiteracy when the language of signs first began to evolve as an instructional medium in deaf education.) The right "H" hand, palm facing left, is brought down on the left "H" hand, palm facing right.

NAMED, *v.* (NAME, indicating who is named.) The sign for NAME is made: The right "H" hand, palm facing left, is brought down on the left "H" hand, palm facing right. The hands, in this position, move forward a few inches. See also CALLED.

NARRATE (nă rāt', năr' āt), *v.*, -RATED, -RATING. (The unraveling or stretching out of words or sentences.) Both open hands are held close to each other, with fingers open and palms facing and almost

touching. As the hands are drawn apart, the thumb
and index finger of each hand come together to form
circles. This is repeated several times. See also
STORY, TALE.

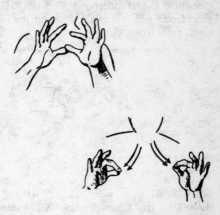

NARRATIVE (năr′ ə tĭv), *n.* See NARRATE.

NATION (nā′ shən), *n.* (An established area.) The
right "N" hand, palm down, executes a clockwise
circle above the downturned prone left hand. The
tips of the "N" fingers then move straight down and
come to rest on the back of the left hand. See also
COUNTRY 2, LAND 2.

NEAR (nĭr), *adv., prep.* (One hand is near the other.) The left hand, cupped, fingers together, is held before the chest, palm facing the body. The right hand, also cupped, fingers together, moves a very short distance back and forth, as it is held in front of the left. See also CLOSE (TO) 2.

NECESSARY (nĕs′ ə sĕr′ ĭ), *adj.* (Being pinned down.) The right hand, in the "X" position, palm down, moves forcefully up and down once or twice. An expression of determination is frequently assumed. See also HAVE TO, MUST, NEED 1, OUGHT TO, SHOULD.

NECESSITY (nə sĕs′ ə tĭ), *n.* See NECESSARY 1.

NECKING (nĕk′ ĭng), *(sl.), n.* (Necks interlocked.) The "S" hands, palms facing, are crossed at the wrists. They swing up and down while the wrists remain in contact. See also MAKE LOVE.

NEED 1 (nēd), *n., v.,* NEEDED, NEEDING. (Being pinned down.) The right hand, in the "X" position, palm down, moves forcefully up and down once or twice. An expression of determination is frequently assumed. See also HAVE TO, MUST, NECESSARY 1, NECESSITY, OUGHT TO, SHOULD.

NEED 2, *n.* (Grasping something and pulling it in.) The upturned "5" hands, held side by side before the chest, close slightly into a grasping position as they move in toward the body. See also DESIRE 1, WANT, WISH 1.

NEPHEW (něf' ū), *n.* (The initial "N;" the upper or masculine portion of the head.) The right "N" hand, held near the right temple, shakes slightly or pivots at the wrist.

NERVOUS (nûr' vəs), *adj.* (The trembling fingers.) Both "5" hands, held palm down, tremble noticeably.

NEVER (něv' ər), *adv.* The open right hand, fingers together and palm facing out, moves in a short arc from left to right, and then straight down. The movement is likened to forming a question mark or an "S" in the air.

NEVERTHELESS (nĕv´ ər <del>t</del>ᵺə lĕs´), *adv.* Both hands, in the "5" position, are held before the chest, fingertips facing each other. With an alternate back-forth movement, the fingertips are made to strike each other. See also HOWEVER 2.

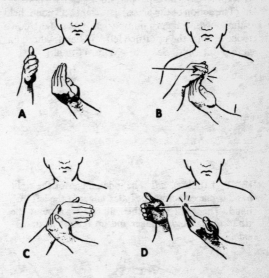

NEW (nū, nōō), *adj.* (Turning over a new leaf.) With both hands held palm up before the body, the right hand sweeps in an arc into the left, and continues up a bit.

NEWS (nūz, nōōz), *n.* See NEW.

NEWSPAPER (nūz′ pā′ pər, nōōz′ -, nūs,′- nōōs′ -), *n.* (The action of the press.) The right "5" hand, held palm down, fingers pointing left, is brought down twice against the upturned left "5" hand, whose fingers point right. See also PAPER, PUBLISH.

NEXT 1 (nĕkst), *adj.* The index finger of the right hand is placed across the index finger of the left "L" hand. The right hand then flips over, around the tip of the left index finger and up against its underside.

NEXT 2, *adj., adv.* The right hand is lifted over the left.

NEXT WEEK *adv. phrase.* The upright, right "D" hand is placed palm-to-palm against the left "5" hand, whose palm faces right. The right "D" hand moves along the left palm from base to fingertips and then beyond in an arc.

NEXT YEAR, *adv. phrase.* (A year in the future.) The right "S" hand, palm facing left, is brought forcefully down to rest on the upturned thumb edge of the left "S" hand, which is held with palm facing right. (See also YEAR.) From this position the right hand moves forward with index finger extended and pointing ahead.

NICE (nīs), *adj.* (Everything is wiped off the hand, to emphasize an uncluttered or clean condition.) The right hand slowly wipes the upturned left palm, from wrist to fingertips. See also CLEAN, PLAIN 2, PURE, PURITY.

NIECE (nēs), *n.* (The initial "N"; the lower of feminine portion of the head.) The right "N" hand, held near the right side of the jaw, shakes slightly, or pivots at the wrist.

NIGHT (nīt), *n.* (The sun drops beneath the horizon.) The left hand, palm down, is positioned at chest height. The downturned right hand, held an inch or so above the left, moves over the left hand in an arc, as the sun setting beneath the horizon.

NO (nō), *interj.* (The letters "N" and "O.") The index and middle fingers of the right "N" hand are held raised, and are then lowered against the extended right thumb, in a modified "O" position.

NOISE (noiz), *n.* (A shaking which disturbs the ear.) After placing the index finger on the ear, both hands assume the "S" position, palms down. They move alternately back and forth, forcefully.

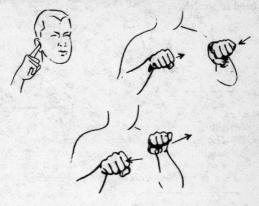

NOISY (noi′ zĭ), *adj.* See NOISE.

NONE 1 (nŭn), *adj.* (The zeros.) Both "O" hands, palms facing, are thrown out and down into the "5" position. See also NOTHING 1.

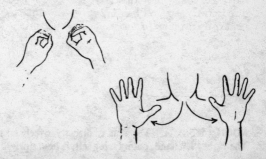

NONE 2, *adj.* (The "O" hands.) Both "O" hands are crossed at the wrists before the chest, thumb edges toward the body. From this position the hands draw apart, the right hand moving to the right and the left hand to the left.

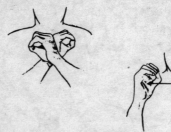

NONSENSE (nŏn′ sĕns), *n.* (Thoughts flickering back and forth.) The right "Y" hand, thumb almost touching the forehead, is shaken back and forth across the forehead several times. See also FOOLISH, RIDICULOUS, SILLY.

NOON (nōͦon), *n.* (The sun is directly overhead.) The right "B" hand, palm facing left, is held upright in a vertical position, its elbow resting on the back of the open left hand. See also MIDDAY.

NOSY (nō′ zǐ), *(sl.)*, *adj.* (A big nose.) The right index finger, after resting on the tip of the nose, moves forward and then back to the nose, in an oval, as if tracing a long extension of the nose.

NOT 1 (not), *adv.* (Crossing the hands—a negative gesture.) The downturned open hands are crossed. They are drawn apart rather quickly.

NOT 2, *adv.* The right "A" hand is placed with the tip of the upturned thumb under the chin. The hand draws out and forward in a slight arc.

NOTHING 1 (nŭth′ ĭng), *n.* (The zeros.) Both "O" hands, palms facing, are thrown out and down into the "5" position. See also NONE 1.

NOTHING 2, *n.* (The zeros.) Both "O" hands, palms facing, move back and forth a number of times, the right hand to the right and the left hand to the left.

NOTIFY (nō′ tə fī′), *v.*, -FIED, -FYING. (Taking knowledge from the mind and giving it out to all.) The fingertips are positioned on either side of the forehead. Both hands then swing down and out, opening into the upturned "5" position. See also INFORM, INFORMATION 1, LET KNOW.

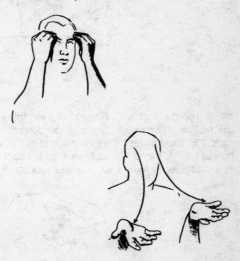

NOT YET, *phrase.* (Hanging back.) The "5" hand and forearm, hanging loosely and straight down from the elbow, move back and forth under the armpit. See also LATE.

NOW (nou), *adv.* (Something right in front of you.) The upturned right-angle hands drop down rather sharply. The "Y" hands may also be used. See also PRESENT 3.

NUDE (nūd, nōōd), *adj.* (Devoid of everything on the surface.) The middle finger of the downturned right "5" hand sweeps over the back of the downturned left "A" or "S" hand, from wrist to knuckles, and continues beyond a bit. See also NAKED.

NUMEROUS (nū′ mər əs, nōō′ -), *adj.* (Many fingers are indicated.) The upturned "S" hands are thrown up, opening into the "5" position, palms up. This may be repeated. See also MANY, QUANTITY.

O

OBEDIENCE (ō bē′ dǐ əns), *n.* (The hands are thrown open as an act of obeisance.) Both "A" hands, palms facing, are positioned at either side of the head. They are thrown open and out, ending in the "5" position, palms up. The head is bowed slightly at the same time.

OBEDIENT (ō bē′ dǐ ənt), *adj.* See OBEDIENCE.

OBEY (ō bā′), *v.,* OBEYING, OBEYED. See OBEDIENT.

OBJECT (əb jĕkt′), *v.,* -JECTED, -JECTING. (The hand is thrust into the chest to force a complaint out.) The curved fingers of the right hand are thrust forcefully into the chest. See also COMPLAIN, COMPLAINT, PROTEST.

OBJECTION (əb jĕk′ shən), *n.* See OBJECT.

OBSERVE (əb zûrv′), *v.*, -SERVED, -SERVING. (The vision is directed forward.) The tips of the right "V" fingers point to the eyes. The right hand is then swung around and forward a bit. See also WITNESS.

OBVIOUS (ŏb′ vĭ əs), *adj.* (Rays of light clearing the way.) Both hands are held at chest height, palms out, all fingertips together. They open into the "5" position in unison, the right hand moving toward the right and the left toward the left. The palms of both hands remain facing out. See also CLEAR, PLAIN 1.

OCCASIONAL (ə kā′ zhən əl), *adj.* (The "1" finger is brought up very slowly.) The right index finger, resting in the open left palm, which is facing right, swings up slowly from its position to one in which it is pointing straight up. The movement is repeated slowly, after a pause. See also ONCE IN A WHILE, SOMETIME(S).

OCCASIONALLY (ə kā′ zhən ə lĭ), *adv.* See OCCASIONAL.

ODD (ŏd), *adj.* (Something which distorts the vision.) The "C" hand describes a small arc in front of the face. See also CURIOUS 1, STRANGE, WEIRD.

ODOR (ō′ dər), *n*. (Bringing something up to the nose.) The upturned right hand moves slowly up to and past the nose, and the signer breathes in as the hand sweeps by. See also SMELL.

OFFER (ôf′ ər), *v.*, -FERED, -FERING. (An offering; a presenting.) Both hands, slightly cupped, palms up, are held close to the chest. They move up and out in unison, describing a very slight arc. See also PRESENT 1, PROPOSE, SUGGEST.

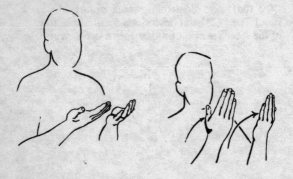

OFFERING (ôf′ ər ĭng), *n*. See OFFER.

OFTEN (ôf′ ən, ŏf′ ən), *adv.* The left hand, open in the "5" position, palm up, is held before the chest. The right hand, in the right-angle position, fingers pointing up, arches over and into the left palm. This is repeated several times. See also FREQUENT.

O.K. 1 (ō′ kā′), *adj., adv.* (A straightening out.) The right hand, fingers together and palm facing left, is placed in the upturned left palm, whose fingers point away from the body. The right hand slides straight out along the left palm, over the left fingers, and stops with its heel resting on the left fingertips. See also ALL RIGHT, RIGHT 1, RIGHTEOUS, YOU'RE WELCOME 2.

O.K. 2 (*adj., adv.* ō′ kā′; *v., n.* ō′ kā′), *(colloq.),* *phrase.* The letters "O" and "K" are fingerspelled.

OLD (ōld), *adj.* (The beard of an old man.) The right hand grasps an imaginary beard at the chin and pulls it downward.

_____

ON (ŏn, ôn), *prep.* (Placing one hand on the other.) The right hand is placed on the back of the down-turned left hand.

_____

ONCE IN A WHILE, *adv. phrase.* (The "1" finger is brought up very slowly.) The right index finger, resting in the open left palm, which is facing right, swings up slowly from its position to one in which it is pointing straight up. The movement is repeated slowly, after a pause. See also OCCASIONAL, OCCASIONALLY, SOMETIME(S).

_____

ONE ANOTHER, *pron. phrase.* (Mingling with.) Both hands are held in modified "A" positions, thumbs out. The left hand is positioned with its

thumb pointing straight up, and the right hand, with
its thumb pointing down, revolves above the left
thumb in a counterclockwise direction. See also
EACH OTHER, FELLOWSHIP, MINGLE.

ONLY (ōn' lĭ), *adv.* (One, wandering around in a
circle.) The index finger, pointing straight up, palm
facing the body (the number *one*), is rotated before
the face in a counterclockwise direction. See also
ALONE, LONE.

OPEN (ō' pən), *adj., v.,* OPENED, OPENING. (The
natural sign.) The "B" hands, palms out, are held
with index finger edges touching. They swing apart
so that the palms now face each other.

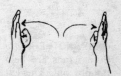

OPEN THE DOOR, *v. phrase.* (The opening and closing of the door.) The "B" hands, palms out and
edges touching, are drawn apart and then come together again. See also DOOR, DOORWAY.

OPEN THE WINDOW, *phrase.* (The opening of the
window.) With both palms facing the body, the little
finger edge of the right hand rests atop the index
finger edge of the left hand. The right hand then
moves straight up. See also WINDOW.

OPERATION 1 (ŏp´ ə rā′ shən), *n.* (The action of the
scalpel.) The thumb of the right "A" hand is drawn
straight down across the upright left palm.

OPERATION 2, *n.* (The action of a scalpel.) The thumbtip of the right "A" hand, palm facing down, moves a short distance across the lower chest or stomach region.

OPINION (ə pĭn′ yən), *n.* (The "O" hand, circling in the head.) The right "O" hand circles before the forehead several times.

OPPONENT (ə pō′ nənt), *n.* (At sword's point.) The two index fingers, after pointing to each other, are drawn sharply apart. This is followed by the sign for INDIVIDUAL: Both open hands, palms facing each other, move down the sides of the body, tracing its outline to the hips. See also ENEMY.

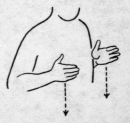

OPPORTUNITY (ŏp´ ər tū´ nə tĭ), *n.* (The letters "O" and "P"; pushing through.) Both "O" hands are held palms down, side by side. They swing up a bit as they assume the "P" position.

OPPOSE (ə´ pōz), *v.,* OPPOSED, OPPOSING. (Opposed to; restraint.) The tips of the right fingers, held together, are thrust purposefully into the open left palm, whose fingers are also together and pointing forward. See also AGAINST.

OPPOSITE (ŏp´ ə zĭt), *adj., n.* (Separateness.) The tips of the extended index fingers touch before the chest, the right finger pointing left and the left finger pointing right. The fingers then draw apart sharply to either side. See also CONTRAST.

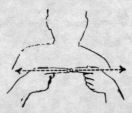

OR (ôr; *unstressed* ər), *conj.* (Considering one thing against another.) The "A" hands, palms facing and thumbs pointing straight up, move alternately up and down before the chest. See also EITHER 3, WHETHER, WHICH.

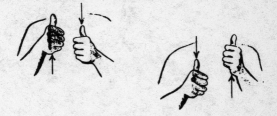

ORANGE 1 (ôr′ ĭnj, ŏr′-), *n., adj.* (The action of squeezing an orange to get its juice into the mouth.) The right "C" hand is held at the mouth. It opens and closes deliberately, as if squeezing an orange.

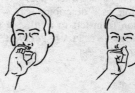

ORANGE 2, *n.* (The peeling of the fruit.) The thumbtip of the right "Y" hand moves over the back of the left "S" hand, which is held palm down or palm facing the body.

ORDER 1 (ôr′ dər), *n., v.,* -DERED, -DERING. (An issuance from the mouth.) The tip of the index finger of the "D" hand, palm facing the body, is placed at the closed lips. It moves around and out, rather forcefully.

ORDER 2, *n., v.* (Placing things in order.) The hands, palms facing, fingers together and pointing away from the body, are positioned at the left side and held about a foot apart. With a slight up-down motion, as if describing waves, the hands travel in unison from left to right. See also ARRANGE, ARRANGEMENT, PLAN, PREPARE 1, PUT IN ORDER, READY 1.

ORGANIZATION 1 (ôr′ gən ə zā′ shən), *n.* (A grouping together.) Both "C" hands, palms facing, are held a few inches apart at chest height. They are swung around in unison, so that the palms now face the body. See also CLASS, CLASSED, COMPANY, GROUP 1.

ORGANIZATION 2, *n.* (The letter "O"; a group or class.) Both "O" hands are held with palms facing out and thumb edges touching. The hands swing apart, around, and come together again with little finger edges touching.

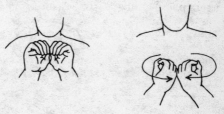

ORIGIN (ôr′ ə jĭn, ŏr′ -), *n.* (Turning a key to open up a new venture.) The right index finger, resting between the left index and middle fingers, executes a half turn, once or twice. See also BEGIN, START.

OTHER (ŭŧħ′ ər), *adj.* (Moving over to another position.) The right "A" hand, thumb up, is pivoted from the wrist and swung over to the right, so that the thumb now points to the right. See also AN-OTHER.

OUGHT TO (ôt), *v. aux.* (Being pinned down.) The right hand, in the "X" position, palm down, moves forcefully up and down once or twice. An expression of determination is frequently assumed. See also HAVE TO, MUST, NECESSARY, NECESSITY, NEED 1, SHOULD.

OUR (our), *pron.* (An encompassing, including oneself and others.) The right "C" hand, palm facing left, is placed at the right shoulder. It swings around to the left shoulder, its palm now facing right.

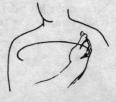

OURSELVES (our sĕlvz′), *pron. pl.* (An encompassing; the thumb representing *self,* *i.e.,* oneness.) The right "A" hand, thumb held straight up, is placed at the right shoulder. It executes the same movement as in OUR.

OUT (out), *adv.* (The natural motion of withdrawing, *i.e.,* taking *out,* of the hand.) The downturned open right hand, grasped loosely by the left, is drawn up and out of the left hand's grasp. As it does so, the fingers come together with the thumb. The left hand, meanwhile, closes into the "O" position, palm facing right.

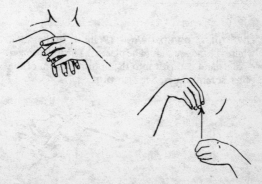

OVER (ō′ vər), *prep.* (A crossing over.) The left hand is held before the chest, palm down and fingers together. The right hand, fingers together, glides over the left, with the right little finger touching the top of the left hand. See also ACROSS, CROSS 2.

OVERCOME (ō′ vər kŭm′), *v.*, -CAME, -COME, -COMING. (Forcing the head into a bowed position.) The right "S" hand, placed across the left "S" hand, moves over and down a bit. See also BEAT 2, DEFEAT.

OWE (ō), *v.*, OWED, OWING. (Pointing to the palm, where the money should be placed.) The index finger of one hand is thrust into the upturned palm of the other several times. See also DUE.

P

PACKAGE (păk′ ĭj), *n., v.,* -AGED, -AGING. (The dimensions are indicated.) The open hands, palms facing and fingers pointing out, are dropped an inch or two simultaneously. They then shift their relative positions so that both palms face the body, with one hand in front of the other. In this new position they again drop an inch or two simultaneously. See also BOX, ROOM 1.

PAIN (pān), *n.* (A stabbing pain.) The "D" hands, index fingers pointing to each other, are rotated in elliptical fashion before the chest—simultaneously but in opposite directions. See also HARM, HURT, INJURE, INJURY.

PALE (pāl) *adj., v.,* PALED, PALING. The sign for WHITE is made: The fingertips of the "5" hand are placed against the chest. The hand moves straight out from the chest, while the fingers and thumb all come together. Then both hands, fingers spread, rise up and over the cheeks.

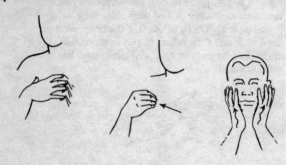

PANTS (pănts), *n. pl.* (The natural sign.) The open hands are drawn up along the thighs, starting at the knees.

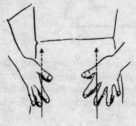

PAPER (pā' pər), *n.* (The action of the press.) The right "5" hand, held palm down, fingers pointing left, is brought down twice against the upturned left

"5" hand, whose fingers point right. See also NEWS-
PAPER, PUBLISH.

PARDON (pär′ dən), *n.* (A wiped-off and cleaned
slate.) The right hand wipes off the left palm several
times. See also APOLOGIZE 2, APOLOGY 2, EXCUSE,
FORGIVE.

PART (pärt), *n., adj.* (Cutting off or designating a
part.) The little finger edge of the open right hand
moves straight down the middle of the upturned left
palm. See also PIECE, PORTION, SOME.

PARTY 1 (pär' tǐ), *n.* (The swinging of tambourines.) Both open hands, held somewhat above the
head, are pivoted back and forth repeatedly, as if
swinging a pair of tambourines.

PARTY 2, *n.* (The rhythmic swaying of the feet.)
The downturned index and middle fingers of the
right "V" hand swing rhythmically back and forth
over the upturned left palm. See also DANCE.

PASS (păs), *v.*, PASSED, PASSING. (One hand
passes the other.) Both "A" hands, palms facing
each other, are held before the body, the right behind
the left. The right hand moves forward, its knuckles
brushing those of the left, and continues forward a
bit beyond the left.

PAST (păst), *adj., n., adv.* (Something past, behind.) The upraised right hand, in the "5" position with palm facing the body, is held just above the right shoulder and is thrown back over it. See also PREVIOUS, PREVIOUSLY, WAS, WERE.

PATIENT (pā′ shənt), *n.* (The letter "P"; the red cross on the hospital gown's sleeve.) The thumb and middle fingers of the right "P" hand trace a small cross on the upper left arm.

PAY (pā), *v.,* PAID, PAYING. (Giving forth of money.) The right index finger, resting in the up-turned left palm, swings forward and up a bit.

PAY ATTENTION (TO), *v. phrase.* (Directing one's attention forward; applying oneself; concentrating.) Both hands, fingers pointing up and together, are held at the sides of the face. They move straight out from the face. See also CONCENTRATE, CONCENTRATION, FOCUS, MIND 2.

PEACE (pēs), *n.* (The hands are clasped as a gesture of harmony or *peace;* the opening signifies quiet or calmness.) The hands are clasped both ways, and then open and separate, assuming the "5" position, palms down.

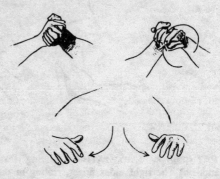

PENALTY (pĕn′ əl tĭ), *n.* (Nicking into one.) The knuckle of the right "X" finger is nicked against the palm of the left hand, held in the "5" position, palm

facing right. See also COST, EXPENSE, FINE 2, PRICE,
TAX, TAXATION.

PEOPLE (pē′ pəl), *n. pl.* (The letter "P" in continuous motion, to indicate plurality.) The "P" hands, side by side, are moved alternately in continuous counterclockwise circles.

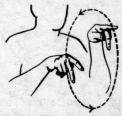

PERCEIVE (pər sēv′), *v.,* -CEIVED, -CEIVING. (The eyesight is directed forward.) The right "V" hand, palm facing the body, is placed so that the fingertips are just under the eyes. The hand swings around and out, so that the fingertips are now pointing forward. See also LOOK 1, SEE, SIGHT, WATCH.

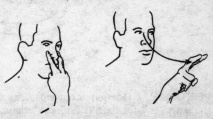

PERCEPTION (pər sĕp' shən), *n.* See PERCEIVE 1.

PERFECT (*adj., n.* pûr' fĭkt; *v.* pər fĕkt'), -FECTED, -FECTING. (The letter "P"; the hands come into precise contact.) The "P" hands face each other. The right executes a clockwise circle above the stationary left, and then moves down so that the thumb and middle fingers of each hand come into precise contact.

PERFORM 1 (pər fôrm'), *v.,* -FORMED, -FORMING. (An activity.) Both open hands, palms down, are swung right and left before the chest. See also DO.

PERFORM 2, *v.* (Motion or movement, modified by the letter "A" for "act.") Both "A" hands, palms out, are held at shoulder height and rotate alternately toward the head. See also ACT 1, PLAY 2, SHOW 2.

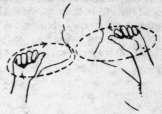

PERFORMANCE 1 (pər fôr′ məns), *n.* See PERFORM 1.

PERFORMANCE 2, *n.* See PERFORM 2.

PERHAPS (pər hăps′), *adv.* (Weighing one thing against another.) The upturned open hands move alternately up and down. See also MAY 1, MAYBE, MIGHT 2, POSSIBILITY, POSSIBLY, PROBABLE, PROBABLY.

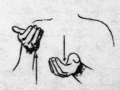

PERMANENT (pûr' mə nənt), *adj.* (Steady, uninterrupted movement.) The "A" hands are held with palms out, thumbs extended and touching, the right behind the left. In this position the hands move forward in a straight, steady line. See also CONTINUE, ENDURE 2, EVER 1, LAST 3, LASTING, PERSEVERE, PERSIST, REMAIN, STAY 1, STAY STILL.

PERMISSION 1 (pər mǐsh' ən), *n.* (A permissive upswinging of the hands, as if giving in.) Both hands, palms facing and fingers pointing away from the body, are held at chest level, almost a foot apart. With an upward movement, using their wrists as pivots, the hands sweep up until the fingers point almost straight up. See also ALLOW, GRANT 1, LET, LET'S, LET US, MAY 3.

PERMISSION 2, *n.* (The "P" hands are used.) The same sign as in PERMISSION 1 is used, except with the "P" hands.

PERMIT 1 (pər mit'), *v.*, -MITTED, -MITTING. See PERMISSION 1.

PERMIT 2, *n., v.* See PERMISSION 2.

PERSEVERE (pûr´ sə vĭr´), *v.*, -VERED, -VERING. (Steady, uninterrupted movement.) The "A" hands are held with palms out, thumbs extended and touching, the right behind the left. In this position the hands move forward in a straight, steady line. See also CONTINUE, ENDURE 2, EVER 1, LAST 3, LASTING, PERMANENT, PERSIST, REMAIN, STAY 1, STAY STILL.

PERSIST (pər sĭst′, -zĭst′), *v.*, -SISTED, -SISTING. (Steady, uninterrupted movement.) The "A" hands are held with palms out, thumbs extended and touching, the right behind the left. In this position the hands move forward in a straight, steady line. See also CONTINUE, ENDURE 2, EVER 1, LAST 3, LASTING, PERMANENT, PERSEVERE, REMAIN, STAY 1, STAY STILL.

PERSON (pûr′ sən), *n.* (The letter "P"; an individual is indicated.) The "P" hands, side by side, move straight down a short distance, as if outlining the sides of an unseen individual.

"PERSON" ENDING. Both open hands, palms facing each other, move down the sides of the body, tracing its outline to the hips.

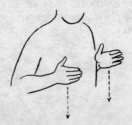

PERSPIRATION 1 (pûr´ spə rā´ shən), *n.* See PER-
SPIRE 1.

_____

PERSPIRATION 2, *n.* See PERSPIRE 2.

_____

PERSPIRE 1 (pər spīr´), *v.,* -SPIRED, -SPIRING.
(Wiping the brow.) The bent right index finger is
drawn across the forehead from left to right and then
shaken to the side, as if getting rid of the sweat.

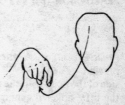

_____

PERSPIRE 2, *v.* (Perspiration dripping from the
brow.) The index finger edge of the open right hand
wipes across the brow, and the same open hand then
continues forcefully downward off the brow, its
fingers wiggling, as if shaking off the perspiration
gathered.

PERSUADE (pər swād'), *v.,* -SUADED, -SUADING. (Shaking someone, to implant one's will into another.) Both "A" hands, palms facing, are held before the chest, the left slightly in front of the right. In this position the hands move back and forth a short distance. See also URGE 2.

PERSUASION (pər swā' zhən), *n.* See PERSUADE.

PHONE (fōn), *n., v.,* PHONED, PHONING. (The natural sign.) The right "Y" hand is placed at the right side of the head with the thumb touching the ear and the little finger touching the lips. This is the more modern telephone receiver. See also TELEPHONE.

PHOTOGRAPH (fō' tə grăf), *n., v.,* -GRAPHED, -GRAPHING. (Recording an image.) The right "C" hand is held in front of the face, with thumb edge near the face and palm facing left. The hand is then brought sharply around in front of the open left hand and is struck firmly against the left palm,

which is held facing forward with fingers pointing
up. See also PICTURE.

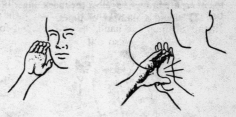

PICK 1 (pĭk), *v.*, PICKED, PICKING. (The natural
motion of selecting something from the hand.) The
thumb and index fingers of the outstretched right
hand grasp an imaginary object on the upturned left
palm. The right hand then moves straight up.

PICK 2, *v.* (The natural sign.) The fingertips and
thumbtip of the downturned open right hand come
together, and the hand moves up a short distance, as
if picking something.

PICK ON (pĭk), *v., phrase.* (The hen's beak pecks.)
The index finger and thumb of the right hand, held
together, are brought against the index finger of the
left "D" hand a number of times.

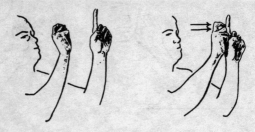

PICK UP 1, *v. phrase.* (To take up.) Both hands, held
palms down in the "5" position, are at chest level.
With a grasping upward movement, both close into
"S" positions before the face. See also ASSUME,
TAKE UP.

PICK UP 2, *v. phrase.* See PICK 2.

PICTURE (pĭk' chər), *n., v.,* -TURED, -TURING. (Recording an image.) The right "C" hand is held in
front of the face, with thumb edge near the face and

palm facing left. The hand is then brought sharply around in front of the open left hand and is struck firmly against the left palm, which is held facing forward with fingers pointing up. See also PHOTO-GRAPH.

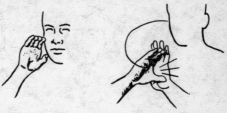

PIE (pī), *n.* (Slicing a wedge-shaped piece of pie.) The upturned left hand represents the pie. The little finger edge of the open right hand goes through the motions of slicing a wedge-shaped piece from the pie.

PIECE (pēs), *n., v.,* PIECED, PIECING. (Cutting off or designating a part.) The little finger edge of the open right hand moves straight down the middle of the upturned left palm. See also PART, PORTION, SOME.

PIG (pĭg), *n.* (The snout digs into the trough.) The downturned right prone hand is placed under the chin, fingers pointing forward. The hand, in this position, swings alternately up and down.

PITY (pĭt′ ĭ), *n., v.,* PITIED, PITYING. (Feelings from the heart, conferred on others.) The middle fingertip of the open right hand touches the chest over the heart. The same open hand then moves in a small, clockwise circle before the right shoulder, with palm facing forward and fingers pointing up. See also MERCY, SYMPATHY.

PLACE (plās), *n.* (The letter "P"; a circle or square is indicated, to show the locale or place.) The "P" hands are held side by side before the body, with middle fingertips touching. From this position, the hands separate and outline a circle (or a square), before coming together again closer to the body. See also LOCATION, POSITION.

PLAIN 1 (plān), *adj.* (Rays of light clearing the way.) Both hands are held at chest height, palms out, all fingertips together. They open into the "5" position in unison, the right hand moving toward the right and the left toward the left. The palms of both hands remain facing out. See also CLEAR, OBVIOUS.

PLAIN 2, *adj.* (Everything is wiped off the hand, to emphasize an uncluttered or clean condition.) The right hand slowly wipes the upturned left palm, from wrist to fingertips. See also CLEAN, NICE, PURE, PURITY.

PLAN (plăn), *n., v.,* PLANNED, PLANNING. (Placing things in order.) The hands, palms facing, fingers together and pointing away from the body, are positioned at the left side and held about a foot apart. With a slight up-down motion, as if describing waves, the hands travel in unison from left to right. See also ARRANGE, ARRANGEMENT, ORDER 2, PREPARE 1, PUT IN ORDER, READY 1.

PLANE 1 (plān), *n.* (The wings of the airplane.) The "Y" hand, palm down and drawn up near the shoulder, moves forward, up and away from the body. Either hand may be used. See also AIRPLANE, FLY 1.

PLANE 2, *n.* (The wings and fuselage of the airplane.) The hand assumes the same position as in PLANE 1, but the index finger is also extended, to represent the fuselage of the airplane. Either hand

may be used, and the movement is the same as in
PLANE 1. See also FLY 2.

PLAY 1 (plā), v., PLAYED, PLAYING. (Shaking tambourines.) The "Y" hands, held aloft, are shaken
back and forth, pivoted at the wrists.

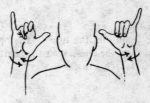

PLAY 2, n. (Motion or movement, modified by the
letter "A" for "act.") Both "A" hands, palms out,
are held at shoulder height and rotate alternately
toward the head. See also ACT 1, PERFORM 2, PER-
FORMANCE 2, SHOW 2.

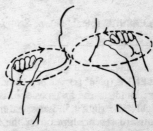

PLEASANT (plĕz′ ənt), *adj.* (A crinkling-up of the face.) Both hands, in the "5" position, palms facing back, are placed on either side of the face. The fingers wiggle back and forth, while a pleasant, happy expression is worn. See also CHEERFUL, FRIENDLY.

PLEASE (plēz), *v.*, PLEASED, PLEASING. (A pleasurable feeling on the heart.) The open right hand is circled on the chest, over the heart. See also ENJOY, ENJOYMENT, LIKE 3.

PLEASURE (plĕzh′ ər), *n.* See PLEASE.

PLENTY (plĕn′ tĭ), *n., adj., adv.* (A full cup.) The left hand, in the "S" position, is held palm facing right. The right "5" hand, palm down, is brushed outward several times over the top of the left, in-

dicating a wiping off of the top of a cup. See also
ENOUGH.

PLUS (plŭs), *prep., n.* (A mathematical symbol.)
The two index fingers are crossed at right angles. See
also POSITIVE.

POLICE (pə lēs′), *n., v.,* -LICED, -LICING. (The letter
"C" for "cop"; the shape and position of the badge.)
The right "C" hand, palm facing left, is placed
against the heart. See also COP.

POLITE (pə līt′), *adj.* (The ruffled shirt front of a gentleman of old.) The thumb of the right "5" hand is thrust into the chest. The hand then pivots down, with thumb remaining in place. This latter part of the sign, however, is optional.

POOR (po͝or), *adj.* (Ragged elbows.) The open right hand is placed at the left elbow. It moves down and off, closing into the "O" position.

POP (pŏp), *n.* (Corking a bottle.) The left "O" hand is held with thumb edge up, representing a bottle. The thumb and index finger of the right "5" hand represent a cork, and are inserted into the circle formed by the "O" hand. The palm of the open right hand then strikes down on the upturned edge of the "O" hand, as if forcing the cork into the bottle. See also SODA POP, SODA WATER.

POP UP, *(colloq.)*, *v.* (Popping up before the eyes.) The right index finger, pointing up, pops up between the index and middle fingers of the left hand, whose palm faces down. See also APPEAR 2.

PORTION (pōr′ shən), *n.* (Cutting off or designating a part.) The little finger edge of the open right hand moves straight down the middle of the upturned left palm. See also PART, PIECE, SOME.

POSITION (pə zĭsh′ ən), *n.* (The letter "P"; a circle or square is indicated, to show the locale or place.) The "P" hands are held side by side before the body, with middle fingertips touching. From this position, the hands separate and outline a circle (or a square) before coming together again closer to the body. See also LOCATION, PLACE.

POSITIVE *adj.* (A mathematical symbol.) The two index fingers are crossed at right angles in the sign for PLUS. See also PLUS.

POSSIBILITY (pŏs′ ə bĭl′ ə tĭ), n. (Weighing one thing against another.) The upturned open hands move alternately up and down. See also MAY 1, MAYBE, MIGHT 2, PERHAPS, PROBABLE, PROBABLY.

 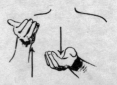

POSSIBLE (pŏs′ ə bəl), *adj.* (An affirmative movement of the hands, likened to a nodding of the head, to indicate ability or power to accomplish something.) Both "A" hands, held palms down, move down in unison a short distance before the chest. See also CAN, CAPABLE, MAY 2.

POSSIBLY (pŏs′ ə blǐ), *adv.* See POSSIBILITY.

POSTPONE (pōst pōn′), *v.,* -PONED, -PONING. (Putting off; moving things forward repeatedly.) The "F" hands, palms facing and fingers pointing out from the body, are moved forward simultaneously in a series of short movements. See also DELAY, PROCRASTINATE, PUT. OFF.

POUND (pound), *n.* (The balancing of the scale is described.) The fingers of the right "H" hand are centered on the left index finger and rocked back and forth. See also WEIGH, WEIGHT.

POVERTY (pŏv′ ər tĭ), *n.* (The knuckles are rubbed, to indicate a condition of being worn down.) The knuckles of the curved index and middle fingers of both hands are rubbed up and down against each other. Instead of the up-down rubbing, they may rub against each other in an alternate clockwise-counterclockwise manner. See also DIFFICULT 1, DIFFICULTY, HARD 1, HARDSHIP, PROBLEM 2.

POWER 1 (pou′ ər), *n.* (Flexing the muscles.) With fists clenched, palms facing back, the signer raises both arms and shakes them once, with force. See also MIGHT 1, MIGHTY 1, STRONG.

POWER 2, *n.* (The curve of the flexed biceps is indicated.) The left hand, clenched into a fist, is held up, palm facing the body. The index finger of the right "D" hand moves in an arc over the left biceps muscle, from shoulder to crook of the elbow.

POWERFUL 1 (pou′ ər fəl), *adj.* See POWER 1.

POWERFUL 2, *adj.* See POWER 2.

PRACTICE (prăk′ tĭs), *n., v.,* -TICED, -TICING. (Polishing or sharpening up.) The knuckles of the downturned right "A" hand are rubbed briskly back and forth over the side of the hand and index finger of the left "D" hand. See also TRAIN 2.

PRAISE (prāz), *n., v.,* PRAISED, PRAISING. (Good words coming from the mouth; clapping hands.) The fingertips of the right hand, palm flat and facing the body, are brought up to the lips so that they touch (part of the sign for GOOD, *q.v.*). The hands are then clapped together several times. See also APPLAUD, APPLAUSE, CONGRATULATE 1, CONGRATULATIONS 1.

PRECISE (prĭ sīs′), *adj.* (The fingers come together precisely.) The thumb and index finger of each hand, palms facing, the right above the left, form circles. They are brought together with a deliberate movement, so that the fingers and thumbs now touch. Sometimes the right hand, before coming together with the left, executes a slow clockwise circle above the left. See also EXACT, EXACTLY, SPECIFIC.

PREFER (prĭ fûr′), *v.*, -FERRED, -FERRING. (More good.) The fingertips of one hand are placed at the lips, as if tasting something (*vide*, GOOD). Then the hand is moved up to a position just above the head, where it assumes the "A" position, thumb up. See also BETTER.

PREPARE 1 (prĭ pâr′), *v.*, -PARED, -PARING. (Placing things in order.) The hands, palms facing, fingers together and pointing away from the body, are positioned at the left side and held about a foot apart. With a slight up-down motion, as if describing waves, the hands travel in unison from left to right.

See also ARRANGE, ARRANGEMENT, ORDER 2, PLAN, PUT IN ORDER, READY 1.

PREPARE 2 *v.* (Set out.) The "A" hands are crossed, with the right resting on top of the left. The right palm faces left and the left palm faces right. Both hands suddenly open and swing apart to the palm-down position. See also READY 3.

PRESENT 1 (prĕz′ ənt), *n.* (An offering; a presenting.) Both hands, slightly cupped, palms up, are held close to the chest. They move up and out in unison, describing a very slight arc. See also OFFER, OFFERING, PROPOSE, SUGGEST.

PRESENT 2 (*n.* prĕz′ ənt; *v.* prĭ zĕnt′), -SENTED, -SENTING. (A giving of something.) Both "A" hands, with index fingers somewhat draped over the tips of the thumbs, are held palms facing in front of the chest. They are pivoted forward and down in unison, from the wrists. See also CONTRIBUTE, GIFT.

PRESENT 3, *adj.* (Something right in front of you.) The upturned right-angle hands drop down rather sharply. The "Y" hands may also be used. See also NOW.

PRESERVE (prĭ zûrv′), *v.,* -SERVED, -SERVING. (Slow, careful movement.) The "K" hands are crossed, the right above the left, little finger edges down. In this position the hands are moved up and down a short distance. See also CARE 2, CAREFUL 2, KEEP, MAINTAIN 1, TAKE CARE OF.

PRESIDENT (prĕz' ə dənt), *n.* The "C" hands, held palms out at either temple, close over imaginary horns and move up a bit to either side, tracing the shape of the horns.

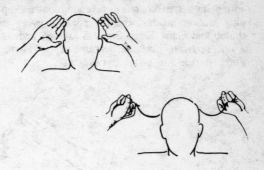

***

PRETTY (prĭt' ĭ), *adj.* (Literally, a good face.) The right hand, fingers closed over the thumb, is placed at or just below the lips (indicating a tasting of something GOOD, *q.v.*). It then describes a counterclockwise circle around the face, opening into the "5" position, to indicate the whole face. At the completion of the circling movement the hand comes to rest in its initial position, at or just below the lips. See also BEAUTIFUL, BEAUTY.

PREVENT (prĭ vĕnt′), *v.*, -VENTED, -VENTING. (Obstruct, block.) The left hand, fingers together and palm flat, is held before the body, facing somewhat down. The little finger side of the right hand, held with palm flat, makes one or several up-down chopping motions against the left hand, between its thumb and index finger. See also ANNOY, ANNOYANCE, BOTHER, DISTURB, INTERFERE, INTERFERENCE, INTERFERE WITH, INTERRUPT.

PREVENTION (prĭ vĕn′ shən), *n.* See PREVENT.

PREVIOUS (prē′ vĭ əs), *adj.* (Something past, behind.) The upraised right hand, in the "5" position with palm facing the body, is held just above the right shoulder and is thrown back over it. See also PAST, WAS, WERE.

PREVIOUSLY, *adv.* See PREVIOUS.

PRICE (prīs), *n., v.,* PRICED, PRICING. (Nicking into one.) The knuckle of the right "X" finger is nicked against the palm of the left hand, held in the "5" position, palm facing right. See also COST, EXPENSE, FINE 2, PENALTY, TAX, TAXATION.

PRIDE (prīd), *n., v.,* PRIDED, PRIDING. (The feelings rise up.) The thumb of the right "A" hand, palm down, moves up along the right side of the chest. A haughty expression is assumed. See also PROUD.

PRINCIPLE (prin' sə pəl), *n.* (A collection or listing is indicated by the open palm, representing a page.) The right "P" hand is placed against the upper part of the open left hand, which faces right, fingers pointing upward. The right "P" hand swings down to the lower part of the left palm.

PRIVACY (prī' və sĭ), *n.* (The sealing of the lips; keeping the words back.) The back of the thumb of the right "A" hand is placed firmly against the closed lips. The thumb, in this position, may move off the lips slightly and return again to the lips. As an optional addition, the thumb may swing down under the downturned cupped left hand, after being placed on the lips as above.

PRIVATE 1 (prī' vĭt), *adj.* See PRIVACY.

PRIVATE 2, *adj.* (Closed.) Both open hands are held before the body, fingers pointing out, right palm facing left and left facing right. The right hand, held above the left, comes down against the index finger edge of the left a number of times.

PROBABLE (prŏb' ə bəl), *adj.* (Weighing one thing against another.) The upturned open hands move alternately up and down. See also MAY 1, MAYBE, MIGHT 2, PERHAPS, POSSIBILITY, POSSIBLY.

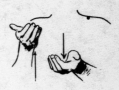

PROBABLY (prŏb′ ə blĭ), *adv.* See PROBABLE.

PROBLEM 1 (prŏb′ ləm), *n.* (A clouding over; a troubling.) Both "B" hands, palms facing each other, are rotated alternately before the forehead. See also TROUBLE, WORRIED, WORRY 1.

PROBLEM 2, *n.* (The knuckles are rubbed, to indicate a condition of being worn down.) The knuckles of the curved index and middle fingers of both hands are rubbed up and down against each other. Instead of the up-down rubbing, they may rub against each other in an alternate clockwise-counterclockwise manner. See also DIFFICULT 1, DIFFICULTY, HARD 1, HARDSHIP, POVERTY.

PROCEED (prə sēd′), *v.*, -CEEDED, -CEEDING. (Moving forward.) Both right-angle hands, palms facing each other and knuckles facing forward, move forward simultaneously. See also GO AHEAD.

PROCRASTINATE (prō krăs′ tə nāt′), *v.*, -NATED, -NATING. (Putting off; moving things forward repeatedly.) The "F" hands, palms facing and fingers pointing out from the body, are moved forward simultaneously in a series of short movements. See also DELAY, POSTPONE, PUT OFF.

PRODUCE (prə dūs′), *v.,* -DUCED, -DUCING. (Fashioning something with the hands.) The right "S" hand, palm facing left, is placed on top of its left counterpart, whose palm faces right. The hands are twisted back and forth, striking each other slightly after each twist. See also CREATE, MAKE, MEND.

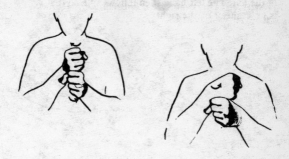

PROGRAM (prō′ grăm, -gram), *n.* (The letter "P"; a listing on both sides of the page.) The thumb side of the right "P" hand is placed against the palm of the open left hand, which is facing right. The right "P" hand moves down the left palm. The left hand then swings around so that its palm faces the body. The right "P" hand then moves down the back of the left hand.

PROGRESS (*n.* prŏg' rĕs; *v.* prə grĕs'), -GRESSED, -GRESSING. (Moving forward, step by step.) Both hands, in the right angle position, palms facing, are held before the chest, a few inches apart, with the right hand slightly behind the left. The right hand is brought up, over and forward, so that it is now ahead of the left. The left hand then follows suit, so that it is now ahead of the right.

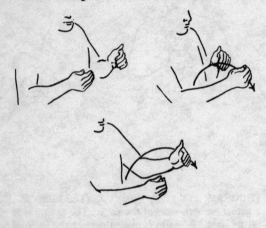

PROHIBIT (prō hĭb' ĭt), *v.,* -ITED, -ITING. (A modification of LAW, *q.v.;* "against the law.") The downturned right "D" or "L" hand is thrust forcefully into the left palm. See also FORBID 1, FORBIDDEN 1.

PROMINENT (prŏm' ə nənt), *adj.* (One's fame radiates far and wide.) The extended index fingers rest on the lips (or on the temples). Moving in small, continuous spirals, they move up and to either side of the head. See also FAME, FAMOUS.

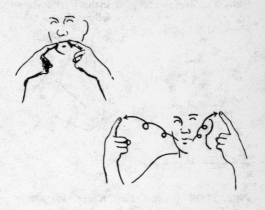

PROMISE (prŏm' ĭs), *n., v.,* -ISED, -ISING. (The arm is raised.) The right index finger is placed at the lips. The right arm is then raised, palm out and elbow resting on the back of the left hand. See also SWEAR 1.

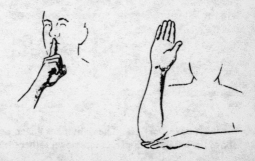

PROMOTE (prə mōt'), *v.*, -MOTED, -MOTING. (Something high up.) Both hands, in the right angle position, are held before the face, about a foot apart, palms facing. They are raised abruptly about a foot, in a slight outward curving movement. See also HIGH 1.

PROMOTION (prə mō' shən), *n.* See PROMOTE.

PROOF (pro͞of), *n.* (Laying out the proof for all to see.) The back of the open right hand is placed with a flourish on the open left palm. The index finger may first touch the lips.

PROPER (prŏp' ər), *adj.* The right index finger, held above the left index finger, comes down rather forcefully so that the bottom of the right hand comes to rest on top of the left thumb joint. See also CORRECT 1, RIGHT 3.

PROPOSE (prə pōz′), v., -POSED, -POSING. (An offering; a presenting.) Both hands, slightly cupped, palms up, are held close to the chest. They move up and out in unison, describing a very slight arc. See also OFFER, OFFERING, PRESENT 1, SUGGEST.

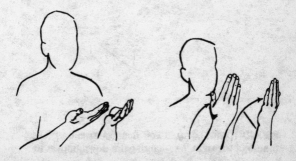

PROTECT (prə těkt′), *v.*, -TECTED, -TECTING. (Hold down firmly; cover and strengthen.) The "S" hands, downturned, are held side by side in front of the body, the arms almost horizontal, and the left hand in front of the right. Both arms move a short distance forward and slightly downward. See also DEFEND, DEFENSE, GUARD, SHIELD.

PROTECTION (prə těk′ shən), *n.* See PROTECT.

PROTEST (*n.* prō′ těst; *v.* prə těst′), -TESTED, -TESTING. (The hand is thrust into the chest to force a complaint out.) The curved fingers of the right hand are thrust forcefully into the chest. See also COMPLAIN, COMPLAINT, OBJECT, OBJECTION.

PROUD (proud), *adj.* (The feelings rise up.) The thumb of the right "A" hand, palm down, moves up along the right side of the chest. A haughty expression is assumed. See also PRIDE.

PROVE (prōōv), *v.*, PROVED, PROVEN, PROVING. See PROOF.

PROVIDE (prə vīd′) *v.*, -VIDED, -VIDING. (Handing over.) The "AND" hands are held upright with palms toward the body. From this position they swing forward and down, opening up as if giving something out.

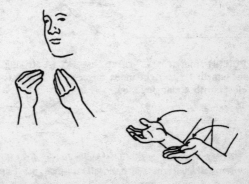

PUBLISH (pŭb' lĭsh), *v.,* -LISHED, -LISHING. (The action of the press.) The right "5" hand, held palm down, fingers pointing left, is brought down twice against the upturned left "5" hand, whose fingers point right. See also NEWSPAPER, PAPER.

PUNCH 1 (pŭnch), *n., v.,* PUNCHED, PUNCHING. (The natural sign.) The right "S" hand strikes its knuckles forcefully against the open left palm, which is held facing right. See also STRIKE.

PUNCH 2, *n., v.* (The natural sign.) The right fist strikes the chin.

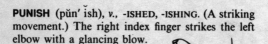

PUNISH (pŭn' ĭsh), *v.,* -ISHED, -ISHING. (A striking movement.) The right index finger strikes the left elbow with a glancing blow.

PURE (pyŏŏr), *adj.* (Everything is wiped off the hand, to emphasize an uncluttered or clean condition.) The right hand slowly wipes the upturned left palm, from wrist to fingertips. See also CLEAN, NICE, PLAIN 2.

PURITY (pyŏŏr′ ə tĭ), *n.* See PURE.

PURPOSE (pûr′ pəs), *n.* (Relative standing of one's thoughts.) A modified sign for THINK is made: The right index finger touches the middle of the forehead. The tips of the right "V" hand, palm down, are then thrust into the upturned left palm (as in STAND, *q.v.*). The right "V" hand is then rethrust into the upturned left palm, with right palm now facing the body. See also INTEND, INTENT, INTENTION, MEAN 2, MEANING, SIGNIFICANCE 2, SIGNIFY.

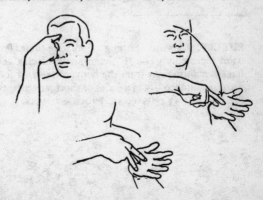

PUT (po͝ot), *v.*, PUT, PUTTING. (Moving from one place to another.) The downturned hands, fingers touching their respective thumbs, move in unison from left to right. See also MOVE.

PUT IN ORDER, *v. phrase.* (Placing things in order.) The hands, palms facing, fingers together and pointing away from the body, are positioned at the left side and held about a foot apart. With a slight up-down motion, as if describing waves, the hands travel in unison from left to right. See also AR-RANGE, ARRANGEMENT, ORDER 2, PLAN, PREPARE 1, READY 1.

PUT OFF, *v. phrase.* (Putting off; moving things forward repeatedly.) The "F" hands, palms facing and fingers pointing out from the body, are moved forward simultaneously in a series of short movements. See also DELAY, POSTPONE, PROCRASTINATE.

Q

QUANTITY (kwŏn′ tə tĭ), *n.* (Many fingers are indicated.) The upturned "S" hands are thrown up, opening into the "5" position, palms up. This may be repeated. See also MANY, NUMEROUS.

QUARREL (kwôr′ əl, kwŏr′ -), *n., v.* -RELED, -RELING. (Repeated rejoinders.) Both "D" hands are held with index fingers pointing toward each other. The hands move up and down alternately, each pivoting in turn at the wrist.

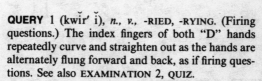

QUERY 1 (kwĭr′ ĭ), *n., v.,* -RIED, -RYING. (Firing questions.) The index fingers of both "D" hands repeatedly curve and straighten out as the hands are alternately flung forward and back, as if firing questions. See also EXAMINATION 2, QUIZ.

QUESTION 1 (kwĕs' chən), *n.* (The natural sign.)
The right index finger draws a question mark in the
air.

QUESTION 2, *n.* See QUERY.

QUESTION MARK, *n.* See QUESTION 1.

QUICK (kwĭk), *adj.* (A quick movement.) The
thumbtip of the upright right hand is flicked quickly
off the tip of the curved right index finger, as if
shooting marbles. See also FAST, IMMEDIATELY,
SPEED, SPEEDY.

QUICKNESS, *n.* See QUICK.

QUIET 1 (kwī' ət), *n., adj., interj., v.,* QUIETED, QUI-
ETING. (The natural sign.) The index finger is

brought up against the pursed lips. See also BE
QUIET 1, SILENCE 1, SILENT.

QUIET 2, *n., adj., interj., v.* (Quiet and peace.) The
open hands are crossed before the mouth, the right
palm facing left, left facing right. Then both hands,
held palms down, move down from the mouth, curving outward to either side of the body. See also BE
QUIET 2, BE STILL, CALM, SILENCE 2.

QUIT (kwĭt), *v.,* QUIT, QUITTING. (Pulling out.) The
index and middle fingers of the right "H" hand are
grasped by the left hand. The right hand pulls out of
the left. See also RESIGN, WITHDRAW 2.

QUIZ (kwĭz), *v.*, *n.* (Firing questions.) The index fingers of both "D" hands repeatedly curve and straighten out as the hands are alternately flung forward and back, as if firing questions. See also ASK 3, EXAMINATION 2, QUERY 1, QUESTION 2.

QUOTATION (kwō tā′ shən), *n.* (The quotation marks are indicated.) The curved index and middle fingers of both hands, held palms out, move slightly to either side of the body, as if drawing quotation marks in the air. See also SO-CALLED, SUBJECT, TITLE, TOPIC.

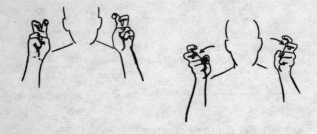

QUOTE (kwōt), *n.*, *v.*, QUOTED, QUOTING. See QUOTATION.

RACE (rās), *n., v.,* RACED, RACING. (Opposing objects.) The "A" hands are held side by side before the chest, palms facing each other and thumbs pointing forward. In this position the hands move alternately back and forth, toward and away from the body. See also COMPETE 2, COMPETITION 2.

RAGE (rāj), *n., v.,* RAGED, RAGING. (A violent welling-up of the emotions.) The curved fingers of the right hand are placed in the center of the chest, and fly up suddenly and violently. An expression of anger is worn. See also ANGER, ANGRY 2, FURY, MAD.

RAILROAD (rāl′ rōd′), *n.* (The letter "R.") The right "R" hand, palm down, moves down an inch or two, and moves to the right in a small arc.

RAISE (rāz), *n., v.,* RAISED, RAISING. (Adding on.) The index and middle fingers of the right "H" hand, palm up, are swung up and over until they come to rest on the index and middle fingers of the left "H" hand, held palm down. See also ADD 2, ADDITION, GAIN, INCREASE.

REACTION (rĭ ăk′ shən), *n.* (The letter "R"; coming out of the mouth.) Both "R" hands are held before the face, with the right "R" hand at the lips and behind the left "R" hand. Both hands move forward simultaneously, describing a small upward arc. See also RESPONSE 2.

READ (rēd), *v.*, READ, READING. (The eyes scan the page.) The left hand is held before the body, palm up and fingers pointing to the right. This represents the page. The right "V" hand then moves down as if scanning the page.

READY (rĕd′ ĭ), *adj.*, *v.*, READIED, READYING. (Placing things in order.) The hands, palms facing, fingers together and pointing away from the body, are positioned at the left side and held about a foot apart. With a slight up-down motion, as if describing waves, the hands travel in unison from left to right. See also ARRANGE, ARRANGEMENT, ORDER 2, PLAN, PREPARE 1, PUT IN ORDER.

READY 2, *adj.*, *adv.* (The "R" hands.) The same sign as for READY 1, *q.v.*, is made, except that the "R" hands are used. With palms facing down, they move simultaneously from left to right.

READY 3, *adj., v.* (Set out.) The "A" hands are crossed, with the right resting on top of the left. The right palm faces left and the left palm faces right. Both hands suddenly open and swing apart to the palm-down position. See also PREPARE 2.

REAL (rē′ əl, rēl), *adj.* (Coming forth directly from the lips; true.) The index finger of the right "D" hand, palm facing left, is placed against the lips. It moves up an inch or two and then describes a small arc forward and away from the lips. See also SURE, SURELY, TRUE, TRULY, TRUTH.

REALLY (rē′ ə lĭ, rē′ lĭ), *adv.* See REAL.

REASON (rē′ zən), *n.* (The letter "R"; the thought.) The fingertips of the right "R" hand describe a small counterclockwise circle in the middle of the forehead.

RECALL (rĭ kôl′), *v.*, -CALLED, CALLING. (Knowledge which remains.) The sign for KNOW is made: The right fingertips are placed on the forehead. The sign for REMAIN then follows: The "A" hands are held with palms toward the body, thumbs extended and touching, the right behind the left. In this position the hands move forward in a straight, steady line, or straight down. See also REMEMBER.

RECEIVE (rĭ sēv′), *v.*, -CEIVED, -CEIVING. (A grasping and bringing forward to oneself.) Both hands, in the "5" position, fingers curved, are crossed at the wrists, with the left palm facing right and the right palm facing left. They are brought in toward the chest, while closing into a grasping "S" position. See also GET.

RECENT (rē′ sənt), *adj.* (The slight movement represents a slight amount of time.) With the closed right hand held with knuckles against the right cheek, the thumbtip flicks off the tip of the curved index finger a number of times. The eyes squint a bit and the lips are drawn out in a slight smile. The hand remains against the cheek during the flicking movement. Sometimes, instead of the flicking movement, the tip of the curved index finger scratches slightly up and down against the cheek. In this case, the palm faces back toward the shoulder. The same expression is used as in the flicking movement. See also WHILE AGO, A 1.

RECENTLY, *adv.* See RECENT.

RED (rĕd), *adj., n.* (The lips, which are red, are indicated.) The tip of the right index finger moves down across the lips. The "R" hand may also be used.

REDUCE (rĭ dūs', -dōōs'), *v.*, -DUCED, -DUCING. (The diminishing size or amount.) With palms facing, the right hand is held above the left. The right hand moves slowly down toward the left, but does not touch it. See also DECREASE, LESS.

REFUSE (rĭ fūz'), *v.*, -FUSED, -FUSING. (Holding back.) The right "A" hand, palm facing left, moves up sharply to a position above the right shoulder. See also WON'T.

REGRET (rĭ grĕt′), *n.*, *v.*, -GRETTED, -GRETTING. (The heart is circled, to indicate feeling, modified by the letter "S," for SORROW.) The right "S" hand, palm facing the body, is rotated several times over the area of the heart. See also APOLOGIZE 1, APOL- OGY 1, SORROW, SORROWFUL 2, SORRY.

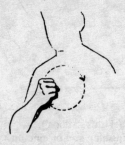

REGRETFUL (rĭ grĕt′ fəl), *adj.* See REGRET.

REGULAR (rĕg′ yə lər), *adj.* (Coming together with regular frequency.) Both "D" hands are held with index fingers pointing forward, the right hand above the left. The right "D" hand is brought down on the left several times in rhythmic succession as both hands move forward.

REJOICE (rĭ jois′), *v.*, -JOICED, -JOICING. (Waving of flags.) Both upright hands, grasping imaginary

flags, wave them in small circles. See also CELE-
BRATE, CELEBRATION, CHEER, VICTORY 1, WIN 1.

RELAX 1 (rĭ lăks'), v., -LAXED, -LAXING. (The
folded arms; a position of rest.) With palms facing
the body, the arms are folded across the chest. See
also REST 1, RESTFUL 1.

RELAX 2, n. (The "R" hands.) The sign for REST
1, q.v., is made, but with the crossed "R" hands. See
also REST 2, RESTFUL 2.

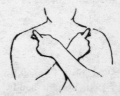

RELY (rĭ lī′), *v.*, -LIED, -LYING. (Hanging on to.) With the right index finger resting across its left counterpart, both hands drop down a bit. See also DEPEND 1, DEPENDABLE.

REMAIN (rĭ mān′), *v.*, -MAINED, -MAINING. (Steady, uninterrupted movement.) The "A" hands are held with palms out, thumbs extended and touching, the right behind the left. In this position the hands move forward in a straight, steady line. See also CONTINUE, ENDURE 2, EVER 1, LAST 3, LASTING, PERMANENT, PERSEVERE, PERSIST, STAY 1, STAY STILL.

REMAINDER (rĭ mān′ dər), *n.* (The remainder is left behind.) The "5" hands, palms facing each other and fingers pointing forward, are dropped simultaneously a few inches, as if dropping something on the table. See also LEFT.

REMEMBER (rĭ mĕm′bər), *v.,* -BERED, -BERING. (Knowledge which remains.) The sign for KNOW is made: The right fingertips are placed on the forehead. The sign for REMAIN then follows: The "A" hands are held with palms toward the body, thumbs extended and touching, the right behind the left. In this position the hands move forward in a straight, steady line, or straight down. See also RECALL.

REMOVE (rĭ mo͞ov′), *v.,* -MOVED, -MOVING. (Removing.) The right "A" hand, resting in the palm of the left "5" hand, moves slightly up and away, describing a small arc. It is then cast downward, opening into the "5" position, palm down, as if removing something from the left hand and casting it down. See also DEDUCT.

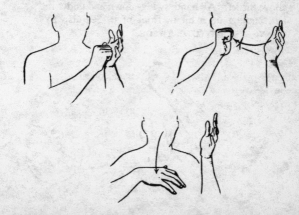

REPEAT (rĭ pēt′), *v.*, -PEATED, -PEATING. The left hand, open in the "5" position, palm up, is held before the chest. The right hand, in the right angle position, fingers pointing up, arches over and into the left palm. See also AGAIN.

REPEATEDLY, *adv.* (Repeating over and over again.) The sign for REPEAT is made several times.

REPLACE (rĭ plās′), *v.*, -PLACED, -PLACING. (Exchanging places.) The right "A" hand, positioned above the left "A" hand, swings down and under the left, coming up a bit in front of it. See also EXCHANGE, SUBSTITUTE, TRADE.

REPLY (rĭ plī′), *n., v.,* **-PLIED, -PLYING.** (Directing a reply from the mouth to someone.) The tip of the right index finger, held in the "D" position, palm facing the body, is placed on the lips, while the left "D" hand, palm also facing the body, is held about a foot in front of the right hand. The right index finger, swinging around, moves toward and stops in a pointing position a few inches from the left index fingertip. See also ANSWER, RESPOND, RESPONSE 1.

REPRESENT (rĕp′ rĭ zĕnt′), *v.,* **-SENTED, -SENTING.** (Directing the attention to something, and bringing it forward.) The right index finger points into the left palm, held facing out before the body. The left palm moves straight out. For the passive form of this verb, *i.e.,* BE SHOWN, the movement is reversed: The left hand, palm facing in, is moved in toward the body, while the right index finger remains pointing into the left palm. See also DEMONSTRATE, DISPLAY, EXAMPLE, EXHIBIT, EXHIBITION, SHOW 1.

REQUEST (rĭ kwĕst′), *n., v.,* -QUESTED, -QUESTING. (Pray tell.) Both hands, held upright about a foot in front of the chest, with palms facing and fingers pointing straight up, are positioned about a foot apart. Moving toward the chest, they come together until they touch, as if in prayer. See also ASK 1.

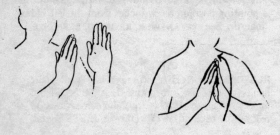

REQUIRE (rĭ kwīr′), *v.,* -QUIRED, -QUIRING. (Something specific is moved in toward oneself.) The palm of the left "5" hand faces right. The right index finger is thrust into the left palm, and both hands are drawn sharply in toward the chest. See also DEMAND.

RESCUE (rĕs′ kū), *v.,* -CUED, -CUING, *n.* (Breaking the bonds.) The "S" hands, crossed in front of the body, swing apart and face out. See also FREE 1, INDEPENDENCE, INDEPENDENT, SAFE, SAVE 1.

RESERVATION (rĕz′ ər vā′ shən), *n.* (Binding the hands down.) The downturned, right "S" hand makes a single, clockwise circle and comes down to rest on the back of the downturned, left "S" hand.

RESERVE (rĭ zûrv′), *v.* -SERVED, -SERVING. See RESERVATION.

RESIGN (rĭ zīn′), *v.,* -SIGNED, -SIGNING. (Pulling out.) The index and middle fingers of the right "H" hand are grasped by the left hand. The right hand pulls out of the left. See also QUIT, WITHDRAW 2.

RESPECT (rĭ spĕkt′), *n., v.,* -SPECTED, -SPECTING. (The letter "R"; bowing the head.) The right "R" hand swings up in an arc toward the head, which bows somewhat as the hand moves up toward it. The hand's movement is sometimes reversed, moving down and away from the head in an arc, while the head bows.

RESPOND (rĭ spŏnd′), *v.,* -PONDED, -PONDING. (Directing a reply from the mouth to someone.) The tip of the right index finger, held in the "D" position, palm facing the body, is placed on the lips, while the left "D" hand, palm also facing the body, is held about a foot in front of the right hand. The right index finger, swinging around, moves toward and stops in a pointing position a few inches from the left index fingertip. See also ANSWER, REPLY.

RESPONSE 1 (rĭ spŏns′), *n.* See RESPOND.

RESPONSE 2, *n.* (The letter "R"; coming out of the mouth.) Both "R" hands are held before the face, with the right "R" hand at the lips and behind the left "R" hand. Both hands move forward simultaneously, describing a small upward arc. See also REACTION, REPORT.

RESPONSIBILITY 1 (rĭ spŏn´ sə bĭl´ ə tĭ), n. (Something which weighs down or burdens one with responsibility.) The fingertips of both hands, placed on the right shoulder, bear down

RESPONSIBILITY 2, n. (Something which weighs down or burdens, modified by the letter "R," for "responsibility.") The "R" hands bear down on the right shoulder, in the same manner as RESPONSIBILITY 1.

RESPONSIBLE 1 (rĭ spŏn′ sə bəl), *adj.* See RESPON-SIBILITY 1.

_____

RESPONSIBLE 2, *adj.* See RESPONSIBILITY 2.

_____

REST 1 (rĕst), *n.* (The folded arms; a position of rest.) With palms facing the body, the arms are folded across the chest. See also RELAX 1.

_____

REST 2, *n.* (The "R" hands.) The sign for REST 1 is made, but with the crossed "R" hands. See also RELAX 2.

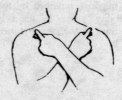

_____

RESTFUL 1 (rĕst′ fəl), *adj.* See REST 1.

RESTFUL 2, *adj.* See REST 2.

RESTRICT (rĭ strĭkt'), *v.,* -STRICTED, -STRICTING.
(The upper and lower limits are defined.) The right-
angle hands, palms facing, are held before the body,
the right above the left. They swing out 45 degrees
simultaneously, pivoted from their wrists. See also
LIMIT.

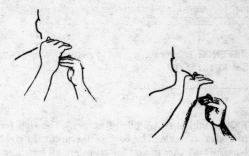

RETALIATE (rĭ tăl' ĭ āt'), *v.,* -ATED, -ATING.
(Birds pecking back and forth at each other.) The
right index finger and thumb, pressed together,
strike their counterparts with force.

RETALIATION (rĭ tăl' ĭ ā' shən), *n.* See RETALIATE.

RETIRE (rĭ tīr′), *v.*, -TIRED, -TIRING. (A position of idleness.) With thumbs tucked in the armpits, the remaining fingers of both hands wiggle. See also VA-CATION.

REVENGE (rĭ vĕnj′), *n., v.,* -VENGED, -VENGING. See RETALIATE.

RICH (rĭch), *adj.* (A pile of money.) The sign for MONEY is made: The back of the upturned right hand, whose thumb and fingertips are all touching, is placed in the upturned left palm. The right hand then moves straight up, as it opens into the "5" position, palm facing down and fingers somewhat curved. See also WEALTH, WEALTHY.

RIDICULOUS (rĭ dĭk′ yə ləs), *adj.* (Thoughts flickering back and forth.) The right "Y" hand, thumb almost touching the forehead, is shaken back and

forth across the forehead several times. See also
FOOLISH, NONSENSE, SILLY.

RIGHT 1 (rīt), *adj.* (A straightening out.) The right
hand, fingers together and palm facing left, is placed
in the upturned left palm, whose fingers point away
from the body. The right hand slides straight out
along the left palm, over the left fingers, and stops
with its heel resting on the left fingertips. See also
ALL RIGHT, O.K. 1, YOU'RE WELCOME 2.

RIGHT 2, *adj., adv.* (The letter "R"; the movement.)
The right "R" hand moves toward the right.

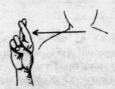

RIGHT 3, *adj., adv.* The right index finger, held above the left index finger, comes down rather forcefully so that the bottom of the right hand comes to rest on top of the left thumb joint. See also CORRECT 1, PROPER.

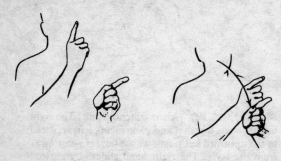

ROAD (rōd), *n.* (The winding movement.) Both hands, palms facing and fingers together and extended straight out, move in unison away from the body, in a winding manner. See also STREET.

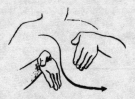

ROB 1 (rŏb), *v.,* ROBBED, ROBBING. (The hand, partly concealed, takes something surreptitiously.) The index and middle fingers of the right hand, somewhat curved, are placed under the left elbow.

As they move slowly along the left forearm toward the left wrist, they close a bit. See also STEAL 1, THEFT, THIEF 1, THIEVERY.

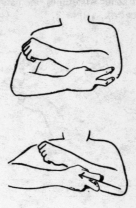

ROB 2, *(colloq.)*, *v.* (A sly, underhanded movement.) The right open hand, palm down, is held a bit behind the body at waist level. Beginning with the little finger, the hand closes finger by finger into the "A" position, as if wrapping itself around something. See also STEAL 2.

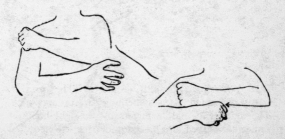

ROB 3, *v.* (A mustachioed thief.) The fingertips of both "H" hands, palms facing the body, are placed above the lips and are drawn slowly apart, describing a mustache. Sometimes one hand only is used. See also CROOK, THEFT 2.

ROOM 1 (rōōm, rŏŏm), *n.* (The dimensions are indicated.) The open hands, palms facing and fingers pointing out, are dropped an inch or two simultaneously. They then shift their relative positions so that both palms face the body, with one hand in front of the other. In this new position they again drop an inch or two simultaneously. See also BOX, PACKAGE.

ROOM 2, *n.* (The "R" hands.) This is the same sign as for ROOM 1, except that the "R" hands are used.

ROUGH (rŭf), *adj.* (The "roughness," in the form of ridges, described.) The tips of the curved right fingers trace imaginary ridges over the upright left palm, from the base of the hand to the fingertips. The action is repeated several times. See also RUDE, SCOLD 1.

RUDE (rōōd), *adj.* (The "roughness," of words is described.) The tips of the curved right fingers trace imaginary ridges over the upright left palm, from the base of the hand to the fingertips. The action is repeated several times. See also ROUGH, SCOLD 1.

RUDENESS (rōōd′ nĭs), *n*. See RUDE.

RUIN (rōō′ ĭn), *n*. (Wiping off.) The left "5" hand, palm up, is held slightly above the right "5" hand, held palm down. The right hand swings up, just brushing over the left palm. Both hands close into the "S" position, and the right is brought back with force to its initial position, striking a glancing blow against the left knuckles as it returns. See also DE-STROY.

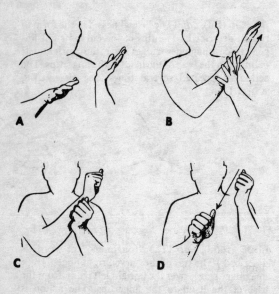

A

B

C

D

RULE (rōōl), *n*., *v*., RULED, RULING. (Holding the reins over all.) The "A" hands, palms facing, move alternately back and forth, as if grasping and manipulating reins. See also CONTROL 1, GOVERN, MANAGE.

RUN (rŭn), *v.*, RAN, RUN, RUNNING. The open left hand is held pointing out, palm down. The open right hand is held beneath it, facing up. The right hand is thrown forward rather quickly so the palm brushes repeatedly across the palm of the left.

RUN AWAY, *v. phrase.* (Slipping out and away.) The right index finger is held pointing upward between the index and middle fingers of the prone left hand. From this position the right index finger moves to the right, slipping out of the grasp of the left fingers and away from the left hand.

S

SAD (săd), *adj.* (The facial features drop.) Both "5" hands, palms facing the eyes and fingers slightly curved, drop simultaneously to a level with the mouth. The head drops slightly as the hands move down, and an expression of sadness is assumed. See also GLOOM, GLOOMY, GRIEF, SORROWFUL 1.

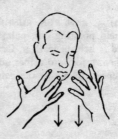

SAFE (sāf), *adj., n.* (Breaking the bonds.) The "S" hands, crossed in front of the body, swing apart and face out. See also FREE 1, INDEPENDENCE, INDEPENDENT, RESCUE, SAVE 1.

SAID (sĕd), *v.* (Words tumbling from the mouth.) The right index finger, pointing left, describes a con-

tinuous small circle in front of the mouth. See also
HEARING, MENTION, SAY, SPEAK, SPEECH 1, TALK
1, TELL.

SALE (sāl), *n*. (Transferring ownership of an object.) Both "AND" hands, fingers touching their respective thumbs, are held palms down before the body. The hands are pivoted simultaneously outward and away from the body, once or several times. See also SELL.

SALT (sôlt), *n*. (The act of tapping the salt from a knife edge.) Both "H" hands, palms down, are held before the chest. The fingers of the right "H" hand tap those of the left several times.

SAME 1 (sām), *adj.* (Matching fingers are brought together.) The outstretched index fingers are brought together, either once or several times. See also ALIKE, LIKE 2, SIMILAR.

SAME 2, *(colloq.), adj.* (Two figures are compared, back and forth.) The right "Y" hand, palm facing left, is moved alternately toward and away from the body. See also ME TOO.

SATISFACTION (săt´ ĭs făk´ shən), *n.* (The inner feelings settle down.) Both "B" hands (or "5" hands, fingers together) are placed palms down against the chest, the right above the left. Both move down simultaneously a few inches. See also CONTENT, CONTENTED.

SATISFIED, *adj.* See SATISFACTION.

SATISFY 1 (săt′ ĭs fĭ), *v.*, -FIED, -FYING. See SATIS-
FACTION.

SATISFY 2, *v.* This is the same sign as for SATISFY
1 but with only one hand used.

SAVE 1 (sāv), *v.*, SAVED, SAVING. (Breaking the
bonds.) The "S" hands, crossed in front of the body,
swing apart and face out. See also FREE 1, INDEPEN-
DENCE, INDEPENDENT, RESCUE, SAFE.

SAVE 2, *v.* (Holding back.) The right "V" fingers are
tapped once or twice across the back of their left
counterparts. Both palms face the chest.

SAY (sā), *v.*, SAID, SAYING. (Words tumbling from the mouth.) The right index finger, pointing left, describes a continuous small circle in front of the mouth. See also HEARING, MENTION, SAID, SPEAK, SPEECH 1, TALK 1, TELL.

SCARE(D) (skâr), *v.*, SCARED, SCARING, *n.* (The heart is suddenly covered with fear.) Both hands, fingers together, are placed side by side, palms facing the chest. They quickly open and come together over the heart, one on top of the other. See also AFRAID, FEAR 1, FRIGHT, FRIGHTEN, TERROR 1.

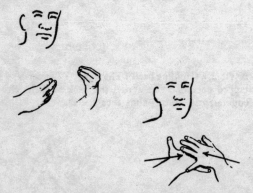

SCHOOL (skōōl), *n.* (The teacher's hands are clapped for attention.) The hands are clapped together several times.

SCIENCE (sī' əns), *n.* (Pouring alternately from test tubes.) The upright thumbs of both "A" hands swing over alternately, as if pouring out the contents of a pair of test tubes.

SCOLD 1 (skōld), *(colloq.), v.,* SCOLDED, SCOLDING. (Rough language.) The tips of the curved right fingers trace imaginary ridges over the upright left palm, from the base of the hand to the fingertips. The action is repeated several times. See also ROUGH, RUDE.

SCOLD 2, *(sl.)*, *v.* (Big, i.e. curse, words tumble out.) The right "Y" hand moves forward in a wavy manner along the left index finger, which is pointing forward. The action is repeated several times. The wide space between the thumb and little finger of the "Y" hand represents the length of the words, and the forward movement the tumbling out of the words in anger.

SCREAM (skrēm), *v.*, SCREAMED, SCREAMING. (Harsh words thrown out.) The right hand, as in CURSE 1, appears to claw words out of the mouth. This time, however, it turns and throws them out, ending in the "5" position. See also CURSE 2, SHOUT.

SEARCH (sûrch), *v.*, SEARCHED, SEARCHING. (Directing the vision from place to place.) The right "C" hand, palm facing left, moves from right to left across the line of vision, in a series of counterclockwise circles. The signer's gaze remains concentrated

and his head turns slowly from right to left. See also
EXAMINE, LOOK FOR, SEEK.

SEAT (sēt), *n.*, *v.*, SEATED, SEATING. (The act of
sitting.) The extended right index and middle fingers
are draped across the back of the same two fingers
of the downturned left hand. The hands then move
straight downward a short distance. See also BE
SEATED, CHAIR, SIT.

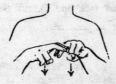

SECOND 1 (sĕk′ ənd), *adj.* (The second finger is
indicated.) The tip of the index finger of the right
"D" hand is placed on the tip of the middle finger
of the left "V" hand. The right hand then executes
a short pivotal movement in a clockwise direction.
The left "L" hand may be substituted for the left
"V" hand, with the right index fingertip placed on
the left index fingertip.

SECOND 2, *n.* (The ticking off of seconds on the clock.) The index finger of the right "D" hand executes a series of very short movements in a clockwise manner as it rests against the left "S" hand, which is facing right.

SECONDARY (sĕk′ ən dĕr´ ĭ), *adj.* See SECOND 1.

SECONDLY (sĕk′ ənd lĭ), *adv.* See SECOND 1.

SEE (sē), *v.*, SAW, SEEN, SEEING. (The eyesight is directed forward.) The right "V" hand (the French *voir*), palm facing the body, is placed so that the fingertips are just under the eyes. The hand swings around and out, so that the fingertips are now pointing forward. The hand often moves straight out, without turning around. See also LOOK 1, PERCEIVE, PERCEPTION, SIGHT, WATCH.

SEEK (sēk), *v.*, SOUGHT, SEEKING. (Directing the vision from place to place.) The right "C" hand, palm facing left, moves from right to left across the line of vision, in a series of counterclockwise circles. The signer's gaze remains concentrated and his head turns slowly from right to left. See also EXAMINE, LOOK FOR, SEARCH.

SEEM (sēm), *v.*, SEEMED, SEEMING. (Something presented before the eyes.) The open right hand, palm flat and facing out, with fingers together and pointing up, is positioned at shoulder level. Pivoting from the wrist, the hand is swung around so that the palm now faces the eyes. Sometimes the eyes glance at the newly presented palm. See also LOOK 2.

SELECT 1 (sĭ lĕkt′), *v.*, -LECTED, -LECTING. (The natural motion of selecting something from the hand.) The thumb and index fingers of the outstretched right hand grasp an imaginary object on the upturned left palm. The right hand then moves straight up. See also FIND, PICK 1.

SELECT 2, *v.* (Taking unto oneself.) The right hand, palm out, is extended before the chest, index finger and thumb in an open position, the other fingers separated and pointing up. The hand is drawn in toward the chest, and the index and thumb close at the same time, indicating something taken to oneself. See also CHOOSE, TAKE.

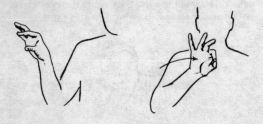

-SELF (sĕlf), *n. used with a gender prefix as a reflexive and intensive pronoun; adj.* (The individual is indicated with the thumb.) The right hand, held in the "A" position, thumb up, moves several times in the direction of the person indicated: *myself, your-*

self, himself, herself, itself, oneself, ourselves, your-
selves, themselves.

SELFISH 1 (sĕl' fĭsh), *adj.* (Pulling things toward
oneself.) Both prone open or "V" hands are held in
front of the body with fingers bent. The hands are
then drawn quickly and forcefully inward, as if raking things toward oneself. See also GREEDY 1,
STINGY 1.

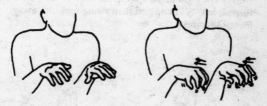

SELFISH 2, *adj.* (Scratching the palm in greed.) The
right fingers scratch the upturned left palm several
times. A frowning expression is often used. See also
GREEDY 2, STINGY 2.

SELL (sĕl), *v.*, SOLD, SELLING. (Transferring ownership of an object.) Both "AND" hands, fingers
touching their respective thumbs, are held palms
down before the body. The hands are pivoted simultaneously outward and away from the body, once or
several times. See also SALE.

SEND 1 (sĕnd), *v.*, SENT, SENDING. (Sending away
from.) The right fingertips tap the back of the downturned, left "S" hand and then swing forward, away
from the hand.

SEND 2, *v.* (Sending something forth.) The right
"AND" hand is held palm out. It then opens and
moves forcefully outward, in a throwing motion.

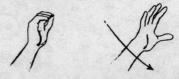

SENSITIVE (sĕn′ sə tĭv), *adj.* (A nimble touch.) The middle finger of the right hand touches the chest over the heart very briefly and lightly, and is then flicked off.

SENSITIVITY (sĕn′ sə tĭv′ ə tĭ), *n.* See SENSITIVE.

SENTENCE (sĕn′ təns), *n., v.,* -TENCED, -TENCING. (A series of letters spelled out on the printed page.) The downturned "F" hands are positioned with thumbs and index fingertips touching. The hands move straight apart to either side in a wavy or straight motion. See also LANGUAGE 1.

SEPARATE 1 (*v.* sĕp′ ə rāt′; *adj., n.* sĕp′ ə rĭt),
-RATED, -RATING. (The hands are moved apart.)
Both hands, in the "A" position, thumbs up, are
held together, with knuckles touching. With a delib-
erate movement they come apart. See also APART,
DIVORCE 1.

SEPARATE 2, *v., adj., n.* (Separating to classify.)
Both hands, in the right angle position, are placed
palms down before the body, knuckles to knuckles.
They pull apart or separate, once or a number of
times.

SEVERAL (sĕv′ ər əl), *adj.* (The fingers are presented in order, to convey the concept of "several.")

The right "A" hand is held palm facing up. One by
one the fingers open, beginning with the index finger
and ending with the little finger. Some use only the
index and middle fingers. See also FEW.

SEXUAL INTERCOURSE, *n. phrase.* (The motions
of the legs during the sexual act.) The upturned left
"V" hand remains motionless, while the downturned right "V" hand comes down repeatedly on
the left.

SHAME 1 (shām), *n.*, *v.*, SHAMED, SHAMING. (The color rises in the cheek; an attempt is made to hide the head.) The backs of the fingers of the right hand, held in the right angle position, are placed against the right cheek. The hand moves up along the cheek, pivoting at the wrist, so that the fingers finally point to the rear. See also ASHAMED, BASHFUL, SHAMEFUL, SHAME ON YOU, SHY 1.

SHAME 2, *n.* Similar to SHAME 1, but both hands are used, at either cheek. See also SHY 2.

SHAMEFUL (shām′ fəl), *adj.* See SHAME 1.

SHAME ON YOU, *phrase.* See SHAME 1.

SHAPE (shāp), *n.*, *v.*, SHAPED, SHAPING. (Contours are indicated or outlined.) Both "A" hands, held about a foot apart before the face, with palms facing each other, move down simultaneously in a wavy, undulating motion. See also FIGURE 2, FORM, STATUE.

SHE (shē), *pron.* (Pointing at a female.) The FEMALE prefix sign is made: The right "A" hand's thumb moves down along the line of the right jaw, from ear almost to chin. The right index finger then points at an imaginary female. If in context the gender is clear, the prefix sign is usually omitted. See also HER.

SHIELD (shēld), *n., v.,* SHIELDED, SHIELDING. (Hold down firmly; cover and strengthen.) The "S" hands, downturned, are held side by side in front of the body, the arms almost horizontal, and the left hand in front of the right. Both arms move a short distance forward and slightly downward. See also DEFEND, DEFENSE, GUARD, PROTECT, PROTECTION.

SHINE (shīn), *v.*, SHINED, SHINING, SHONE. (Reflected glistening of light rays.) The left hand, held supinely before the chest, palm down, represents the object from which the rays glisten. The right hand, in the "5" position, touches the back of the left lightly and moves up toward the right, pivoting slightly at the wrist, with fingers wiggling.

SHINING, *adj.* See SHINE.

SHIRT (shûrt), *n.* (Draping the clothes on the body.) With fingertips resting on the chest, both hands move down simultaneously. The action is repeated. See also CLOTHES, CLOTHING, DRESS, GOWN, WEAR.

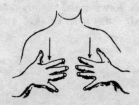

SHIVER (shĭv′ ər), *v.*, -ERED, -ERING. (The trembling from cold.) Both "S" hands, palms facing, are placed at the sides of the body. In this position the arms and hands shiver. See also COLD 1, WINTER 1.

SHOCKED (shŏkt), *v.* (The mind is frozen; the thought is frozen.) The index finger of the right "D" hand, palm facing the body, touches the forehead (modified THINK sign, *q. v.*). Both hands, in the "5" position, palms down, are then suddenly and deliberately dropped down in front of the body. A look of surprise is assumed at this point, and the head jerks back slightly.

SHOP (shŏp), *n.*, *v.*, SHOPPED, SHOPPING. (Paying out money.) The right hand, palm up and all fingertips touching the thumb, is placed in the upturned left hand. From this position it moves forward and off the left hand a number of times. The right fingers usually remain against the thumb, but they may be opened very slightly each time the right hand moves forward.

SHOPPING (shŏp' ĭng), *n.* See SHOP.

SHORT 1 (shôrt), *adj.* (To make short; to measure off a short space.) The index and middle fingers of the right "H" hand are placed across the top of the index and middle fingers of the left "H" hand, and move a short distance back and forth, along the length of the left index finger. See also BRIEF.

SHORT 2, *adj.* (A shortness of height is indicated.)
The right hand, in right-angle position, pats an
imaginary head at approximately chest level.
SMALL 2.

SHORTEN (shôr′ tən), *v.*, -ENED, -ENING. See
SHORT 1.

SHOULD (sho͝od), *v.* (Being pinned down.) The
right hand, in the "X" position, palm down, moves
forcefully up and down once or twice. An expression
of determination is frequently assumed. See also
HAVE TO, MUST, NECESSARY, NECESSITY, NEED 1,
OUGHT TO.

SHOUT (shout), *v.*, SHOUTED, SHOUTING. (Harsh words thrown out.) The right hand, as in CURSE 1, appears to claw words out of the mouth. This time, however, it turns and throws them out, ending in the "5" position. See also CURSE 2, SCREAM.

SHOW 1 (shō), *n., v.*, SHOWED, SHOWING. (Directing the attention to something, and bringing it forward.) The right index finger points into the left palm, held facing out before the body. The left palm moves straight out. For the passive form of this verb, *i.e.,* BE SHOWN, the movement is reversed: The left hand, palm facing in, is moved in toward the body, while the right index finger remains pointing into the left palm. See also DEMONSTRATE, DISPLAY, EXAMPLE, EXHIBIT, EXHIBITION, REPRESENT.

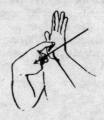

SHOW 2, *n.* (Motion or movement, modified by the letter "A" for "act.") Both "A" hands, palms out, are held at shoulder height and rotate alternately

toward the head. See also ACT 1, PERFORM 2, PER-
FORMANCE 2, PLAY 2.

SHUT (shŭt), *adj., v.,* SHUT, SHUTTING. (The act of closing.) Both "B" hands, held palms out before the body, come together with some force. See also CLOSE 1.

SHY 1 (shī), *adj.* (The color rises in the cheek; an attempt is made to hide the head.) The backs of the fingers of the right hand, held in the right angle position, are placed against the right cheek. The hand moves up along the cheek, pivoting at the wrist, so that the fingers finally point to the rear. See also ASHAMED, BASHFUL, SHAME 1, SHAMEFUL, SHAME ON YOU.

SHY 2, *adj.* Similar to SHY 1, but both hands are used, at either cheek. See also SHAME 2.

SICK (sĭk), *adj., adv.* (The sick parts of the anatomy are indicated.) The right middle finger rests on the forehead, and its left counterpart is placed against the stomach. The signer assumes an expression of sadness or physical distress. See also ILL.

SIGHT (sīt), *n.*, SAW, SEEN, SEEING. (The eyesight is directed forward.) The right "V" hand, palm facing the body, is placed so that the fingertips are just under the eyes. The hand swings around and out, so that the fingertips are now pointing forward. See also LOOK 1, PERCEIVE, PERCEPTION, SEE, WATCH 1.

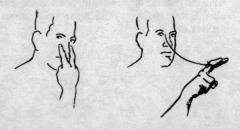

SIGNIFICANCE 1 (sĭg nĭf′ ə kəns), *n.* Both "F" hands, palms facing each other, move apart, up, and together in a smooth elliptical fashion, coming together at the tips of the thumbs and index fingers of both hands. See also IMPORTANT, VALUABLE, VALUE, WORTH, WORTHWHILE, WORTHY.

SIGNIFICANCE 2, *n.* (Relative standing of one's thoughts.) A modified sign for THINK is made: The right index finger touches the middle of the forehead. The tips of the right "V" hand, palm down, are then thrust into the upturned left palm (as in STAND, *q.v.*). The right "V" hand is then re-thrust into the upturned left palm, with right palm now facing the body. See also INTEND, INTENT, INTENTION, MEAN 2, MEANING, PURPOSE.

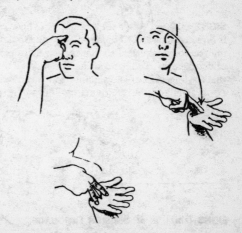

SIGNIFICANT (sĭg nĭf′ ə kənt), *adj.* See SIGNIFICANCE 1.

SIGNIFY (sĭg′ nə fī′), *n.* See SIGNIFICANCE 2.

SIGN LANGUAGE, *n.* (LANGUAGE 1, *q.v.,* and hand/arm movements.) The "D" hands, palms facing and index fingers pointing back toward the face, describe a series of continuous counterclockwise circles toward and away from the face, imitating the foot motions in bicycling. This is followed by the sign for LANGUAGE: The downturned "F" hands are positioned with thumbs and index fingertips touching. The hands move straight apart to either side in a wavy motion. The LANGUAGE part is often omitted. See also LANGUAGE OF SIGNS.

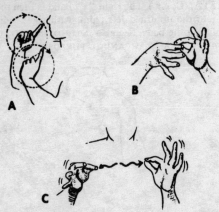

SIGNS (sīnz), *n. pl.* See SIGN LANGUAGE.

SILENCE 1 (sī′ ləns), *interj., n., v.,* -LENCED, -LENC-
ING. (The natural sign.) The index finger is brought
up against the pursed lips. See also BE QUIET 1,
QUIET 1.

SILENCE 2, *n., interj., v.* (Quiet and peace.) The
open hands are crossed before the mouth, the right
palm facing left, the left facing right. Then both
hands, held palms down, move down from the
mouth, curving outward to either side of the body.
See also BE QUIET 2, BE STILL, CALM, QUIET 2.

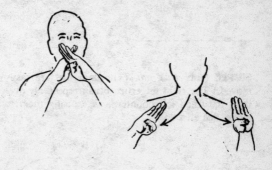

SILENT (sī′ lənt), *adj.* See SILENCE 1.

SILLY (sĭl' ĭ), *adj.* (Thoughts flickering back and forth.) The right "Y" hand, thumb almost touching the forehead, is shaken back and forth across the forehead several times. See also FOOLISH, NONSENSE, RIDICULOUS.

SIMILAR (sĭm' ĭ lər), *adj.* (Matching fingers are brought together.) The outstretched index fingers are brought together, either once or several times. See also ALIKE, LIKE 2, SAME 1.

SIMPLE (sĭm' pəl), *adj.* (The fingertips are easily moved.) The right fingertips brush repeatedly over their upturned left counterparts, causing them to move. See also EASY.

SINCE (sĭns), *adv., prep., conj.* (From a point up and over.) In the "D" position, palms down, both index fingers touch the right shoulder and then are brought up and over, ending in a palm-up position, pointing straight ahead of the body. See also ALL ALONG, ALL THE TIME, EVER SINCE, SO FAR, THUS FAR.

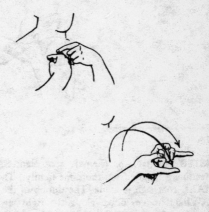

SINCERE (sĭn sĭr′), *adj.* (The letter "H," for HONEST; a straight and true path.) The index and middle fingers of the right "H" hand, whose palm faces left, move straight forward along the upturned left palm. See also HONEST, HONESTY.

SING (sĭng), *v.*, SANG or SUNG, SUNG, SINGING, *n.*
(A rhythmic, wavy movement of the hand, to indicate a melody; the movement of a conductor's hand
in directing a musical performance.) The right "5"
hand, palm facing left, is waved back and forth over
the downturned left hand, in a series of elongated
figure-eights. See also MUSIC, SONG.

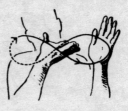

SISTER (sĭs′ tər), *n.* (Female root sign; SAME.
Meaning a female from the same family.) The FE-
MALE root sign is made: The thumb of the right
"A" hand moves down along the right jawbone,
almost to the chin. This is followed by the sign for
SAME: The outstretched index fingers are brought
together, either once or several times.

SIT (sĭt), *v.*, SAT, SITTING. (The act of sitting.) The
extended right index and middle fingers are draped
across the back of the same two fingers of the downturned left hand. The hands then move straight

downward a short distance. See also BE SEATED,
CHAIR, SEAT.

SKEPTIC (skĕp′ tĭk), *n.* (Warding off.) The sign for
SKEPTICAL is formed. This is followed by the sign
for INDIVIDUAL.

SKEPTICAL (skĕp′ tə kəl), *adj.* (Throwing the fist.)
The right "S" hand is held before the right shoulder,
elbow bent out to the side. The hand is them thrown
forward several times, as if striking at someone.

SKILL (skĭl), *n.* (A sharp-edged hand.) The right
hand grasps the little finger edge of the left firmly.
As it leaves this position, moving down and out, it
assumes the "A" position, palm facing left. See also
EXPERIENCE 1, EXPERT.

SKILLFUL (skĭl′ fəl), *adj.* See SKILL.

SKINNY (skĭn′ ĭ), *(sl.), adj.* (A thin, tapering object is described with the little fingers, the thinnest of all.) The tips of the little fingers, touching, one above the other, are drawn apart. The cheeks may also be drawn in for emphasis. See also THIN 2.

SLEEP 1 (slēp), *v.*, SLEPT, SLEEPING, *n.* (The eyes are closed.) The fingers of the right open hand, facing the forehead, are placed on the forehead. The hand moves down and away from the head, with the fingers closing so that they all touch. The eyes meanwhile close, and the head bows slightly, as in sleep. See also ASLEEP.

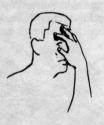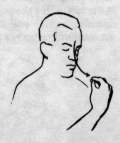

SLEEP 2, *n., v.* (The natural sign.) The signer's head leans to the right and rests in the upturned palm of the open right hand.

SLEEPY (slē′ pĭ), *adj.* (Drooping eyelids.) The right fingers are wiggled in front of the face, and the head is bowed forward.

SLOW (slō), *adj.* (The movement indicates the slowness.) The right hand is drawn slowly over the back of the downturned left hand, from fingertips to wrist.

SMALL 1 (smôl), *adj.* (Indicating a small mass.) The extended right thumb and index finger are held slightly spread. They are then moved slowly toward each other until they almost touch. See also TINY.

SMALL 2, *adj.* (A shortness of height is indicated.) The right hand, in right-angle position, pats an imaginary head at approximately chest level. See also SHORT 2.

SMART (smärt), *adj.* (The mind is bright.) The middle finger is placed at the forehead, and then the hand, with an outward flick, turns around so that the palm faces outward. This indicates a brightness flowing from the mind. See also INTELLIGENT.

SMELL (smĕl), v., SMELLED, SMELLING, n. (Bringing something up to the nose.) The upturned right hand moves slowly up to and past the nose, and the signer breathes in as the hand sweeps by. See also ODOR.

SMILE (smīl), v., SMILED, SMILING, n. (Drawing the lips into a smile.) The right index finger is drawn back over the lips, toward the ear. As the finger moves back, the signer breaks into a smile. (Both index fingers may also be used.)

SO-CALLED (sō′ kôld′), adj. (The quotation marks are indicated.) The curved index and middle fingers of both hands, held palms out, move slightly to either side of the body, as if drawing quotation marks in the air. See also QUOTATION, QUOTE, SUBJECT, TITLE, TOPIC.

SODA POP, *n.* (Corking a bottle.) The left "O" hand is held with thumb edge up, representing a bottle. The thumb and index finger of the right "5" hand represent a cork, and are inserted into the circle formed by the "O" hand. The palm of the open right hand then strikes down on the upturned edge of the "O" hand, as if forcing the cork into the bottle. See also POP 1.

SODA WATER, *n. phrase.* See SODA POP.

SO FAR, *adv. phrase.* (From a point up and over.) In the "D" position, palms down, both index fingers touch the right shoulder and then are brought up and over, ending in a palm-up position, pointing straight ahead of the body. See also ALL ALONG, ALL THE TIME, EVER SINCE, SINCE, THUS FAR.

SOME (sŭm; *unstressed* səm), *adj.* (Cutting off or designating a part.) The little finger edge of the open right hand moves straight down the middle of the upturned left palm. See also PART, PIECE, PORTION.

SOMETIME(S) (sŭm′ tīmz′), *adv.* (The "1" finger is brought up very slowly.) The right index finger, resting in the open left palm, which is facing right, swings up slowly from its position to one in which it is pointing straight up. The movement is repeated slowly, after a pause. See also OCCASIONAL, OCCASIONALLY, ONCE IN A WHILE.

SON (sŭn), *n.* (Male, baby.) The sign for MALE is made: The thumb and extended fingers of the right hand are brought up to grasp an imaginary cap brim. This is followed by the sign for BABY: The arms are held with one resting on the other, as if cradling a baby.

 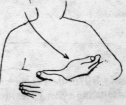

SONG (sông, sŏng), *n.* (A rhythmic, wavy movement of the hand, to indicate a melody; the movement of a conductor's hand in directing a musical performance.) The right "5" hand, palm facing left, is waved back and forth over the downturned left hand, in a series of elongated figure-eights. See also MUSIC, SING.

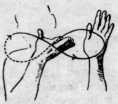

SORROW (sŏr' ō, sôr' ō), *n.* (The heart is circled, to indicate feeling, modified by the letter "S," for SORRY.) The right "S" hand, palm facing the body, is rotated several times over the area of the heart. See also APOLOGIZE 1, APOLOGY 1, REGRET, REGRETFUL.

SORROWFUL 1 (sŏr' ə fəl, sôr' -), *adj.* (The facial features drop.) Both "5" hands, palms facing the

eyes and fingers slightly curved, drop simultaneously
to a level with the mouth. The head drops slightly
as the hands move down, and an expression of sadness is assumed. See also GLOOM, GLOOMY, GRIEF,
SAD.

SORROWFUL 2, *adj.* See SORROW.

SORRY (sŏr' ĭ, sôr' ĭ), *adj.* See SORROW.

SPEAK (spēk), *v.*, SPOKE, SPOKEN, SPEAKING.
(Words tumbling from the mouth.) The right index
finger, pointing left, describes a continuous small
circle in front of the mouth. See also HEARING, MEN-
TION, SAID, SAY, SPEECH 1, TALK 1, TELL.

SPECIAL (spĕsh′ əl), *adj.* (Selecting a particular item from among several.) The index finger and thumb of the right hand grasp and pull up the left index finger. See also EXCEPT, EXCEPTION.

SPECIALIZE (spĕsh′ ə līz′), *v.*, -IZED, -IZING. (A straight, *i.e.*, special, path.) The hands are held in the "B" position, one above the other, with left palm facing right and right palm facing left. The little finger edge of the right hand moves straight forward along the index finger edge of the left.

SPECIALTY (spĕsh′ əl tĭ), *n.*, *pl.* -TIES. See SPECIAL-IZE.

SPECIFIC (spĭ sĭf′ ĭk), *adj.* (The fingers come to-gether precisely.) The thumb and index finger of each hand, palms facing, the right above the left, form circles. They are brought together with a delib-erate movement, so that the fingers and thumbs now

touch. Sometimes the right hand, before coming together with the left, executes a slow clockwise circle
above the left. See also EXACT, EXACTLY, PRECISE.

SPECULATE 1 (spĕk′ yə lāt′), *v.*, -LATED, -LATING.
(A thought is turned over in the mind.) The index
finger makes a small circle on the forehead. See also
CONSIDER 1, THINK, THOUGHT, THOUGHTFUL.

SPECULATE 2, *v.* (Turning thoughts over in the
mind.) Both index fingers, pointing to the forehead,
describe continuous alternating circles. See also
CONSIDER 2, WONDER.

SPECULATION 1 (spĕk′ yə lā′ shən), *n.* See SPECU-LATE 1.

SPECULATION 2, *n.* See SPECULATE 2.

SPEECH 1 (spēch), *n.* (Words tumbling from the mouth.) The right index finger, pointing left, describes a continuous small circle in front of the mouth. See also HEARING, MENTION, SAID, SAY, SPEAK, TALK 1, TELL.

SPEECH 2 *n.* (A gesture of an orator.) The right open hand, palm facing left, is held above and to the right of the head. It pivots, forward and backward, on the wrist several times. See also LECTURE, TALK 2.

SPEECHLESS (spēch′ lĭs), *(colloq.)*, *adj.* (The mouth drops open.) The fingertips of both "V" hands are held curved and touching before the body, one hand above the other. Then the hands are suddenly drawn apart, and at the same instant the mouth drops open and the eyes open wide.

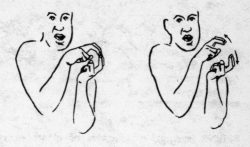

SPEED (spēd), *n.*, *v.*, SPED, or SPEEDED, SPEEDING. (A quick movement.) The thumbtip of the upright right hand is flicked quickly off the tip of the curved right index finger, as if shooting marbles. See also FAST, IMMEDIATELY, QUICK, QUICKNESS.

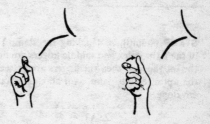

SPEEDY (spē′ dĭ), *adj.* See SPEED.

SPEND (spĕnd), *v.*, SPENT, SPENDING. (Repeated giving forth.) The back of the upturned right hand, thumb touching fingertips, is placed in the upturned left palm. The right hand moves off and away from the left once or several times, each time opening into the "5" position, palm up. See also WASTE 1.

SPRING (sprĭng), *n.* (Flowers or plants emerge from the ground.) The right fingers, pointing up, emerge from the closed left hand, and they spread open as they do. The action may be repeated. See also GROW, GROWN.

STAMP (stămp), *n.* (Licking the stamp.) The tips of the right index and middle fingers are licked with the tongue, and then the fingers are pressed against the upturned left palm, as if affixing a stamp to an envelope.

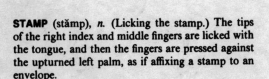

STAND 1 (stănd), *v.*, STOOD, STANDING, *n.* (The feet planted on the ground.) The downturned right "V" fingers are thrust into the upturned left palm.

STAND 2, *v.*, *n.* (Getting onto one's feet.) The upturned index and middle fingers of the right hand, representing the legs, are swung up and over in an arc, coming to rest in the upturned left palm. See also GET UP.

STANDING (stăn' dĭng), *n.* See STAND 1.

STAND UP, *v. phrase.* See STAND 2.

START (stärt), *v.*, STARTED, STARTING. (Turning a key to open up a new venture.) The right index finger, resting between the left index and middle fingers, executes a half turn, once or twice. See also BEGIN, ORIGIN.

STARVATION (stär vā' shən), *n.* (The upper alimentary tract is outlined.) The right "C" hand, palm facing the body, is placed with fingertips touching mid-chest. In this position it moves down a bit. See also WISH 2.

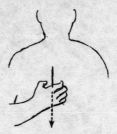

STARVE (stärv), *v.*, STARVED, STARVING. See STARVATION.

STARVED *v.* See STARVATION.

STATUE (stăch′ ōō), *n.* (Contours are indicated or outlined.) Both "A" hands, held about a foot apart before the face, with palms facing each other, move down simultaneously in a wavy, undulating motion. See also FIGURE 2, FORM, SHAPE.

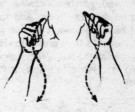

STAY 1 (stā), *n., v.,* STAYED, STAYING. (Steady, uninterrupted movement.) The "A" hands are held with palms out, thumbs extended and touching, the right behind the left. In this position the hands move forward in a straight, steady line. See also CON-TINUE, ENDURE 2, EVER 1, LAST 3, LASTING, PER-MANENT, PERSEVERE, PERSIST, REMAIN.

STAY 2, *v.* (Remaining in place.) One "Y" hand, held palm down, drops down a few inches.

STAY STILL, *v. phrase.* See STAY 1.

STEAL 1 (stēl), *n., v.,* STOLE, STOLEN, STEALING.
(The hand, partly concealed, takes something surreptitiously.) The index and middle fingers of the
right hand, somewhat curved, are placed under the
left elbow. As they move slowly along the left forearm toward the left wrist, they close a bit. See also
ROB 1, THEFT, THIEF 1, THIEVERY.

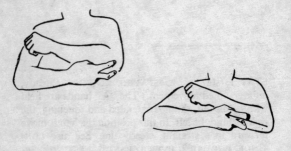

STEAL 2, *(colloq.),* v. (A sly, underhanded movement). The right open hand, palm down, is held a bit
behind the body at waist level. Beginning with the
little finger, the hand closes finger by finger into the
"A" position, as if wrapping itself around something. See also ROB 2.

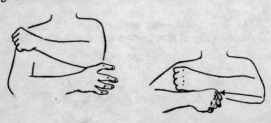

STILL (stĭl), *adv., conj.* (Duration of movement from past to present.) The right "Y" hand is held palm down in front of the right shoulder and is then moved slowly down and forward in a smooth curve.

STINGY 1 (stĭn' jĭ), *adj.* (Pulling things toward oneself.) Both prone open or "V" hands are held in front of the body with fingers bent. The hands are then drawn quickly and forcefully inward, as if raking things toward oneself. See also GREEDY 1, SELFISH 1.

STINGY 2, *adj.* (Scratching the palm in greed.) The right fingers scratch the upturned left palm several times. A frowning expression is often used. See also GREEDY 2, SELFISH 2.

STOP (stŏp), *v.*, STOPPED, STOPPING, *n.* (A stopping or cutting short.) The little finger edge of the right hand is thrust abruptly into the upturned left palm, indicating a cutting short.

STORY (stōr' ĭ), *n.* (The unraveling or stretching out of words or sentences.) Both open hands are held close to each other, with fingers open and palms facing and almost touching. As the hands are drawn apart, the thumb and index finger of each hand come together to form circles. This is repeated several times. See also NARRATE, NARRATIVE, TALE.

STRANGE (strănj), *adj.* (Something which distorts the vision). The "C" hand describes a small arc in front of the face. See also CURIOUS, ODD, WEIRD.

STREET (strēt), *n.* (The path.) Both hands, palms facing and fingers together and extended straight out, move in unison away from the body, in a straight or winding manner. See also ROAD.

STRENGTH (strĕngkth, strĕngth), *n.* (Strength emanating from the body.) Both "5" hands are placed palms against the chest. They move out and away, forcefully, closing and assuming the "S" position. See also BRAVE, BRAVERY, HEALTH, HEALTHY, MIGHTY 2, WELL.

STRIKE (strīk), *v.*, STRUCK, STRIKING. (The natural sign.) The right "S" hand strikes its knuckles forcefully against the open left palm, which is held facing right. See also PUNCH 1.

STRONG (strông, strŏng), *adj.* (Flexing the muscles.) With fists clenched, palms facing down or back, the signer raises both arms and shakes them

once, with force. See also MIGHT 1, MIGHTY 1,
POWER 1, POWERFUL 1.

STUBBORN (stŭb′ ərn), *adj*. (The donkey's broad
ear; the animal is traditionally a stubborn one.) The
open hand, or the "B" hand, is placed at the side of
the head, with palm out and fingers pointing straight
up. The hand moves forward and back, pivoting at
the wrist, as in the case of a donkey's ears flapping.
Both hands may also be used, at either side of the
head.

STUCK (stŭk), *adj*. (Impaled on a stick, as a snake's
head.) The "V" fingers are thrust into the throat.

STUDENT (stū′ dənt, sto͞o′ -), *n*. (One who learns.) The sign for LEARN is made: The downturned fingers of the right hand are placed on the upturned left palm. They close, and then the hand rises and the right fingertips are placed on the forehead. This is followed by the sign for INDIVIDUAL: Both open hands, palms facing each other, move down the sides of the body, tracing its outline to the hips.

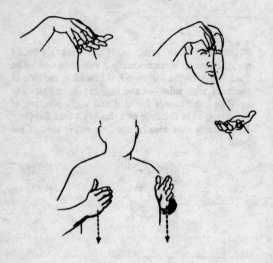

STUPID (stū′ pĭd, sto͞o′ -), *adj*. (Knocking the head to indicate its empty state.) The "S" hand, palm facing the body, knocks against the forehead.

SUBJECT (sŭb′ jĭkt), *n.* (The quotation marks are indicated.) The curved index and middle fingers of both hands, held palms out, move slightly to either side of the body, as if drawing quotation marks in the air. See also QUOTATION, QUOTE, SO-CALLED, TITLE, TOPIC.

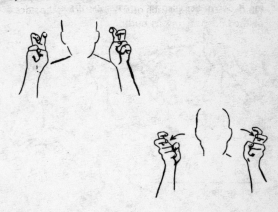

SUBSTITUTE (sŭb′ stə tūt′), *n., v.,* -TUTED, -TUTING. (Exchanging places.) The right "A" hand, positioned above the left "A" hand, swings down and under the left, coming up a bit in front of it. See also EXCHANGE, REPLACE, TRADE.

SUBTRACT (səb trăkt′), *v.*, -TRACTED, -TRACTING. (Removing.) The right "A" hand, resting in the palm of the left "5" hand, moves slightly up and away, describing a small arc. It is then cast downward, opening into the "5" position, palm down, as if removing something from the left hand and casting it down. See also DEDUCT, REMOVE.

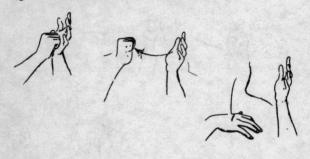

SUBTRACTION (səb trăk′ shən), *n.* See SUBTRACT.

SUCCEED (sək sēd′), *v.*, -CEEDED, -CEEDING. (Penetrating the heights.) The "D" hands, palms back, are held at each side of the head, near the temples. With a pivoting motion of the wrists, the hands swing up and around, simultaneously, to a position above the head, with palms facing out. See also TRIUMPH 2.

SUCCESS (sək sĕs′), *n*. See SUCCEED.

SUCCESSFUL (sək sĕs′ fəl), *adj*. See SUCCEED.

SUFFER (sŭf′ ər), *v*., -FERED, -FERING. (A clenching of the fists; the rise and fall of pain.) Both "S" hands, tightly clenched, revolve about each other, slowly and deliberately, while a pained expression is worn. See also ENDURE 1.

SUGAR (shoŏg′ ər), *n*. (Titillating to the taste.) The fingertips of the right "U" hand, palm facing the body, brush against the chin a number of times beginning at the lips. See also CUTE 1, SWEET.

SUGGEST (səg jĕst′), *v.*, -GESTED, -GESTING. (An offering; a presenting.) Both hands, slightly cupped, palms up, are held close to the chest. They move up and out in unison, describing a very slight arc. See also OFFER, OFFERING, PRESENT 1, PROPOSE.

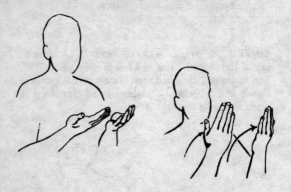

SUM (sŭm), *n., v.*, SUMMED, SUMMING. (To bring up all together.) The two open hands, palms and fingers facing each other, with the left hand above the right, are brought together, with all fingers closing simultaneously. This sign is used mainly in the sense of adding up figures or items. See also ADD 1, ADDITION.

SUMMARIZE 1 (sŭm´ ə rīz´), *v.*, -RIZED, -RIZING.
(To squeeze or condense into a small space.) The
"C" hands face each other, with the right hand
nearer to the body than the left. Both hands draw
together and close deliberately, squeezing an imaginary object. See also MAKE BRIEF.

SUMMARIZE 2, *v.* See SUM.

SUMMARY 1 (sŭm´ ə rĭ), *n., adj.* See SUMMARIZE 1.

SUMMARY 2, *n.* See SUM.

SUMMER (sŭm′ ər), *n.* (Wiping the brow.) The downturned right index finger, slightly curved, is drawn across the forehead from left to right.

SUM UP, *v. phrase.* See SUM.

SUN (sŭn), *n., v.,* SUNNED, SUNNING. (The round shape and the rays.) The right index finger, pointing forward and held above the face, describes a small clockwise circle. The right hand, all fingers touching the thumb, then drops down and forward from its position above the head. As it does so, the fingers open to the "5" position.

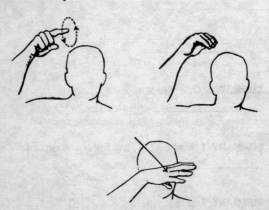

SUNRISE (sŭn′ rīz′), *n.* (The natural sign.) The downturned left arm, held horizontally, represents the horizon. The right thumb and index finger form a circle, and this circle is drawn up from a position in front of the downturned left hand.

———————

SUNSET (sŭn′ sĕt′), *n.* (The natural sign.) The movement described in SUNRISE is reversed, with the right hand moving down below the downturned left hand.

———————

SUNSHINE (sŭn′ shīn′), *n.* See SUN.

———————

SUPERVISE (sōō′ pər vīz′), *v.*, -VISED, -VISING. (The eyes sweep back and forth.) The "V" hands, held crossed, describe a counterclockwise circle before the chest.

SUPPORT (sə pōrt'), *n., v.* -PORTED, -PORTING.
(Holding up.) The right "S" hand pushes up the left
"S" hand. See also ENDORSE 1, SUSTAIN, SUSTE-
NANCE.

SURE (shŏŏr), *adj., adv.* (Coming forth directly
from the lips; true.) The index finger of the right "D"
hand, palm facing left, is placed against the lips. It
moves up an inch or two and then describes a small
arc forward and away from the lips. See also REAL,
REALLY, TRUE, TRULY, TRUTH.

SURELY (shŏŏr' lĭ), *adv.* See SURE.

SURPRISE (sər prīz'), *v.,* -PRISED, -PRISING, *n.* (The
eyes pop open in amazement.) Both hands are held
in modified "O" positions with thumb and index

fingers of each hand near the eyes. These fingers suddenly flick open, and the eyes simultaneously pop open wide. See also AMAZE, AMAZEMENT, ASTONISH, ASTONISHED, ASTONISHMENT, ASTOUND.

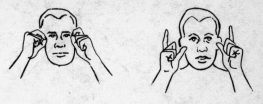

SURRENDER (sə rĕn′ dər), *v.*, -DERED, -DERING. (Throwing up the hands in a gesture of surrender.) Both "A" hands are held palms down before the chest and then thrown up in unison, ending in the "5" position. See also GIVE UP.

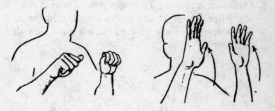

SUSPEND (sə spĕnd′), *v.*, -PENDED, -PENDING. (The natural sign.) The curved right index finger "hangs" on the extended left index finger.

SUSTAIN (sə stān'), *v.*, -TAINED, -TAINING. (Holding up.) The right "S" hand pushes up the left "S" hand. See also ENDORSE 1, SUPPORT.

SUSTENANCE (sŭs' tə nəns), *n.* See SUSTAIN.

SWEAR 1 (swâr), *v.* SWORE, SWORN, SWEARING. (The arm is raised.) The right index finger is placed at the lips. The right arm is then raised, palm out and elbow resting on the back of the left hand. See also PROMISE 1.

SWEAR 2, *v.* (Harsh words and a threatening hand.) The right hand appears to claw words out of the mouth. It ends in the "S" position, above the

head, shaking back and forth in a threatening manner. See also CURSE 1.

SWEET (swēt), *adj., n.* (Titillating to the taste.) The
fingertips of the right "U" hand, palm facing the
body, brush against the chin a number of times beginning at the lips. See also CUTE 1, SUGAR.

SWEETHEART (swēt′ härt′), *(colloq.), n.* (Heads
nodding toward each other.) The "A" hands are
placed together before the body with thumbs up.
The thumbs wiggle up and down. See also LOVER.

SYMPATHY (sĭm′ pə thĭ), *n.* (Feelings from the heart, conferred on others.) The middle fingertip of the open right hand touches the chest over the heart. The same open hand then moves in a small, clockwise circle before the right shoulder, with palm facing forward and fingers pointing up. See also MERCY, PITY.

T

TAKE (tāk), *v.* TOOK, TAKEN, TAKING, *n.* (Taking
unto oneself.) The right hand, palm out, is extended
before the chest, index finger and thumb in an open
position, the other fingers separated and pointing up.
The hand is drawn in toward the chest, and the
index and thumb close at the same time, indicating
something taken to oneself. See also CHOOSE, SE-
LECT 2.

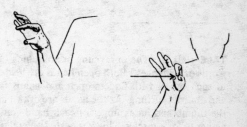

TAKE CARE OF *v. phrase.* (Slow, careful movement.) The "K" hands are crossed, the right above
the left, little finger edges down. In this position the
hands are moved up and down a short distance. See
also CARE 2, CAREFUL 2, KEEP, MAINTAIN 1, PRE-
SERVE.

513

TAKE UP, *v. phrase.* (Responsibility.) Both hands, held palms down in the "5" position, are at chest level. With a grasping upward movement, both close into "S" positions before the face. See also ASSUME, PICK UP 1.

TALE (tāl), *n.* (The unraveling or stretching out of words or sentences.) Both open hands are held close to each other, with fingers open and palms facing and almost touching. As the hands are drawn apart, the thumb and index finger of each hand come together to form circles. This is repeated several times. See also NARRATE, NARRATIVE, STORY.

TALK 1 (tôk), *v.,* TALKED, TALKING. (Words tumbling from the mouth.) The right index finger, pointing left, describes a continuous small circle in front of the mouth. See also HEARING, MENTION, SAID, SAY, SPEAK, SPEECH 1, TELL.

_____

TALK 2, *n., v.* (A gesture of an orator.) The right open hand, palm facing left, is held above and to the right of the head. It pivots on the wrist, forward and backward, several times. See also LECTURE, SPEECH 2.

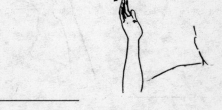

_____

TALK 3, *n., v.* (Movement forward from, and back to, the mouth.) The tips of both index fingers, held pointing up, move alternately forward from, and back to, the lips. See also CONVERSATION 1, CONVERSE.

TALL 1 (tôl), *adj.* (The height is indicated.) The index finger of the right "D" hand moves straight up against the palm of the left "5" hand. See also HEIGHT 1.

TALL 2, *adj.* (The height is indicated.) The right right-angle hand, palm facing the left, is held at the height the signer wishes to indicate. See also BIG 2, HEIGHT 2, HIGH 2.

TAX (tăks), *n., v.,* TAXED, TAXING. (Nicking into one.) The knuckle of the right "X" finger is nicked against the palm of the left hand, held in the "5" position, palm facing right. See also COST, EXPENSE, FINE 2, PENALTY, PRICE.

TAXATION 1 (tăks ā′ shən), *n.* See TAX 1.

TEA 1 (tē), *n.* (Dipping the teabag.) The right index finger and thumb raise and lower an imaginary teabag into a "cup" formed by the left "C" or "O" hand, held thumb side up.

TEA 2, *n.* (Stirring the teabag.) The hand positions in TEA 1 are assumed, but the right hand executes a circular, stirring motion instead.

TEACH (tēch), *v.*, TAUGHT, TEACHING. (Giving forth from the mind.) The fingertips of each hand are placed on the temples. They then swing out and open into the "5" position. See also EDUCATE, INSTRUCT, INSTRUCTION.

TELEPHONE (tĕl′ ə fōn′), *n.*, *v.*, -PHONED, -PHON-
ING. (The natural sign.) The right "Y" hand is
placed at the right side of the head with the thumb
touching the ear and the little finger touching the
lips. This is the more modern telephone receiver. See
also PHONE.

TELL (tĕl), *v.*, TOLD, TELLING. (Words tumbling
from the mouth.) The right index finger, pointing
left, describes a continuous small circle in front of
the mouth. See also HEARING, MENTION, SAID, SAY,
SPEAK, SPEECH 1, TALK 1, VERBAL.

TELL ME, *phrase.* (The natural sign.) The tip of the
index finger of the right "D" hand, palm facing the

body, is first placed at the lips and then moves down
to touch the chest.

TEMPERATURE (tĕm′ pər ə chər, -prə chər), *n.* (The
rise and fall of the mercury in the thermometer.) The
index finger of the right "D" hand, pointing left,
moves slowly up and down the index finger of the left
"D" hand, which is held pointing up.

TEMPT (tĕmpt), *v.*, TEMPTED, TEMPTING. (Tapping one surreptitiously at a concealed place.) With
the left arm held palm down before the chest, the
curved right index finger taps the left elbow a number of times.

TEMPTATION (tĕmp tā′ shən), *n.* See TEMPT.

TEND (tĕnd), *v.,* TENDED, TENDING. (The feelings of the heart move toward a specific object.) The tip of the right middle finger touches the heart. The open right hand, palm facing the body, then moves away from the heart toward the palm of the open left hand.

TENDENCY (tĕn′ dən sĭ), *n.* See TEND.

TERRIBLE (tĕr′ ə bəl), *adj.* (Throwing out the hands.) Both hands, their fingertips touching their respective thumbs, are held, palms facing each other, near the temples. They are thrown out before the face, assuming "5" positions, palms still facing. See also AWFUL, TRAGEDY.

TERROR 1 (tĕr′ ər), *n.* (The heart is suddenly covered with fear.) Both hands, fingers together, are placed side by side, palms facing the chest. They quickly open and come together over the heart, one on top of the other. See also AFRAID, FEAR 1, FRIGHT, FRIGHTEN, SCARE(D).

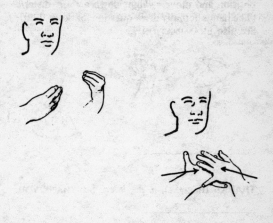

TERROR 2, *n.* (The hands attempt to ward off something which causes fear.) The "5" hands, right behind left, move downward before the body, in a wavy motion. See also FEAR 2.

TEST (tĕst), *n., v.,* TESTED, TESTING. (A series of questions, spread out on a page.) Both "D" hands, palms down, simultaneously execute a single circle, the right hand moving in a clockwise direction and the left in a counterclockwise direction. Upon completion of the circle, both hands open into the "5" position and move straight down a short distance. (The hands actually draw question marks in the air.) See also EXAMINATION 1.

THANKS (thăngks), *n. pl., interj.* See THANK YOU.

THANK YOU, *phrase.* (Words extended politely from the mouth.) The fingertips of the right "5" hand are placed at the mouth. The hand moves away from the mouth to a palm-up position before the body. The signer meanwhile usually nods smilingly. See also YOU'RE WELCOME 1.

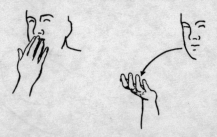

THAT (t̶h̶at, *unstressed* t̶h̶ət), *pron.* (Something specific.) The downturned right "Y" hand is placed on the upturned left palm. See also THIS.

THEFT 1 (thĕft), *n.* (The hand, partly concealed, takes something surreptitiously.) The index and middle fingers of the right hand, somewhat curved, are placed under the left elbow. As they move slowly along the left forearm toward the left wrist, they close a bit. See also ROB 1, STEAL 1, THIEF 1, THIEVERY.

THEFT 2, *n.* (A mustachioed thief.) The fingertips of both "H" hands, palms facing the body, are placed above the lips and are drawn slowly apart, describing a mustache. Sometimes one hand only is used. See also CROOK, ROB 3.

THEIR(S) (*ŧħâr, unstressed ŧħər*), *pron.* (Belonging to; pushed toward.) The open right hand, palm facing out and fingers together and pointing up, moves out a short distance from the body. This is repeated several times, with the hand moving an inch or two toward the right each time. The hand may also be swept in a short left-to-right arc in this position.

THEM (*ŧħĕm, unstressed ŧħəm*), *pron.* (The natural sign.) The right index finger points in turn to a number of imaginary persons or objects. See also THEY.

THEMSELVES (ŧħəm sĕlvz'), *pron. pl.* (The thumb indicates an individual, *i.e.,* a *self;* several are indicated.) The right hand, in the "A" position with thumb pointing up, makes a series of short forward movements as it sweeps either from right to left, or from left to right.

THEN 1 (ŧħĕn), *adv.* (Going from one specific point in time to another.) The left "L" hand is held palm facing right and thumb pointing left. The right index finger, positioned behind the left thumb, moves in an arc over the left thumb and comes to rest on the tip of the left index finger.

THEN 2, *adv.* (Same basic rationale as for THEN 1, but modified to incorporate the concept of nearness, *i.e.,* NEXT. The sign, then, is "one point [in time] to the next.") The left hand is held as in THEN 1. The extended right index finger rests on the ball of the thumb. The right hand then opens and arcs over, coming to rest on the back of the left hand, whose index finger has now closed.

THERE 1 (*thâr*), *adv.* (The natural sign.) The right index finger points to an imaginary object, usually at or slightly above eye level, *i.e.*, "yonder."

THERE 2, *adv.* (Something brought to the attention.) The right hand is brought forward, simultaneously opening into the palm-up position.

THEY (*thā*), *pron.* (The natural sign.) The right index finger points in turn to a number of imaginary persons or objects. See also THEM.

THIEF 1 (thēf), *n.* (The hand, partly concealed, takes something surreptitiously.) The index and middle fingers of the right hand, somewhat curved, are placed under the left elbow. As they move slowly along the left forearm toward the left wrist, they close a bit. This is followed by INDIVIDUAL, as in THIEF 2. See also ROB 1, STEAL 1, THEFT.

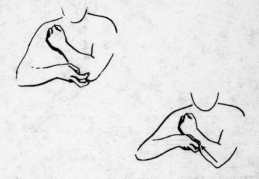

THIEVERY (thē'və rǐ), *n.* See THIEF 1.

THIN 1 (thǐn), *adj.* (The drawn face.) The thumb and index finger run down the cheeks, which are drawn in.

THIN 2, *(sl.), adj.* (A thin, tapering object is described with the little fingers, the thinnest of all.) The tips of the little fingers, touching, one above the other, are drawn apart. The cheeks may also be drawn in for emphasis. See also SKINNY.

THING (thĭng), *n.* (Something shown in the hand.) The outstretched right hand, palm up and held before the chest, is dropped slightly and brought over a bit to the right.

THINK (thĭngk), *v.,* THOUGHT, THINKING. (A thought is turned over in the mind.) The index finger makes a small circle on the forehead. See also CON-

SIDER 1, SPECULATE 1, SPECULATION 1, THOUGHT, THOUGHTFUL.

THIRST (thûrst), *n.* (The parched throat.) The index finger moves down the throat a short distance.

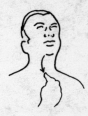

THIRSTY (thûrs' tĭ), *adj.* See THIRST.

THIS (thĭs), *pron., adj.* (Something specific.) The downturned right "Y" hand is placed on the up-turned left palm. See also THAT.

THIS MONTH, *phrase.* (Now, month.) The sign for NOW is made: The upturned right-angle hands drop down rather sharply. The "Y" hands may also be used. This is followed by the sign for MONTH: The extended right index finger moves down along the upturned, extended left index finger. The two signs are sometimes given in reverse order. For the phrases THIS WEEK and THIS YEAR, substitute the signs for WEEK or YEAR *(q.v.)* for MONTH, as shown above.

THOUGHT (thôt), *n.* (A thought is turned over in the mind.) The index finger makes a small circle on the forehead. See also CONSIDER 1, SPECULATE 1, SPECULATION 1, THINK.

THOUGHTFUL (thôt′ fəl), *adj.* See THOUGHT.

THOUSAND (thou′ zənd), *n.* ("M" for the Latin *mille,* thousand.) The tips of the right "M" hand are thrust into the upturned left palm.

THRILL (thrĭl), *(colloq.), n., v.,* THRILLED, THRILL-ING. (The feelings well up and come out.) The open hands are placed near the chest, with middle fingers resting on the chest. Both hands move up and out simultaneously. A happy expression is assumed. See also WHAT'S NEW?, WHAT'S UP?

THROUGH (thrōō), *adv., prep., adj.* (The natural movement.) The open right hand is pushed between either the middle and index or the middle and third fingers of the open left hand.

THUS FAR, *adv. phrase.* (From a point up and over.) In the "D" position, palms down, both index fingers touch the right shoulder and then are brought up and over, ending in a palm-up position, pointing straight ahead of the body. See also ALL ALONG, ALL THE TIME, EVER SINCE, SINCE, SO FAR.

TICKET (tǐk ǐt), *n.* (A baggage check or ticket.) The sign for TICKET 1 is made. Then the middle knuckles of the second and third fingers of the right hand squeeze the outer edge of the left palm, as a conductor's ticket punch.

TILL (tǐl), *prep.* (From one point to the next.) The extended right index finger moves forward slowly and comes to rest on the tip of the extended, upturned left index finger. See also TO, TOWARD, UNTIL, UNTO, UP TO, UP TO NOW.

TIME 1 (tīm), *n.* (Time by the clock, indicated by the ticking of the clock or watch.) The curved right index finger taps the back of the left wrist several times.

TIME 2, *n*. (Time in the abstract, indicated by the rotating of the "T" hand on the face of a clock.) The right "T" hand is placed palm to palm in the open left hand. It describes a clockwise circle and comes to rest again in the left palm.

TINY (tī′ ni), *adj.* (Indicating a small mass.) The extended right thumb and index finger are held slightly spread. They are then moved slowly toward each other until they almost touch. See also SMALL 1.

TIRE (tīr), *v*., TIRED, TIRING. (The hands collapse in exhaustion.) Both "C" hands are placed either on the lower chest or at the waist. The palms face the body. They fall away into a palms-up position. At the same time, the shoulders suddenly sag in a very pronounced fashion. An expression of weariness may be used for emphasis.

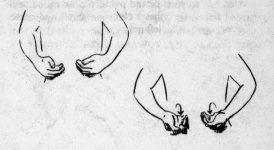

TIRED (tīrd), *adj*. See TIRE.

TITLE (tī′ təl), *n.* (The quotation marks are indicated.) The curved index and middle fingers of both hands, held palms out, move slightly to either side of the body, as if drawing quotation marks in the air. See also QUOTATION, QUOTE, SO-CALLED, SUBJECT, TOPIC.

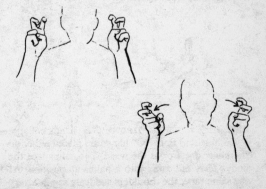

TO (tōō), *prep.* (From one point to the next.) The extended right index finger moves forward slowly and comes to rest on the tip of the extended, up-turned left index finger. This sign should never be used for an infinitive; it is simply omitted in that case. See also TILL, TOWARD, UNTIL, UNTO, UP TO, UP TO NOW.

TODAY (tə dā'), *n.* (Now, day.) The sign for NOW is made: The upturned right-angle hands drop down rather sharply. The "Y" hands may also be used. This is followed by the sign for DAY: The left arm, held horizontally, palm down, represents the horizon. The right elbow rests on the back of the left hand, with the right arm in a perpendicular position. The right "D" hand, palm facing left, moves in an arc to the left until it is just above the left elbow. The two signs may be reversed.

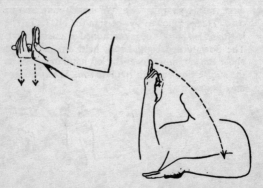

TOILET (toi′ lĭt), *n.* (The letter "T.") The right "T" hand is shaken slightly.

TOMORROW (tə môr′ ō, -mŏr′ ō), *n., adv.* (A single step ahead, *i.e.,* into the future.) The thumb of the right "A" hand, placed on the right cheek, moves straight out from the face, describing an arc.

TONIGHT (tə nīt′), *n.* (Now, night.) The sign for NOW is made: The upturned right-angle hands drop down rather sharply. The "Y" hands may also be used. This is followed by the sign for NIGHT: The left hand, palm down, is positioned at chest height. The downturned right hand, held an inch or so above the left, moves over the left hand in an arc, as the sun setting beneath the horizon. The two signs may be reversed.

TOPIC (tŏp' ĭk), *n.* (The quotation marks are indicated.) The curved index and middle fingers of both hands, held palms out, move slightly to either side of the body, as if drawing quotation marks in the air. See also QUOTATION, QUOTE, SO-CALLED, SUBJECT, TITLE.

TOUCH (tŭch), *n., v.,* TOUCHED, TOUCHING. (The natural movement of touching.) The tip of the middle finger of the downturned right "5" hand touches the back of the left hand a number of times. See also CONTACT 1, FEEL 1.

TOUCHED (tŭcht), *adj.* (A piercing of the heart.) The tip of the middle finger of the right "5" hand is thrust against the heart. The head, at the same time, moves abruptly back a very slight distance. See also FEEL TOUCHED.

TOUCHING (toŭch' ĭng), *adj.* See TOUCHED.

_____

TOWARD (tōrd, tə wôrd'), *prep.* (From one point to the next.) The extended right index finger moves forward slowly and comes to rest on the tip of the extended, upturned left index finger. See also TILL, TO, UNTIL, UNTO, UP TO, UP TO NOW.

_____

TRADE (trād), *n., v.,* TRADED, TRADING. (Exchanging places.) The right "A" hand, positioned above the left "A" hand, swings down and under the left, coming up a bit in front of it. See also EXCHANGE, REPLACE, SUBSTITUTE.

_____

TRAIN 1 (trān), *n.* (Running along the tracks.) The "V" hands are held palms down. The right "V" moves back and forth over the left "V."

TRAIN 2, *v.*, TRAINED, TRAINING. (Polishing or sharpening up.) The knuckles of the downturned right "A" hand are rubbed briskly back and forth over the side of the hand and index finger of the left "D" hand. See also PRACTICE.

TRAVEL (trăv′ əl), *n., v.*, -ELED, ELING. Using the downturned curved "V" fingers, describe a series of small counterclockwise circles as they move in random fashion from right to left.

TREE (trē), *n.* (The shape.) The elbow of the upright right arm rests on the palm of the upturned left hand. This is the trunk. The right "5" fingers wiggle to imitate the movement of the branches and leaves.

TRIUMPH (trī′ əmf), *n.* (Penetrating the heights.)
The "D" hands, palms back, are held at each side of
the head, near the temples. With a pivoting motion
of the wrists, the hands swing up and around, simultaneously, to a position above the head, with palms
facing out. See also SUCCEED, SUCCESS, SUCCESS-
FUL.

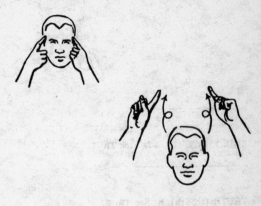

TROUBLE (trŭb′ əl), *n., v.,* -BLED, -BLING. (A
clouding over; a troubling.) Both "B" hands, palms
facing each other, are rotated alternately before the
forehead. See also PROBLEM 1, WORRIED, WORRY 1.

TRUE (trōō), *adj.* (Coming forth directly from the lips; true.) The index finger of the right "D" hand, palm facing left, is placed against the lips. It moves up an inch or two and then describes a small arc forward and away from the lips. See also REAL, REALLY, SURE, SURELY.

TRULY (trōō′ lĭ), *adv.* See TRUE.

TRUTH (trōōth), *n.* See TRUE.

TRY 1 (trī), *n., v.,* TRIED, TRYING. (Trying to push through.) The "A" hands, palms facing before the body, are swung around and a bit down, so that the palms now face out. The movement indicates an attempt to push through a barrier. See also ATTEMPT 1, EFFORT 1.

TRY 2, *v., n.* (Trying to push through, using the "T" hands, for "try.") This is the same sign as TRY 1, except that the "T" hands are employed. See also ATTEMPT 2, EFFORT 2, PERSEVERE.

U

UNCLE (ŭng′ kəl), *n.* (The letter "U"; the "male" or upper portion of the head.) The right "U" hand is held near the right temple and is shaken slightly.

UNDER 1 (ŭn′ dər), *prep.* (Underneath something.) The right hand, in the "A" position, thumb pointing straight up, moves down under the left hand, held outstretched, fingers together, palm down. See also BELOW 2.

UNDER 2, *prep.* (The area below.) The right "A" hand, thumb pointing up, moves in a counterclockwise fashion under the downturned left hand. See also BELOW 3.

UNDERNEATH (ŭn´ dər nēth´, -nĕ̱th), *prep.* See
UNDER 1.

UNDERSTAND (ŭn´ dər stănd´), *v.,* -STOOD,
-STANDING. (An awakening of the mind.) The right
"S" hand is placed on the forehead, palm facing the
body. The index finger suddenly flicks up into the
"D" position.

UNTIL (ŭn tĭl´), *prep.* (From one point to the next.)
The extended right index finger moves forward
slowly and comes to rest on the tip of the extended,
upturned left index finger. See also TILL, TO, TO-
WARD, UP TO, UP TO NOW.

UNTO (ŭn´ tōō), *prep.* See UNTIL.

UP TO, *prep. phrase.* (From one point to the next.) The extended right index finger moves forward slowly and comes to rest on the tip of the extended, upturned left index finger. See also TILL, TO, TOWARD, UNTIL, UNTO.

UP TO NOW, *adv. phrase.* See UP TO.

URGE 1 (ûrj), *v.,* URGED, URGING, *n.* (Pushing forward.) Both "5" hands are held, palms out, the right fingers facing right and the left fingers left. The hands move straight forward in a series of short movements. See also ENCOURAGE, MOTIVATE, MOTIVATION.

URGE 2, *v.* (Shaking someone, to implant one's will into another.) Both "A" hands, palms facing, are held before the chest, the left slightly in front of the right. In this position the hands move back and forth a short distance. See also PERSUADE, PERSUASION.

US (ŭs), *pron.* (The letter "U"; an encompassing gesture.) The right "U" hand, palm facing the body, swings from right shoulder to left shoulder.

USE (*n.* ūs; *v.* ūz), USED, USING. (The letter "U.") The right "U" hand describes a small clockwise circle.

USED (ūzd), *v.* See USE.

USEFUL (ūs′ fəl), *adj.* See USE.

UTILIZE (ū′ tə līz′), *v.,* -LIZED, -LIZING. See USE.

V

VACATION (vā kā' shən), *n.* (A position of idleness.) With thumbs tucked in the armpits, the remaining fingers of both hands wiggle. See also RETIRE.

VALUABLE (văl' yōō ə bəl, văl' yə bəl), *adj.* Both "F" hands, palms facing each other, move apart, up, and together in a smooth elliptical fashion, coming together at the tips of the thumbs and index fingers of both hands. See also IMPORTANT, SIGNIFICANCE 1, SIGNIFICANT, WORTH, WORTHWHILE, WORTHY.

VALUE (văl' ū), *n.* See VALUABLE.

VARIED (vâr' ĭd), *adj.* (Separated many times; different.) The "D" hands, palms down, are crossed at the index fingers or are held side by side. They separate and return to their initial position a number of times. See also DIFFERENCE, DIFFERENT, DIVERSE 1, DIVERSITY 1.

VARIOUS (vâr' ĭ əs), *adj.* (The fingertips indicate many things.) Both hands, in the "D" position, palms out and index fingertips touching, are drawn apart. As they move apart, the index fingers wiggle up and down. See also DIVERSE 2, DIVERSITY 2.

VARY (vâr' ĭ), *v.*, VARIED, VARYING. See VARIOUS.

VERY (vĕr' ĭ), *adv.* (The "V" hands, with the sign for MUCH.) The fingertips of the "V" hands are placed together, and then moved apart.

VICTORY 1 (vĭk' tə rĭ), *n.* (Waving of flags.) Both upright hands, grasping imaginary flags, wave them in small circles. See also CELEBRATE, CELEBRATION, CHEER, REJOICE, WIN 1.

VICTORY 2, *n.* (Waving a flag.) The right "A" hand goes through the natural movement of waving a flag in circular fashion. Preceding this, the right hand may go through the motion of grabbing the flagstaff out of the left hand. See also WIN 2.

VIEW (vū), *n., v.,* VIEWED, VIEWING. (Look around.) The sign for LOOK is made: The right "V" hand, palm facing the body, is placed so that the fingertips are just under the eyes. Then both "V" hands are held with palms down and fingers pointing forward in front of the body. In this position the hands move simultaneously from side to side several times.

VISION (vĭzh′ ən), *n.* See VIEW.

VISIT (vĭz′ ĭt), *n., v.,* -ITED, -ITING. (The letter "V"; random movement, *i.e.,* moving around as in visiting.) The "V" hands, palms facing, move alternately in clockwise circles out from the chest.

VOTE (vōt), *n.*, *v.*, VOTED, VOTING. (Placing a ballot in a box.) The right hand, holding an imaginary ballot between the thumb and index finger, places it into an imaginary box formed by the left "O" hand, palm facing right. See also ELECT, ELECTION.

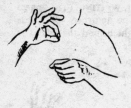

W

WAIT (wāt), *n., v.,* WAITED, WAITING. (The fingers wiggle with impatience.) The upturned "5" hands are positioned with the right behind the left. The fingers of both hands wiggle.

WAKE UP (wāk), *v. phrase.* (Opening the eyes.) Both hands are closed, with thumb and index finger of each hand held together, extended, and placed at the corners of the closed eyes. Slowly they separate, and the eyes open. See also AWAKE, AWAKEN.

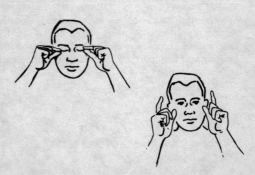

WALK (wôk), *n., v.,* WALKED, WALKING. (The movement of the feet.) The downturned "5" hands move alternately toward and away from the chest.

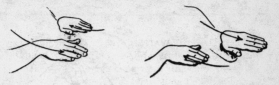

WANT (wŏnt, wônt), *v.,* WANTED, WANTING. (Grasping something and pulling it in.) The upturned "5" hands, held side by side before the chest, close slightly into a grasping position as they move in toward the body. See also DESIRE 1, NEED 2, WISH 1.

WARM (wôrm), *adj., v.,* WARMED, WARMING. (The warmth of the breath is indicated.) The upturned cupped right hand is placed at the slightly open mouth. It moves up and away from the mouth, opening into the upturned "5" position, with fingers somewhat curved.

WARN (wôrn), *v.*, WARNED, WARNING. (Tapping one to draw attention to danger.) The right hand taps the back of the left several times.

WAS (wŏz, wŭz; *unstressed* wəz), *v.* (Something past, behind.) The upraised right hand, in the "5" position with palm facing the body, is held just above the right shoulder and is thrown back over it. See also PAST, PREVIOUS, PREVIOUSLY, WERE.

WASH 1 (wŏsh, wôsh), *n.*, *v.*, WASHED, WASHING. (Rubbing the clothes.) The knuckles of the "A" hands rub against one another, in circles.

WASH 2, *v.* (The natural sign.) The closed hands move up and down against the chest as if scrubbing it. See also BATH, BATHE.

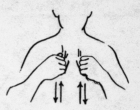

WASH DISHES, *v. phrase.* (The natural sign.) The downturned right "5" hand describes a clockwise circle as it moves over the upturned left "5" hand.

WASTE 1 (wāst), *n., v.,* WASTED, WASTING. (Repeated giving forth.) The back of the upturned right hand, thumb touching fingertips, is placed in the upturned left palm. The right hand moves off and away from the left once or several times, each time opening into the "5" position, palm up. See also SPEND.

WASTE 2, *n., v.* (The "W" is indicated.) The same movement as in WASTE 1 is used, except that the right hand assumes the "W" position and keeps it.

WATCH 1, (wŏch), *n., v.,* WATCHED, WATCHING. (The eyesight is directed forward.) The right "V" hand, palm facing the body, is placed so that the fingertips are just under the eyes. The hand swings around and out, so that the fingertips are now pointing forward. See also LOOK 1, PERCEIVE, PERCEPTION, SEE, SIGHT.

WATCH 2, *n.* (The shape of the wristwatch.) The thumb and index finger of the right hand, forming a circle, are placed on the back of the left wrist. See also WRISTWATCH.

WATER (wô′ tər, wŏt′ ər), *n.* (The letter "W" at the mouth, as in drinking water.) The right "W" hand, palm facing left, touches the lips a number of times.

WE 1 (wē; *unstressed* wĭ), *pron.* (An encompassing movement.) The right index finger points down as it swings over from the right shoulder to the left shoulder.

WE 2, *pron.* (The letter "W.") The right "W" hand, fingers pointing up, goes through the same motion as in WE 1.

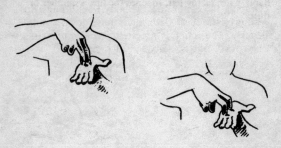

WEAK (wēk), *adj.* (The knees buckle.) The right "V" hand is placed with fingertips resting in the upturned left palm. The knuckles of the "V" fingers buckle a bit. This motion may be repeated.

WEAKNESS (wēk' nĭs), *n.* See WEAK.

WEALTH (wĕlth), *n.* (A pile of money.) The sign for MONEY is made: The back of the upturned right hand, whose thumb and fingertips are all touching, is placed in the upturned left palm. The right hand then moves straight up, as it opens into the "5" position, palm facing down and fingers somewhat curved. See also RICH.

WEALTHY (wĕl' thĭ), *adj.* See WEALTH.

WEAR (wâr), *n., v.,* WORE, WORN, WEARING. (Draping the clothes on the body.) With fingertips resting on the chest, both hands move down simultaneously. The action is repeated. See also CLOTHES, CLOTHING, DRESS, GOWN, SHIRT.

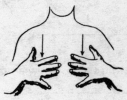

WEDDING (wĕd' ĭng), *n.* (A joining of hands.) The downturned "B" hands are joined together with a flourish.

WEEK (wēk), *n.* The upright, right "D" hand is placed palm-to-palm against the left "5" hand, whose palm faces right. The right "D" hand moves along the left palm from base to fingertips.

WEIGH (wā), *v.*, WEIGHED, WEIGHING. (The balancing of the scale is described.) The fingers of the right "H" hand are centered on the left index finger and rocked back and forth. See also POUND.

WEIGHT (wāt), *n.* See WEIGH.

WEIRD (wĭrd), *adj.* (Something which distorts the vision.) The "C" hand describes a small arc in front of the face. See also CURIOUS 1, ODD, STRANGE.

WELCOME (wĕl′ kəm), *n.*, *v.*, -COMED, -COMING.
(Opening or leading the way toward something.)
The open right hand, held up before the body,
sweeps down in an arc and over toward the left side
of the chest, ending in the palm-up position. Reversing the movement gives the passive form of the verb,
except that the hand does not arc upward but rather
simply moves outward in a small arc from the body.
See also INVITE, INVITED.

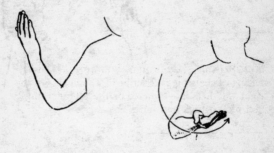

WELL (wĕl), *adj.* (Strength emanating from the
body.) Both "5" hands are placed palms against the
chest. They move out and away, forcefully, closing
and assuming the "S" position. See also BRAVE,
BRAVERY, COURAGE, COURAGEOUS, HEALTH,
HEALTHY, MIGHTY 2, STRENGTH.

WERE (wûr, *unstressed* wər), *v.* (Something past, behind.) The upraised right hand, in the "5" position with palm facing the body, is held just above the right shoulder and is thrown back over it. See also PAST, PREVIOUS, PREVIOUSLY, WAS.

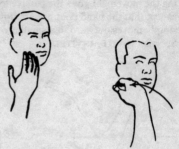

WET (wĕt), *adj., n., v.,* WET or WETTED, WETTING. (The wetness.) The right fingertips touch the lips, and then the fingers of both hands open and close against the thumbs a number of times.

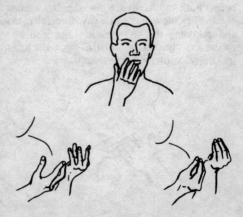

WHAT (hwŏt, hwŭt; *unstressed* hwət), *pron., adj., adv., interj., conj.* (The finger passes over several specifics to bring out the concept of "which one?") The right index finger passes over the fingers of the upturned left "5" hand, from index to little finger.

WHAT IS THE PRICE? (Amount of money is indicated.) The sign for MONEY is made: The upturned right hand, grasping some imaginary bills, is brought down into the upturned left palm a number of times. The right hand then moves straight up, opening into the "5" position, palm up.

WHAT'S NEW? (The feelings well up and come out.)
The open hands are placed near the chest, with middle fingers resting on the chest. Both hands move up and out simultaneously. A happy expression is assumed. See also THRILL.

WHAT'S UP? See WHAT'S NEW?

WHEN (hwĕn), *adv., conj., n.* (Fixing a point in time.) The left "D" hand is held upright, palm facing the body. The right index finger describes a clockwise circle around the left, coming to rest on the left index fingertip.

WHERE 1 (hwâr), *adv.* (Alternate directions are indicated.) The right "D" hand, with palm out and

index finger straight or slightly curved, moves a
short distance back and forth, from left to right.

WHERE 2, *adv.* The open "5" hands, palms up and
fingers slightly curved, move back and forth in front
of the body, the right hand to the right and the left
hand to the left. See also HERE.

WHETHER (hwĕtħ' ər), *conj.* (Considering one
thing against another.) The "A" hands, palms facing
and thumbs pointing straight up, move alternately
up and down before the chest. See also EITHER 3, OR.

WHICH (hwĭch), *pron. (esp. interrog. pron.), adj.*
See WHETHER.

WHILE (hwĭl), *conj. only.* (Parallel time.) Both "D"
hands, palms down, move forward in unison, away
from the body. They may move straight forward or
may follow a slight upward arc. See also DURING,
MEANTIME.

WHILE AGO, A 1, *phrase.* (The slight movement
represents a slight amount of time.) With the closed
right hand held with knuckles against the right
cheek, the thumbtip flicks off the tip of the curved
index finger a number of times. The eyes squint a bit,
and the lips are drawn out in a slight smile. The hand
remains against the cheek during the flicking movement. Sometimes, instead of the flicking movement,
the tip of the curved index finger scratches slightly
up and down against the cheek. In this case, the
palm faces back toward the shoulder. The same expression is used as in the flicking movement. See also
RECENT, RECENTLY.

WHILE AGO, A 2, *phrase.* (Time moved backward a bit.) The right "D" hand, palm facing the body, is placed in the palm of the left hand, which is facing right. The right hand swings back a bit toward the body, with the index finger describing an arc. See also FEW SECONDS AGO, JUST A MOMENT AGO.

WHO (hōō), *pron.* (The pursed lips are indicated.) The right index finger traces a small counterclockwise circle in front of the lips, which are pursed in the enunciation of the word.

WHOM (hōōm), *pron.* See WHO.

WHOSE (hōōz), *pron.* (Who; outstretched open hand signifies possession, as if pressing an item against the chest of the person spoken to.) The sign for WHO is made: The right index finger traces a small counterclockwise circle in front of the lips, which are pursed in the enunciation of the word. Then the right "5" hand, palm facing out, moves straight out toward the person spoken to or about.

WHY (hwī), *adv., n., interj.* (Reason—coming from the mind—modified by the letter "Y," the phonetic equivalent of WHY.) The fingertips of the right hand, palm facing the body, are placed against the forehead. The right hand then moves down and away from the forehead, assuming the "Y" position, palm still facing the body. Expression is an important indicator of the context in which this sign is used. Thus, as an interjection, a severe expression is assumed; while as an adverb or a noun, the expression is blank or inquisitive.

WIDE (wīd), *adj.* (The width is indicated.) The open hands, fingers pointing out and palms facing each

other, separate from their initial position an inch or
two apart.

WIDTH (wĭdth), *n*. See WIDE.

WIFE (wīf), *n*. (A female whose hand is clasped in
marriage.) The FEMALE root sign is made: The
thumb of the right "A" hand moves down along the
right jawbone, almost to the chin. The hands are
then clasped together, right above left.

WILL (wĭl), *v*. (Something ahead or in the future.)
The upright, open right hand, palm facing left,
moves straight out and slightly up from a position
beside the right temple. See also FUTURE, IN THE
FUTURE, LATER 2, LATER ON, WOULD.

WIN 1 (wĭn), *v.*, WON, WINNING, *n.* (Waving of flags.) Both upright hands, grasping imaginary flags, wave them in small circles. See also CELEBRATE, CELEBRATION, CHEER, REJOICE, VICTORY 1.

WIN 2, *v.*, *n.* (Waving a flag.) The right "A" hand goes through the natural movement of waving a flag in circular fashion. Preceding this, the right hand may go through the motion of grabbing the flagstaff out of the left hand. See also VICTORY 2.

WIND (wĭnd), *n.* (The blowing back and forth of the wind.) The "5" hands, palms facing and held up before the body, sway gracefully back and forth, in unison. The cheeks meanwhile are puffed up and the breath is being expelled. The nature of the swaying movement—graceful and slow, fast and violent, etc.

—determines the type of wind. The strength of exhalation is also a qualifying device.

WINDOW (wĭn' dō), *n*. (The opening of the window.) With both palms facing the body, the little finger edge of the right hand rests atop the index finger edge of the left hand. The right hand then moves straight up and down. See also OPEN THE WINDOW.

WINE (wīn), *n*. (The "W" hand indicates a flushed cheek.) The right "W" hand, palm facing the face, rotates at the right cheek, in either a clockwise or a counterclockwise direction.

WINTER 1 (wĭn′ tər), *n.* (The trembling from cold.) Both "S" hands, palms facing, are placed at the sides of the body. In this position the arms and hands shiver. See also COLD 1, SHIVER.

WINTER 2, *n.* (The letter "W.") The upright "W" hands, palms facing or forward, are brought together forcefully before the body one or two times.

WISDOM (wĭz′ dəm), *n.* (Measuring the depth of the mind.) The downturned "X" finger moves up and down a short distance as it rests on mid-forehead.

WISE (wīz), *adj.* See WISDOM.

WISH 1 (wǐsh), *v.*, WISHED, WISHING. (Grasping something and pulling it in.) The upturned "5" hands, held side by side before the chest, close slightly into a grasping position as they move in toward the body. See also DESIRE 1, NEED 2, WANT.

WISH 2, *v.*, *n.* (The upper alimentary tract is outlined.) The right "C" hand, palm facing the body, is placed with fingertips touching mid-chest. In this position it moves down a bit. See also STARVATION, STARVE, STARVED.

WITH (wǐth), *prep.* (The two hands are together, *i.e.*, WITH each other.) Both "A" hands, knuckles together and thumbs up, come together.

WITHDRAW 1 (wĭth drô′, wĭth-), *v.*, -DREW, -DRAWN, -DRAWING. (Pulling away.) The down-turned open hands are held in a line, with fingers pointing to the left, the right hand behind the left. Both hands move in unison toward the right. As they do so, they assume the "A" position. See also DEPART, LEAVE.

WITHDRAW 2, *v.* (Pulling out.) The index and middle fingers of the right "H" hand are grasped by the left hand. The right hand pulls out of the left. See also QUIT, RESIGN.

WITHIN (wĭth ĭn′, wĭth-), *adv., prep.* (The natural sign.) The fingers of the right hand are thrust into the left. See also IN, INSIDE, INTO.

WITHOUT (wĭth out′, wĭth-), *prep., adv.* (The hands fall away from the WITH position.) The sign for WITH is formed. The hands then drop down, open, and part, ending in the palms-down position.

WOMAN (wŏŏm′ ən), *n.* (A big female.) The FE-MALE prefix sign is made: The thumb of the right "A" hand moves down along the line of the right jaw, from ear almost to chin. This outlines the string used to tie ladies' bonnets in olden days. This is a root sign to modify many others. The downturned right hand then moves up to a point above the head, to indicate the relative height.

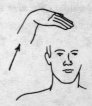

WONDER (wŭn′ dər), *v.*, -DERED, -DERING. (Turning thoughts over in the mind.) Both index fingers, pointing to the forehead, describe continuous alternating circles. See also CONSIDER 2, SPECULATE 2, SPECULATION 2.

WONDERFUL (wŭn′ dər fəl), *adj., interj.* (The feelings are titillated.) With the thumb resting on the upper part of the chest, the fingers are wiggled back and forth. See also ELEGANT, FINE 1.

WON'T (wōnt, wŭnt), *v.* Contraction of *will not.* (Holding back.) The right "A" hand, palm facing left, moves up sharply to a position above the right shoulder. See also REFUSE.

WORD (wûrd), *n.* (A small part of a sentence, *i.e.,* a word.) The tips of the right index finger and thumb, about an inch apart, are placed on the side of the outstretched left index finger, which represents the length of a sentence.

WORK (wûrk), *n., v.,* WORKED, WORKING. (Striking an anvil.) Both "S" hands are held palms down. The right hand strikes against the back of the left a number of times. See also JOB.

WORLD (wûrld), *n.* (The letter "W" in orbit.) The right "W" hand makes a complete circle around the left "W" hand and comes to rest on the thumb edge of the left "W" hand. The left hand frequently assumes the "S" position instead of the "W," to represent the stationary sun.

WORRIED (wûr′ ĭd) *adv., adj.* A clouding over; a troubling.) Both "B" hands, palms facing each other, are rotated alternately before the forehead. See also PROBLEM 1, TROUBLE.

WORRY 1 (wûr′ ĭ), *v.*, -RIED, -RYING. See WOR-RIED.

WORRY 2, *v., n.* (Drumming at the forehead, to represent many worries making inroads on the thinking process.) The right fingertips drum against the forehead. The signer frowns somewhat, or looks very concerned.

WORSE 1 (wûrs), *adj.* The "V" hands, palms facing the body, cross quickly. The comparative degree suffix sign -ER is often used after this sign: The

upright thumb of the right "A" hand is brought
sharply up to a level opposite the right ear.

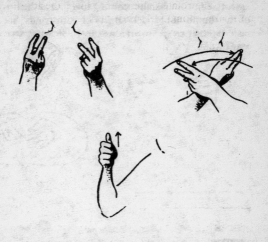

WORSE 2, *adj.* The same movements as in WORSE
1 are used, except that the "W" hands are employed.
The comparative degree suffix sign may likewise follow.

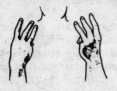

WORTH (wûrth), *adj., n.* Both "F" hands, palms facing each other, move apart, up, and together in a smooth elliptical fashion, coming together at the tips of the thumbs and index fingers of both hands. See also IMPORTANT, SIGNIFICANCE 1, SIGNIFICANT, VALUABLE, VALUE.

_____

WORTHWHILE (wûrth' hwīl'), *adj.* See WORTH.

_____

WORTHY (wûr' t͡hǐ), *adj.* See WORTH.

_____

WOULD (wŏŏd, *unstressed* wəd), *v.* (Something ahead or in the future.) The upright, open right hand, palm facing left, moves straight out and slightly up from a position beside the right temple. See also FUTURE, IN THE FUTURE, LATER 2, LATER ON, WILL 1.

WRISTWATCH, *n.* (The shape of the wristwatch.) The thumb and index finger of the right hand, forming a circle, are placed on the back of the left wrist. See also WATCH 3.

WRITE (rīt), *v.,* WROTE, WRITTEN, WRITING. (The natural movement.) The right index finger and thumb, grasping an imaginary pen, write across the open left palm.

WRONG (rông, rŏng), *adj., n.* (Rationale obscure; the thumb and little finger are said to represent, respectively, right and wrong, with the head poised between the two.) The right "Y" hand, palm facing the body, is brought up to the chin. See also ERROR, MISTAKE.

X

XEROX (zǐr' ŏks), *n.* (The letter "X;" the movement of the light as it moves under the item to be copied.) The "X" finger moves back and forth rather rapidly under the downturned hand.

XMAS, *n.* See CHRISTMAS.

Y

YEAR (yĭr), *n.* (A circumference around the sun.) The right "S" hand, palm facing left, represents the earth. It is positioned atop the left "S" hand, whose palm faces right, and represents the sun. The right "S" hand describes a clockwise circle around the left, coming to rest in its original position.

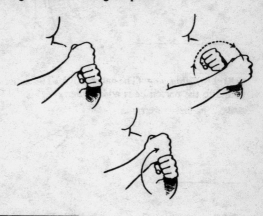

YEARS (yĭrs), *n. pl.* The sign for YEAR is made twice.

YES (yĕs), *(colloq.), adv., n.* (The nodding.) The right "S" hand, imitating the head, "nods" up and down.

YESTERDAY (yĕs′ tər dĭ, -dā ̄), *adv., n.* (A short distance into the past.) The thumbtip of the right "A" or "Y" hand, palm facing left, rests on the right cheek. It then moves back a short distance.

YOU 1 (ŭ), *pron. sing.* (The natural sign.) The signer points to the person he is addressing.

YOU 2, *pron. pl.* (The natural sign.) The signer points to several persons before him, or swings his index finger in an arc from left to right.

YOUNG (yŭng), *adj.* (The spirits bubbling up.) The fingertips of both open hands, placed on either side of the chest just below the shoulders, move up and off the chest, in unison, to a point just above the

shoulders. This is repeated several times. See also
ADOLESCENCE, ADOLESCENT.

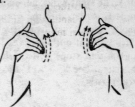

YOUR (yŏŏr), *pron., adj.* (The outstretched open
hand indicates possession, as if pressing an item
against the chest of the person spoken to.) The right
"5" hand, palm facing out, moves straight out toward the person spoken to. This sign is also used for
YOURS.

YOU'RE WELCOME 1. (Words extended politely
from the mouth.) The fingertips of the right "5"
hand are placed at the mouth. The hand moves away
from the mouth to a palm-up position before the
body. The signer meanwhile usually nods smilingly.
See also THANKS, THANK YOU.

YOU'RE WELCOME 2, *phrase.* (A straightening out.) The right hand, fingers together and palm facing left, is placed in the upturned left palm, whose fingers point away from the body. The right hand slides straight out along the left palm, over the left fingers, and stops with its heel resting on the left fingertips. See also ALL RIGHT, O.K. 1, RIGHT 1, RIGHTEOUS.

YOURS (yŏŏrz, yôrz), *pron.* See YOUR.

YOURSELF (yŏŏr sĕlf'), *pron.* The signer moves his upright thumb in the direction of the person spoken to. See SELF.

YOURSELVES (yŏŏr sĕlvz'), *pron. pl.* The signer moves his upright thumb toward several people be-

fore him, in a series of small forward movements
from left to right.

YOUTH (ūth), *n.* See YOUNG.

YOUTHFUL (ūth′ fəl), *adj.* See YOUNG.

Z

ZERO 1 (zĭr′ ō), *(colloq.)*, *n.* (An emphatic movement of the "O," *i.e.*, ZERO, hand.) The little finger edge of the right "O" hand is brought sharply into the upturned left palm.

ZERO 2, *n.* (The natural sign.) The right "O" hand, palm facing left, is held in front of the face. It then moves an inch or two toward the right.